CRITICAL
INSIGHTS
William Faulkner

CRITICAL INSIGHTS

William Faulkner

Editor
Kathryn Stelmach Artuso
Westmont College

SALEM PRESS
A Division of EBSCO Publishing
Ipswich, Massachusetts

GREY HOUSE PUBLISHING

Copyright © 2013, by Salem Press, A Division of EBSCO Publishing, Inc.

Critical Insights: William Faulkner, 2013, published by Grey House Publishing, Inc., Amenia, NY, under exclusive license from EBSCO Publishing, Inc.

∞ The paper used in these volumes conforms to the American National Standard for Permanence of Paper for Printed Library Materials, Z39.48-1992 (R1997).

Library of Congress Cataloging-in-Publication Data

William Faulkner / editor, Kathryn Stelmach Artuso, Westmont College.
    pages cm. -- (Critical Insights)
 Includes bibliographical references and index.
 ISBN 978-1-4298-3828-3 (hardcover)
 1. Faulkner, William, 1897-1962--Criticism and interpretation. I. Artuso, Kathryn Stelmach, editor of compilation.
 PS3511.A86Z9856857 2013
 813'.52--dc23

                                                                    2013008597

ebook ISBN: 978-1-4298-3844-3

PRINTED IN THE UNITED STATES OF AMERICA

Contents_____

Resources

About this Volume

Kathryn Stelmach Artuso

Faced with a staggering mountain of commentary dedicated to the fiction of William Faulkner, critics may well wonder whether anything new is left to be said. Yet this volume proves that close textual analysis and theoretical applications still yield fresh insights that can be communicated to Faulkner's readership. Fostering appreciation of William Faulkner's fiction and encouraging new scholarship, this volume seeks to deepen readers' comprehension of Faulkner's daring and defamiliarizing narrative techniques. The thirteen essays included provide an extensive range of critical perspectives and offer innovative insights on perhaps the most experimental and influential American author of the twentieth century. In this volume, relatively new voices in Faulkner studies join the chorus of well-established scholars; European scholars appear alongside American scholars; and various schools of criticism blend in counterpoint and harmony.

The volume opens with a consideration of Faulkner's career, life, and influence, beginning with an overview of significant themes and techniques in Faulkner's works, paying particular attention to the central section of *Go Down, Moses* (1942) as revelatory of larger themes in Faulkner's oeuvre. This essay is followed by a helpful biographical sketch of Faulkner's life by Lorie Watkins Fulton. The four critical context essays follow and build an introductory scaffolding, ranging broadly from cultural contextualization and critical reception and then narrowing to comparison and close textual analysis. In "'The Past Is Never Dead': Faulkner's Relationship to Southern Culture and History," Karen M. Andrews explores Faulkner's fiction in relation to its historical and cultural context, and especially regarding the legacy of slavery and segregation in the American South. Taylor Hagood conquers the daunting task of navigating and summarizing the expanding ocean of Faulkner criticism in the next essay entitled "William Faulkner's Critical Reception." Following the contextual and reception essays, Doreen Fowler's piece, "Reading Faulkner through Morrison," renders a comparative analysis of racial hybridity in *Absalom, Absalom!* (1936) and Toni Morrison's *Jazz* (1992) in an effort to illuminate the enigmatic motives of Charles Bon. Focusing the critical lens on a single text in "Misreading 'the Other' as a Strategy of Narrative Empathy in *Go Down, Moses*," Patrick E. Horn adopts a narratological and reader-response approach to examine Faulkner's paradoxical narrative strategies that elicit a reader's empathy in the face of white characters' misrepresentations of African Americans.

Like the first four essays and the introductory piece, "On William Faulkner," the nine essays that follow present new scholarship and provide a variety of critical readings that elucidate Faulkner's challenging high modernist fiction. Perhaps it should come as no surprise that the dialogic and intertextual nature of Faulkner's works should provoke a profusion of comparative analyses; in fact, five of the nine articles in this section of critical readings place Faulkner in juxtaposition with various modern and contemporary authors. In "Faulkner the Cannibal: Digesting Conrad," Jacques Pothier makes a strong contribution to postcolonial and global south studies when he explores two of Faulkner's early short stories as well as Sutpen's Haitian experience in *Absalom, Absalom!* to reveal the African "Orientalism" that Faulkner appropriated from Joseph Conrad. The profound influence on Faulkner of James Joyce's stream-of-consciousness technique also comes to mind as readily as Conrad's frame narratives—a topic addressed in "A Furious Echo: Hearing Dublin's Joyce in Faulkner's Yoknapatawpha," as Kieran Quinlan reveals the transatlantic intersections between Ireland and the American South and analyzes the technical parallels between *Ulysses* (1922) and *The Sound and the Fury* (1929). Less recognized than Joyce and Conrad but perhaps equally significant for Faulkner's aesthetic development was Elizabeth Madox Roberts, whose 1926 "plainfolk" novel, *The Time of Man*, demonstrated the complexity of ostensibly provincial characters and wielded immense influence on the verbal texture, mythical resonances, and interior monologues of *As I Lay Dying* (1930), as Mark Lucas relates in his essay, "*As I Lay Dying, The Time of Man*, and the Modern Folk Novel."

Skipping from the 1920s to the 1980s, from Faulkner's influences to those influenced by Faulkner, Bryan Giemza's essay, "'Shall Not the Judge of All the Earth Do Right?' William Faulkner, Cormac McCarthy, and Jurisprudence," compares the use of specialized legal language in the works of the two writers, especially in McCarthy's *Suttree* (1979) and *Blood Meridian* (1985) and Faulkner's *The Town* (1957), where the use of such legal parlance allowed the writers to investigate the limits of communication and the interplay between natural law and human law. Another contemporary writer, Randall Kenan, is juxtaposed with Faulkner in Mary Alice Kirkpatrick's essay, "'Far from Home across the Sea': William Faulkner, Randall Kenan, and Taboo Sexualities." Reconsidering the traditional southern trope of "place," Kirkpatrick's scrutiny of Faulkner's short story, "Divorce in Naples," and Kenan's short story, "Run, Mourner, Run," underscores the ways in which sites of travel and sites such as the stable "homeplace" can both "reorient the boundaries of desire."

If comparative analyses prove the most popular for this volume, a close runner-up would be discussions of Faulkner's highly acclaimed novel *Absalom, Absalom!*, whose dizzying and dazzling complexity inspired several of the contributors, including Fowler, Pothier, Norman W. Jones, and Hans H. Skei, to tackle its challenging contours. While I considered grouping all of these essays together, I sought intermittency and variety instead, although some overlap was inevitable. In "The Haunted House: Faulkner and the Bible," Jones closely explicates passages with biblical resonances from both *Absalom, Absalom!* and *The Sound and the Fury* to support his claim that the Bible operates as a "ghostly presence" or "intertext" in Faulkner's fiction, acting in ambivalent ways as both an ancient text and as a prophetic force on his characters and on his readership. Taking a different approach, Skei, in his essay "'A Summer of Wistaria': Old Tales and Talking, Story, and History in *Absalom, Absalom!*," revisits and seeks to clarify the obscure web of narrative multiplicity and instability in the novel.

The last two essays demonstrate the wide-ranging and popular appeal of Faulkner's demanding and recursive works. Shifting gears from biblical allusions and nearly impenetrable narratives to popular-cultural references, the penultimate essay by D. Matthew Ramsey, "Faulkner and Film: The 1950s Melodramas" discusses several film adaptations of Faulkner's novels, including *The Tarnished Angels* (directed by Douglas Sirk, 1957), *The Long, Hot Summer* (Martin Ritt, 1958), *The Sound and the Fury* (Ritt, 1959), and *Sanctuary* (Tony Richardson, 1961), ultimately emphasizing the ways in which these adaptations both uphold and undermine the patriarchal family values of the United States in the mid-twentieth century. The final essay is a creative nonfiction piece by Amy Weldon, "Hurling Yourself against the Beautiful: Faulkner and Creativity," in which she draws upon her personal experience as a writer to explore various pedagogical approaches to teaching the wildly disorienting section that represents Benjy's stream of consciousness in *The Sound and the Fury*. Including a creative nonfiction piece is a potentially pathbreaking decision, in the spirit of Faulkner's own experimentation that expanded the parameters of American literature and exploded the bounds of American literary criticism. Even in the face of a staggering mountain of commentary, what critics have to say about Faulkner appears to be limitless. The depth and complexity of his works magnetizes his readership, and each rereading brings to light new discoveries. This volume contributes to that ongoing conversation with rigor and originality.

CAREER, LIFE, AND INFLUENCE

On William Faulkner_____

Kathryn Stelmach Artuso

Discovering at the end of *As I Lay Dying* (1930) that Darl Bundren served in World War I and could be experiencing post-traumatic stress disorder, one might recall Septimus Warren Smith in Virginia Woolf's *Mrs. Dalloway* (1925), whose synesthetic capacity forms a parallel with Darl's own visionary abilities. In the wake of World War I, high modernists such as William Faulkner, Woolf, and James Joyce saw that the world was irretrievably broken and fragmented and that artistic representation needed to respond to that fragmentation in an unprecedented way. The long-cherished Enlightenment ideals of the goodness of humanity, the reign of reason, and the inevitability of progress were shattered by the mechanized slaughter and shell shock of modern warfare, the alienation of modern urban life, and the acquisitive mentality of the capitalist marketplace. Faulkner, Woolf, and Joyce no longer conceived of art as a mirror held up to nature that offered an accurate and faithful reflection of reality; like the cubist painters, they instead considered artistic representation to be a broken mirror that refracts reality into a multiplicity of images.

The experimental narrative techniques of the high modernists, including stream of consciousness, interior monologues, free indirect discourse, elusive referents, and multiperspectivalism, have led many critics (including Kieran Quinlan in this volume) to note that one cannot read but only reread the high modernists. Despite the density of modernist works, the rewards are as great as the challenges, and when the reader is fully immersed in their intensely lyrical prose, the high modernists make other authors start to pale in comparison. Each rereading brings to light new discoveries, and one rarely tires of returning to texts that yield such revelations.

The revelations are many. As they seek to re-enchant a desacralized world, Faulkner, Woolf, and Joyce often freeze the frame on moments of epiphany, which coincide with tableau-like moments of aesthetic

On William Faulkner   **3** ekphrasis—verbal representations of visual representations.[1] The latter portion of this essay will return to questions of epiphany and ekphrasis in Faulkner's *Go Down, Moses,* while the middle section will provide an overview of dominant themes in several of Faulkner's exemplary short stories and novels. Yet when encountering Faulkner for the first time, a bewildered reader will likely seek explanations for his disorienting narrative techniques. When encountering Faulkner for the first time, a bewildered reader will likely seek explanations for his disorienting narrative techniques. Unlike Joyce, whose stream-of-consciousness technique is usually relegated to one person's mind at a time, and unlike Woolf, who smoothly weaves in and out of multiple minds, Faulkner writes in a more disruptive and cacophonous way, with jarring shifts in chronology and unexpected transitions between minds.

Faulkner's signature style of nearly interminable sentences raises various questions regarding his syntactic strategies, in which subordinate clauses, extensive appositives, and lengthy parenthetical interjections accrue in such a fashion that one often loses sight of the original subject of the sentence, stumbling upon elusive referents such as an ambiguous "which" or "it" that will require a retracing of steps, sometimes to several pages previous. Consider, for example, a passage from Quentin Compson's section in *The Sound and the Fury* (1929), which requires readers to piece together a prose puzzle:

> "When he was seventeen I said to him one day 'What a shame that you should have a mouth like that it should be on a girl's face' and **can you imagine** *the curtains leaning in on the twilight upon the odor of the apple tree her head against the twilight her arms behind her head kimono-winged the voice that breathed o'er eden clothes upon the bed by the nose seen above the apple* **what he said?** just seventeen, mind. 'Mother' he said 'it often is'." And him sitting there in attitudes regal watching two or three of them through his eyelashes. They gushed like swallows swooping his eyelashes. **Shreve said he always had** *Are you going to look after Benjy and Father*

The less you say about Benjy and Father the better when have you ever considered them Caddy

Promise

You needn't worry about them you're getting out in good shape

Promise I'm sick you'll have to promise **wondered who invented that joke** but then he always had considered Mrs Bland a remarkably preserved woman he said she was grooming Gerald to seduce a duchess sometime. (67, bolded emphasis added)

Embedded within the joke about Gerald's women and Shreve's humorous commentary is Quentin's flashback in italics to his memory of a conversation with Caddy, who is pregnant and getting ready to marry a man who is not the father of her child. The duality of dialogue and memory work together on multiple levels, as the external comedy and internal tragedy intermingle, revealing and indicting the sexual double standard for men and women in the South, even as the Edenic imagery underscores Caddy's fall from innocence. The humor seems to predominate until one remembers that this double standard is no amusing game for Quentin, who internalizes all of it in a deadly serious fashion, and who will not live beyond the end of the day. As Quentin's consciousness grows increasingly unhinged, the reader struggles to piece together and retrace the relationships between subject and object, cause and effect, Caddy's actions and their consequences.

In contrast to Quentin's hypotactic style—which is also Faulkner's signature style—Benjy's section of the novel is paratactic in nature: "Steam came off of Roskus. He was sitting in front of the stove. The oven door was open and Roskus had his feet in it. Steam came off the bowl. Caddy put the spoon into my mouth easy. There was a black spot on the inside of the bowl" (45). Like an Ernest Hemingway hero who lives a simple, straightforward life, Benjy is a perfect spectator and observer of actions ("He tells us what happened, but not why," according to Faulkner), often observing his hands as indicating actors, but without a coordinating consciousness.[2] Ironically revealing the pathological nature of Hemingway's minimalist style, Faulkner displays its extreme objectivity and hyperrepetitiveness in a mentally challenged person.

In the wake of a disenchanted modernity, where the Enlightenment ideals may be fractured beyond repair, both Faulkner and Hemingway call into question direct cause-effect relationships, but the two authors present divergent techniques for subverting causality. Hemingway's terse, declarative, and paratactic style relies primarily on the coordinating conjunction "and"; rarely, if ever, does he link his sentences with a subordinating conjunction such as "because." Faulkner instead often separates the subject so far from the predicate, referent, or object that it becomes difficult to trace back to the original cause of the sentence. In "The Bear," Faulkner composed a six-page, nearly 1800-word sentence—one of the longest in all literature—that seeks to encompass the entire history and tragedy of the South in its relation to God's providence and design, though it proves highly unlikely that readers are convinced of the causal connection between God's design and southern history by the time the end of the sentence is reached. Faulkner's obscurantist techniques extend to the very subjects of his books: Caddy Compson, Addie Bundren, and Thomas Sutpen remain enigmatic figures who unsettle every attempt at analysis of character and comprehension of motivation. Faulkner's complex prose style circles endlessly about these inexplicable figures, never quite piercing to the heart of the matter, never quite giving readers the answers they want or allowing them to comprehend their pervasive mystery.

Time and Change, Maturation and Patriarchy

For first-time readers of Faulkner, his frequently anthologized short stories "A Rose for Emily" and "Barn Burning" are valuable places to start, as they encapsulate several of his reigning themes, particularly the concern with time and change, initiation and maturation, and ceremony and violence. Throughout his fiction, Faulkner continually emphasizes that linearity and chronology are human constructs, and he establishes two contrasting visions of time and memory at the conclusion of "A Rose for Emily," first comparing the past to an unspoiled, eternal meadow: "The very old men—some in their brushed Confederate uniforms—on the porch and the lawn, [were] talking of Miss Emily as if she had been a contemporary of theirs, believing that they had danced with her and courted her perhaps, confusing time with its mathematical progression, as the old do, to whom all the past is not a diminishing road but, instead, a huge meadow which no winter ever quite touches, divided from them now by the narrow bottle-neck of the most recent decade of years" (129). This comforting, nostalgic image is immediately juxtaposed with the shocking revelation that Miss Emily had been sleeping with the corpse of Homer Barron, suggesting an alternative obsession with the past, one that evinces a pathological morbidity. Throughout his oeuvre, Faulkner persistently tackles the South's various representations and misrepresentations of the past, undermining both the rosy nostalgia of the "moonlight and magnolias" myth and the unhealthy obsession with the corpse of the Lost Cause.

"Barn Burning" extends the theme of ambiguous misrepresentations of the past when Sarty Snopes betrays his father as a criminal, even as he seeks to create a more honorable image of him in his imagination: "*My father*, he thought. 'He was brave!' he cried suddenly, aloud but not loud, no more than a whisper: 'He was! He was in the war! He was in Colonel Sartoris' cav'ry!' not knowing that his father had gone to that war a private in the fine old European sense, wearing no uniform, admitting the authority of and giving fidelity to no man or army or flag, going to war as Malbrouck himself did: for booty" (24–25). Refusing to collude with the sins of his father, Sarty instead invents an admirable image that he can emulate as he embarks on a new stage of maturation, free from the cold fury and implacable stiffness of his father: "He was a little stiff, but walking would cure that too as it would the cold, and soon there would be the sun. He went on down the hill, toward the dark woods within which the liquid silver voices of the birds called unceasing—the rapid and urgent beating of the urgent and quiring heart of the late spring night. He did not look back" (25). Though the themes of initiation and ceremonial violence predominate in Faulkner's fiction, such optimistic imagery of springtime's renewal and the forward momentum of maturation rarely reappears and is often undermined by the blighted coming of age experienced by characters such as Quentin Compson and Darl Bundren.

Like Sarty Snopes, Quentin in *The Sound and the Fury* seeks a valiant role model and he attempts to script himself according to his grandfather's example, believing that his grandfather represents a noble, heroic age with a moral code, a code that no longer seems attainable in the modern world. He would rather join his grandfather, even it means death: "I thought of death as a man something like Grandfather a friend of his . . . I always thought of them as being together somewhere all the time waiting for old Colonel Sartoris to come down and sit with them . . . Grandfather wore his uniform and we could hear the murmur of their voices from beyond the cedars they were always talking and grandfather was always right" (111). Refusing to succumb to his father's world-weary cynicism and nihilistic philosophies, Quentin can be viewed as a representative of the Old South, who is clinging desperately to outdated models of aristocratic chivalry, all the while failing to realize that the Old South was no great bastion of idealism. When Caddy loses her virginity, Quentin's father tells him that he is experiencing a temporary state of pain and that time will heal all wounds, but Quentin wants the immediacy of the pain his sister has caused him never to fade away (48, 112–13). If sorrow and loss do in fact fade with time, as symbolized by the fading of the honeysuckle, then Quentin feels that his father's nihilistic philosophies have won the debate, and he refuses to let his father have the last word. Because Quentin freezes the frame on one moment of his life and suspends it there in an apotheosis, his suicide becomes an immobile tableau, one that perhaps challenges the redemptive stasis of moments of epiphany and revelation espoused by Joyce and Woolf.

The famous ambiguity of the conclusion of *The Sound and the Fury* expands the questions of time and stasis to eschatological proportions, embracing the entire sweep of human history and eternity. The Easter sermon at the African American church encompasses the Paschal mystery of the journey from death to rebirth, moving from Christ's incarnation to his crucifixion, resurrection, and second coming. Like the conclusion of Flannery O'Connor's short story "Revelation," the Easter sermon overturns all social hierarchies of class, caste, and status, as it reveals that "the last will be first, and the first will be last" (Matt. 20:16, NIV), according to an eternal perspective. Such a regenerative reconfiguration that includes African Americans, the poverty-stricken, and the disabled is immediately undermined by Faulkner's conclusion, when Benjy's panic attack is triggered by the displacement of his regularly ordered vision. Whether the sermon represents Babel's fragmentation of tongues or Pentecost's linguistic reunification is still up for debate, and whether the Christian theology of redemption or Mr. Compson's philosophy of nihilism emerges victorious in the end remains for the reader to decide.

In contrast to *The Sound and the Fury*, which he called his "most splendid failure," Faulkner dubbed *As I Lay Dying* his most perfect book: "I set out deliberately to write a tour-de-force. Before I ever put pen to paper and set down the first word, I knew what the last word would be and almost where the last period would fall."[3] Faulkner wrote this novel in six weeks on an overturned wheelbarrow while working a night shift in the power plant at the University of Mississippi. The novel's fifty-nine separate interior monologues demonstrate a mosaic of multiple perspectives, and Faulkner refuses to privilege any single voice as the authoritative one. The cacophony of multiple perspectives in endless regress reaches fever pitch in *Absalom, Absalom!* (1936), widely considered to be the South's masterpiece. As Quentin Compson and his Harvard roommate Shreve McCannon imaginatively attempt to reassemble the splintered puzzle of Thomas Sutpen's failed dynasty, the reader enters a dizzying tailspin of obscurity and narrative instability. The entire history and tragedy of the South are ultimately reflected in Sutpen's own life: turned away from the plantation door because of his lower class status, Sutpen reiterates the same tragedy of hierarchies when he later turns away his own son, this time for racial reasons.

Sacrificing the Father(land) in *Go Down, Moses*

The representations of patriarchal authority, with its concomitant abuses and inevitable demolition, perhaps reach the fullest expression in *Go Down, Moses* (1942), which, despite Faulkner's protestations to the contrary, qualifies as an interrelated short-story cycle rather than a novel.[4] Heavily influenced by Joyce's experimental narrative techniques, Faulkner's epiphanic moments in "The Bear" are also indebted to Sigmund Freud's *Totem und Tabu* (1913; *Totem and Taboo*, 1918), which was translated into English and published by Woolf's Hogarth Press. According to Freud, the symbol of a tribe is a totemic animal, which represents not only the tribe's ruling patriarch but also his bloody demise. Comparing primitive society to a primal horde dominated by a single ruthless male figure, Freud postulates that this ruling man enjoyed the sexual privileges of all the women in his clan, including his own daughters (*Totem* 208, 233). When Isaac McCaslin discovers in the plantation ledgers that his grandfather had slept not only with his slave but also with his own daughter, his horror regarding the violation of the incest taboo leads him to renounce all claims to his property and inheritance.[5]

In his myth of the origin of human culture, which also explains the origins of the incest taboo, Freud imagines that two brothers, jealous of their father's exploits, killed and devoured their father, a profane yet sacred act that Freud considered to be humanity's earliest festival and the beginning of social organization and religion (*Totem* 234). This mythical subtext surfaces in Faulkner's "The Bear," in which the bear is the central totemic figure around which the group of men coalesces until they succeed in killing him in a ritualistic fashion, a ritual meant to signify the death of patriarchal rule in the Old South.[6] The wise Chickasaw, Sam Fathers, and his idealistic apprentice, Isaac McCaslin, are direct patrilineal descendants of the original patriarchs who ruthlessly dominated the region, and the nonprogenitive wane of the two protagonists—one to his literal death—follows closely upon the demise of the bear.

Like a totemic emblem, Old Ben "had earned for himself a name, a definite designation like a living man" (185). The first time that an overly eager Isaac hears Old Ben passing by, leaving in his wake a trail of abject dogs, Sam says, "He dont care no more for bears than he does for dogs or men neither. He come to see who's here, who's new in camp this year, whether he can shoot or not, can stay or not. Whether we got the dog yet that can bay and hold him until a man gets there with a gun. *Because he's the head bear. He's the man*" (190, emphasis added). This echoes a passage in "The Old People," which describes Sam's father, Ikkemotubbe, who is nicknamed *Du Homme* (Doom), or The Man. Doom's merciless behavior includes poisoning puppies and poisoning a rival's son in order to gain accession as ruler of the tribe, followed by the sale of his own son, Sam Fathers, to Isaac's grandfather, Carothers McCaslin—who is often named "old" Carothers, much like "Old" Ben (160). Carothers McCaslin is just as ruthless as Doom, if not more so, and the implicit parallels drawn between Ikkemotubbe, old Carothers, and Old Ben suggest the end of an era dominated by primal fathers.

Encountering Old Ben with a courageous feist who brings the bear to bay, Isaac experiences a moment of "familiarity"—a familial relationship with a larger-than-life ancestor: "When he overtook and grasped the shrill, frantically pinwheeling little dog, it seemed to him that he was directly under the bear. He could smell it, strong and hot and rank. Sprawling, he looked up where it loomed and towered over him like a thunderclap. *It was quite familiar*, until he remembered: this was the way he had used to dream about it" (203, emphasis added). While Sam is the "direct son not only of a warrior but of a chief" (161) and Isaac is the grandson of the powerful white patriarch, the job of killing the bear falls to Boon Hogganbeck, who embodies a hybrid blend of various ethnic identities, underscoring the South's movement away from paternalistic supremacy and toward a new intercultural dynamic.[7]

Though his story fails to exhibit an exact one-to-one correspondence with Freud's theories, Faulkner nonetheless relies on various anthropological resonances, which continue into the fourth section of the story, where themes of sacrifice and sovereignty evoke various theories of gift-giving rituals. In *Formes élémentaires de la vie religieuse* (1915; *The Elementary Forms of the Religious Life*, 1965), the French sociologist Emile Durkheim argues that religious belief is the glue of societal collective consciousness and that totemism is the elementary form of religious belief. Durkheim's nephew Marcel Mauss and his eccentric compatriot Georges Bataille researched the ritual known as the potlatch performed by American Indians in the Pacific Northwest, where the sovereign individual or chief would engage in lavish displays of gift-giving, perhaps designed to humiliate the opposing tribe. The sovereign individual, in Bataille's terms, is the one who embodies "life beyond utility" (198) and who can squander everything without a thought for reciprocation, blurring boundaries and creating room for aesthetic play and imaginative exuberance in an anomic world significantly bereft of such capacities.

Following the tutelage of Sam Fathers, Isaac becomes Bataille's sovereign individual because he sacrifices everything he owns without a thought for reciprocation when he relinquishes all claims to his inheritance in the late 1880s. He contends that God has called humans to be stewards of the land, and that humans are cursed because they have insisted on owning property—both land and slaves. Isaac's unswerving commitment to the pivotal moment of his life, in which he repudiates his landownership during a noteworthy discussion of John Keats's ekphrastic poem, "Ode on a Grecian Urn," appears to uphold Alain Badiou's concept of the Event as a rupture that then requires relentless fidelity to the subjective truth that has emerged (42–43). Although numerous literary critics deride Isaac as a hero manqué, viewing his penitential generosity as overly idealistic, naive, and useless, his sacrificial epiphany nonetheless corresponds to the nonutilitarian extravagance of artistic creation, remaining as beautiful as a work of art freely produced in a moment of imaginative exuberance.[8] Art and religion may be antiutilitarian, according to Faulkner, but they provide the primary forms that give meaning to people's lives.

Extending these themes, Faulkner draws parallels between the sacrificial moments of epiphany and ekphrasis during Cass and Isaac's discussion of Keats's "Ode on a Grecian Urn."[9] The figures on the urn are frozen in time, just as Sam and Isaac experienced the old "heart's truth" that surpasses mutability and that encompasses *courage and honor and pride, and pity and love of justice and of liberty. They all touch the heart, and what the heart holds to becomes truth, as far as we know truth*" (249, 284).[10] Cass interprets Isaac and Sam's inability to kill the bear as an example of the timeless transcendence of art, but Isaac's renunciation of his heritage instead ironizes that earlier epiphanic moment, casting it as an inability to break free of the stifling constraints of the towering father figure. When Isaac finally rejects his claims to the land, *this* is the sacrificial act that merges the true and the beautiful as it transcends utility, just as the sacrificial scene on the urn reveals art to be a form of nonutilitarian excess. Although Cass quotes from the second stanza of Keats's "Ode on a Grecian Urn," which exalts the ageless permanence of the immobile lovers ("She cannot fade, though thou hast not thy bliss / Forever wilt thou love, and she be fair"), the discussion regarding Isaac's expiation, coupled with the ritual killing of Old Ben, instead summons to mind the fourth stanza of the "Ode on a Grecian Urn," which describes the unknowable mystery of sacrifice.[11]

In her detailed explication of the fourth stanza of Keats's "Ode on a Grecian Urn," Helen Vendler rightly notes that "once we pass (as museum visitors) beyond a wish for the explanatory factual truths of historical or cultural captions, and beyond the narcissistic stage of being interested only in 'lyric' art which we can see as a reflection of something in ourselves, we can confront art as it is in itself, in its ultimate formal anonymity and otherness" (123–24). The alien nature and complete alterity of Isaac's sacrifice puzzles literary critics, who often demand from Isaac a Calvinist cost-benefit calculus, or at least an entrance into a more active, useful life. Yet there will be no return for Isaac's generous expenditure, and in the spirit of true gift-giving, the reader and the critic are humiliated as recipients, insisting that something else must be done to repay the debt.[12] Or, in the case of Faulkner's recursive, obscurantist techniques, we demand that something else must be explained—if not by Faulkner, then by ourselves. Thus, Isaac's generosity forms a parallel with Faulkner's own artistic gift, a stream of consciousness that embodies the lavish potlatch of literary modernism—the "extravagant display of the artistic word."[13] Such extravagance leaves us bewildered and bemused, exasperated and exhilarated, but with each rereading we encounter new questions, new enigmas, and new revelations that richly reward—even when we fail to penetrate to the heart of the mystery, even as we confront the ultimate alterity of Faulkner's artistic gift.

Notes

1. The affinities between the moments of spiritual epiphany and the moments of aesthetic ekphrasis in the works of Joyce, Woolf, and Faulkner reveal art and religion to be corresponding and synthesizing forces with the power to revivify a disenchanted world. This process often occurs when characters appear to enter a *tableau vivant* that paradoxically freezes the frame on their moments of revelation. Woolf's epiphanic "moments of being," for example, arise in the midst of sacrificial displays of generosity, fusing motion with stasis at the height of energetic expenditure. The fiction of Joyce, which Woolf both admired and ridiculed, also reveals the inextricability of secular and sacred themes, underscoring the difficulties in sustaining the Enlightenment thesis of inevitable secularization. The blurred boundary between the secular and the sacred perhaps applies most readily to Joyce, who has no trouble conceiving of himself as a "pagan priest" who transubstantiates life into art, "a priest of eternal imagination, transmuting the daily bread of experience into the radiant body of everliving life"—a process most clearly typified in the ekphrastic *tableau* of Stephen's "bird-girl" epiphany, which merges Stephen's oscillation between sensuality and spirituality into an aesthetic synthesis (*Portrait* 221). Even as he escaped to the continent and attempted to fly past the Irish "nets" of religion, nationalism, and language, Joyce never completely cast off this triad and instead spent most of his life wrestling with the very issues he wanted to avoid and paying in his person the very debts he did not want to pay—much like Faulkner on his tiny "postage stamp of native soil" (Faulkner, "Interview" 255).
2. See Faulkner, "Interview" 245.

---

3. The quotation about his "most splendid failure" comes from Gwynn and Blotner's *Faulkner in the University* (77), while the longer quotation comes from Faulkner's "Introduction for *The Sound and the Fury*" (226).

4. Novels, as Faulkner knew full well, are easier to sell than short stories. Nonetheless, the generic indeterminacy of Faulkner's short-story cycle allows the hybridity of the form to intersect with thematic questions of interracial hybridity.

5. For an influential psychoanalytic study of Faulkner's fiction, especially of *Absalom, Absalom!* and *The Sound and the Fury*, see Irwin, who views incest as a symbol "of the state of the South after the Civil War . . . of a region turned in upon itself" (59). Polk also addresses various Oedipal conflicts in Faulkner's fiction (*Children* 22–98). In *Faulkner and the Politics of Reading*, Zender charts the evolution of the incest motif in Faulkner's works as a movement away from the South's patriarchal chauvinism—as represented in the father-daughter incest of Carothers McCaslin and Tomasina—to the egalitarian ideals of the early 1940s— as represented by the brother-sister incest of Roth and his lover (xiv, 23–25).

6. In *Faulkner: The Return of the Repressed*, Fowler also views the bear as a "fatherhead" figure, but focuses primarily on a Lacanian interpretation of the story, reading Isaac's "renunciation of his patrimony, which was prefigured by his refusal to kill the old bear, Old Ben, as a figuration of his renunciation of the missing phallus, the object of desire. While Ike submits to the Law of the Father . . . he also finds in the wilderness a substitute for the forbidden maternal relation" (xviii). In contrast, Davis interprets Old Ben as an "extensive use of the Negro as an abstraction," who "cannot be fully comprehended" and "is finally disembodied from the reality of ordinary human life" (Faulkner's *"Negro"* 246), though she revises her views in her later work, *Games of Property*. Brivic concurs with Davis's earlier reading of *Go Down, Moses* (Tears 44). For an early consideration of Old Ben as a totemic animal who symbolizes the wilderness, see Lydenberg (160–67). See also Kerr, who regards the snake at the end of "The Bear" as representative of old Carothers (189).

7. Boon, however, is not the best representative of this new intercultural dynamic, a dynamic that is better expressed by the unnamed woman who visits Isaac in "Delta Autumn" and poignantly reminds him that love can transcend racial boundaries.

8. The critics who disparage Isaac's penitential act are too multitudinous to list, but Brooks in *Yoknapatawpha County* (272–74) and Sundquist (138–39, 151–52) present prototypical discussions of Isaac's ethical failures as an antihero.

9. On classical tropes in "The Bear," particularly ekphrasis and appellation, see Millichap (95–112). He defines ekphrasis as "an extended literary description of some aspect of nature or of art" (33), whereas I am following Heffernan's narrower definition of ekphrasis as a "verbal representation of visual representation" (2–3). See also Brooks's famous explication of Keats's poem in *The Well Wrought Urn* (151–66), as well as Gelfant's and O'Shea's analyses of Faulkner's intertextual allusions to Keats. O'Shea attributes Isaac's ethical failures to his desire to enter the static, unchanging world of art (95).

10. Various examples of the pictorial and ekphrastic motifs emerge throughout the story: the hunt "was like the last act on a set stage" (216), which showcased the "pageant-rite of the old bear's furious immortality" (186). When Boon kills Old Ben, "they almost resembled a piece of statuary: the clinging dog, the bear, the man stride its back, working and probing the buried blade" (231).

11. The Keatsian lines quoted by Cass ironically prefigure Isaac's later marital troubles, even as they reflect back upon the theme of incest and of the jealous rivalry between father and son. Keats's fourth stanza of "Ode on a Grecian Urn" explores the "limits of representational art," as Vendler notes (122):

> Who are these coming to the sacrifice?
> To what green altar, O mysterious priest,
> Lead'st thou that heifer lowing at the skies,
> And all her silken flanks with garlands drest?
> What little town by river or sea shore,
> Or mountain-built with peaceful citadel,
> Is emptied of its folk, this pious morn?
> And, little town, thy streets for evermore
> Will silent be; and not a soul to tell
> Why thou art desolate, can e'er return. (lines 31–40)

12. The conclusion of "Delta Autumn," as many critics have noted, calls into question Isaac's ostensibly noble process of purification and penance. Nonetheless, Isaac tells Cass that "I have got myself to have to live with for the rest of my life and all I want is peace to do it in" (*Go Down, Moses* 275). When asked by a student at the University of Virginia if he thought Ike McCaslin "fulfilled his destiny," Faulkner replied, "I do, yes. They didn't give him success but they gave him something a lot more important, even in this country. They gave him serenity, they gave him what would pass for wisdom—I mean wisdom as contradistinct from the schoolman's wisdom of education. They gave him that" (Gwynn, "Faulkner's Commentary" 113).

13. Vincent Pecora draws upon Durkheim, Bataille, and the anthropological underbelly of modernity to argue that literary modernism's "extravagant displays of the artistic word" parallel the nostalgia for a precapitalistic enchanted economy in which excessive, sacrificial expenditure—a symbolic exchange without production—represented a noble gesture that modernism adopted to oppose to the narrow utilitarianism of a Calvinist marketplace (*Households* xi).

Works Cited

Badiou, Alain. *Ethics: An Essay on the Understanding of Evil.* London: Verso, 2001. Print.

Bataille, Georges. *The Accursed Share.* Trans. Robert Hurley. New York: Urzone, 1989. Print.

Brivic, Shelly. *Tears of Rage: The Racial Interface of Modern American Fiction.* Baton Rouge: Louisiana State UP, 2008. Print.

Brooks, Cleanth. *The Well Wrought Urn: Studies in the Structure of Poetry.* New York: Harcourt, 1947. Print.

___. *William Faulkner: The Yoknapatawpha County.* New Haven: Yale UP, 1963. Print.

Davis, Thadious M. *Faulkner's "Negro": Art and the Southern Context.* Baton Rouge: Louisiana State UP, 1983. Print.

___. *Games of Property: Law, Race, Gender, and Faulkner's* Go Down, Moses. Durham, NC: Duke UP, 2003. Print.

Durkheim, Emile. *The Elementary Forms of the Religious Life.* Trans. Joseph Ward Swain. New York: Free, 1965. Print.

Faulkner, William. "Barn Burning." *The Collected Stories of William Faulkner.* New York: Vintage Books, 1976. 3–25.

___. *Go Down, Moses.* 1942. New York: Vintage Books, 1970.

___. "Interview with Jean Stein vanden Heuvel." *Lion in the Garden: Interviews with William Faulkner, 1926-1962.* Ed. James B. Meriwether and Michael Millgate. New York: Random, 1968. 237–56. Print.

___. "An Introduction for *The Sound and the Fury.*" Introduction. *The Sound and the Fury.* Ed. David Minter. Norton Critical Ed., 2nd ed. New York: Norton, 1994. 225–28. Print.

___. "A Rose for Emily." *The Collected Stories of William Faulkner.* New York: Vintage Books, 1976. 119–130.

___. *The Sound and the Fury.* Ed. David Minter. Norton Critical Ed., 2nd ed. New York: Norton, 1994. Print.

Fowler, Doreen. *Faulkner: The Return of the Repressed.* Charlottesville: UP of Virginia, 1997. Print.

Freud, Sigmund. *Totem and Taboo: Resemblances between the Psychic Lives of Savages and Neurotics.* Trans. A. A. Brill. New York: Moffat, 1918. Print.

Gelfant, Blanche. "Faulkner and Keats: The Ideality of Art in 'The Bear.'" *Southern Literary Journal* 2.1 (1969): 43–65. Print.

Gwynn, Frederick L., and Joseph L. Blotner. "Faulkner's Commentary on *Go Down, Moses.*" *Bear, Man, and God: Eight Approaches to William Faulkner's "The Bear."* Ed. Francis Lee Utley. 2nd ed. New York: Random, 1971. Print.

___. *Faulkner in the University.* Charlottesville: UP of Virginia, 1995. Print.

Heffernan, James. *Museum of Words: The Poetics of Ekphrasis from Homer to Ashbery.* Chicago: U of Chicago P, 1993. Print.

Irwin, John T. *Doubling and Incest/Repetition and Revenge: A Speculative Reading of Faulkner.* Baltimore: Johns Hopkins UP, 1975. Print.

Joyce, James. *A Portrait of the Artist as a Young Man.* Ed. Chester G. Anderson. New York: Penguin, 1977. Print.

Keats, John. "Ode on a Grecian Urn." *The Norton Anthology of English Literature.* Ed. M. H. Abrams, et al. 6th ed. Vol. 2. New York: Norton, 1993. Print.

Kerr, Elizabeth. *William Faulkner's Yoknapatawpha: "A Kind of Keystone in the Universe."* New York: Fordham UP, 1983.

Lydenberg, John. "Nature Myth in Faulkner's 'The Bear.'" *Bear, Man, and God: Eight Approaches to William Faulkner's "The Bear."* Ed. Francis Lee Utley. 2nd ed. New York: Random, 1971. 160–67. Print.

Millichap, Joseph R. *A Backward Glance: The Southern Renascence, the Autobiographical Epic, and the Classical Legacy.* Knoxville: U of Tennessee P, 2009. Print.

O'Shea, José Roberto. "'Ode on a Grecian Urn' and *Go Down, Moses:* an Intertextual Inquiry into John Keats and William Faulkner." *Fragmentos* 25 (2003): 85–101. Print.

Pecora, Vincent. *Households of the Soul.* Baltimore: Johns Hopkins UP, 1997. Print.

Polk, Noel. *Children of the Dark House: Text and Context in Faulkner.* Jackson: UP of Mississippi, 1996. Print.

Sundquist, Eric. *Faulkner: The House Divided.* Baltimore: Johns Hopkins UP, 1985. Print.

Vendler, Helen. *The Odes of John Keats.* Cambridge: Harvard UP, 1983. Print.

Zender, Karl F. *Faulkner and the Politics of Reading.* Baton Rouge: Louisiana State UP, 2002. Print.

Biography of William Faulkner_____

Lorie Watkins Fulton

Although William Faulkner claimed that his "ancestors came from Inverness, Scotland" and that the "principal family lines were Falconer, Murray, McAlpine, and Cameron," there "were more versions of the Falkner origins than the number of families Faulkner himself settled on" (Blotner 3, 4). Eventually, Faulkner's great-grandfather settled in what would later become Tippah County, Mississippi, and lived there for "the rest of his life, siring one of the most unusual southern families ever to be produced in that state and becoming, himself, the inspiration for one of the most extreme, most influential, most amazing legends to emerge from the nineteenth century South" (Duclos 16). This is the legend that Faulkner inherited and, to be sure, incorporated into his fiction. More commonly referred to as "the Old Colonel," Faulkner's great-grandfather, William C. Falkner, serves as the prototype for Colonel John Sartoris in *Flags in the Dust* (1929, as *Sartoris*) and *The Unvanquished* (1938), and Donald Philip Duclos notes that "the entire Sartoris family have their counterparts in the Faulkner family with but little attempt made to disguise them" (6). The old colonel's Civil War exploits and literary successes influenced Faulkner from an early age: Duclos writes that like "Gail Hightower, in *Light in August*, William Faulkner too 'had grown up with a ghost'" (5). When asked what he wanted to be when he grew up, Faulkner told Miss Eades, his third-grade teacher, "I want to be a writer like my great-granddaddy" (Blotner 105). Become a writer he did. Faulkner went on to spend almost thirty years writing fiction set primarily in his native state.

Faulkner's success, however, did not always seem so assured. A high school dropout, he tried to enlist in the US Army for service in World War I after his childhood sweetheart, Estelle Oldham, married another man. The Army rejected Faulkner, but determined to join the war effort, he finally enlisted as a cadet in the Canadian Royal Air Force. The war ended before he saw active duty, although Faulkner sometimes allowed people to assume that he suffered injuries in combat that resulted in a limp and a steel plate being placed in his head. In 1918, Faulkner returned to Oxford and soon enrolled in the University of Mississippi as a war veteran. On campus, Faulkner continued to write poetry, helped found a dramatic club called the Marionettes, wrote material for the club, and submitted artwork, fiction, and poetry to the school yearbook.

Faulkner left the University of Mississippi after three terms and took a series of odd jobs, including becoming postmaster for the university post office and leading the local troop of Boy Scouts. With the help of friend Phil Stone, Faulkner did secure a contract with the Four Seas Company to publish a book of poetry, *The Marble Faun*, in 1924, but that same year the post office dismissed Faulkner because of charges of negligence brought by the postal inspector, and the Boy Scouts discharged him for "moral reasons," presumably related to alcohol. A failure by the standards of most Oxford citizens, Faulkner fortuitously left town for New Orleans with plans to sail for Europe in 1925. In New Orleans, Faulkner befriended Sherwood Anderson, a fellow modernist, who gave Faulkner entrée into the town's literary milieu and later changed the course of Faulkner's career by suggesting that Faulkner write about the material he knew best, the people of Oxford. During this period, Faulkner turned from poetry to fiction. He also began to write for the New Orleans *Times-Picayune*, and, after Faulkner returned from Europe, Boni and Liveright published his first two novels. *Soldiers' Pay* (1926) is a novel born of Faulkner's war experience, and *Mosquitoes* (1927) draws from his experience with the New Orleans literary scene. In his third novel, Faulkner took Anderson's advice and began writing tales of his apocryphal town of Jefferson, fictionally located in Yoknapatawpha County, Mississippi. Jefferson is a thinly veiled version of Faulkner's hometown, Oxford, located in Lafayette County. Faulkner said that in writing *Sartoris* he realized "my own little postage stamp of native soil was worth writing about and that I would never live long enough to exhaust it, and by sublimating the actual into apocryphal I would have complete liberty to use whatever talent I might have to its absolute top" (*Lion in the Garden* 255).

In 1929, Faulkner returned to Oxford and married his childhood sweetheart, Estelle, after she divorced Cornell Franklin. Faulkner, Estelle, and her children from the previous marriage (Malcolm and Victoria) lived in Oxford, and Faulkner continued to take jobs and write profitable short stories that allowed him time to work on his long (and still unprofitable) fiction. With a family to provide for, money became Faulkner's primary concern, especially given his 1930 purchase of the dilapidated antebellum home that he later christened Rowan Oak. Moreover, the Faulkners attempted to begin a family of their own, but the couple's first child, Alabama, died shortly after her premature birth in January of 1931. Nevertheless, these years proved extraordinarily productive as Faulkner quickly published four volumes, including the Compson family saga titled *The Sound and the Fury* in 1929, the story of the Bundren family's tragicomic attempt to bury the family matriarch in *As I Lay Dying* in 1930, and the scandalous tale of violent crime and bootlegging in *Sanctuary* in 1931. Faulkner also published a collection of short stories, *These Thirteen*, in 1931, but his bills continued to outpace the proceeds of his literary production, so in 1932, he went to Hollywood to write for Metro-Goldwyn-Mayer (MGM).

During his several stints in Hollywood, Faulkner received on-screen credit for six screenplays, one of which, *Today We Live*, was based on his own short story "Turnabout." Although the work took time away from what Faulkner thought of as his serious work, the early years in Hollywood were extremely productive. Faulkner published his first novel dealing directly with race, *Light in August*, in 1932; his last volume of poetry, *A Green Bough*, in 1933; another collection of short stories, *Doctor Martino, and Other Stories*, in 1934; an aviation novel set primarily in New Orleans, *Pylon*, in 1935; and the novel that many critics consider his best, *Absalom, Absalom!*, in 1936. His personal life also changed significantly during these years. In June of 1933, Estelle gave birth to Faulkner's only surviving child, his daughter, Jill. Faulkner's familial financial obligations expanded again in 1936 when his brother Dean died in a plane crash. Faulkner took on the role of surrogate father to his niece, also named Dean. Faulkner's life also changed dramatically outside the realm of family during this period. In December of 1934, he met Howard Hawks's secretary, Meta Dougherty Carpenter, a young divorcée from Mississippi. Faulkner soon began the first of his several affairs with younger women when he became involved with Carpenter, and he also struggled with alcohol abuse during these stressful years. In January of 1936, he first checked in to Wright's Sanatorium, a nursing facility in Byhalia, Mississippi, and it proved to be the first of many stays required to recover from alcoholic binges.

With the publication of *The Unvanquished*, a volume that contained many of Faulkner's stories about Bayard Sartoris reworked into novel form, and MGM's subsequent purchase of the screen rights, Faulkner finally secured much-needed revenue in 1938. The profits bought him time to write exclusively, and the next year, Faulkner published one of his most unusual works, *The Wild Palms* (later reissued with Faulkner's original title, *If I Forget Thee, Jerusalem*). The book interweaves two distinctly separate narratives in "The Wild Palms" and "Old Man" sections of the text. In *Faulkner in the University* (1959), Faulkner says that he wrote "Old Man" as a thematic "counterpoint" to "The Wild Palms" (171). The first installment of the Snopes trilogy, *The Hamlet*, appeared in 1940, and in 1942, Faulkner published *Go Down, Moses, and Other Stories* (later versions dropped the phrase "and Other Stories" at Faulkner's insistence that the book was a novel). Faulkner dedicated *Go Down, Moses*, his second major exploration of race, to his former caretaker, Caroline Barr, who died in 1940. Deeply in debt by July of 1942, Faulkner headed back to Hollywood in hopes of becoming solvent.

In 1946, Viking Press published *The Portable Faulkner*, a representative collection of Faulkner's work, and Faulkner soon became more than merely solvent. Often credited with rescuing Faulkner's dwindling reputation, Malcolm Cowley, the volume's editor, helped bring the significant attention Faulkner already enjoyed abroad to bear in the author's home country. Financial stability followed critical recognition when, two years later, Faulkner published *Intruder in the Dust*, a coming-of-age mystery that features Chick Mallison's growing racial awareness via his relationship with Lucas Beauchamp. MGM quickly purchased the movie rights for $50,000, and Faulkner finally achieved some measure of financial independence. Faulkner followed *Intruder in the Dust* with a collection of mystery stories, *Knight's Gambit*, in 1949, and in 1950, the *Collected Stories of William Faulkner* appeared. The pinnacle of this period of success came later that same year when he received the Nobel Prize in Literature.

After winning the Nobel Prize, Faulkner turned his attention to different venues. He went to New York to work on a stage version of *Requiem for a Nun* in 1951, and Random House published the novel that same year. Most significantly, though, the notoriously reclusive Faulkner embarked on a startlingly public period of political activity during this period, lecturing about race relations and civil rights at home and abroad as an ambassador for the State Department. In keeping with this political mind-set, in 1954, Faulkner finally published the book he had worked on for years, *A Fable*. Set during Easter week of 1918, the overtly political novel depicts a mutiny of sorts that results when a corporal in the French army and twelve of his men organize a cease-fire by persuading soldiers on both sides of the conflict to simply lay down their guns. The novel later won both a National Book Award and a Pulitzer Prize.

Although the early 1950s brought acclaim and an unprecedented measure of literary success, they were not happy years for Faulkner. He and Estelle both drank heavily, and Faulkner pursued additional affairs with younger women, including Jean Stein and Joan Williams. However, Faulkner entered into seemingly the most satisfying years of his life during the second half of this decade. A series of events were key to his peace: in 1954, his daughter, Jill, married Paul D. Summers Jr. and moved to Charlottesville, Virginia. Jill soon gave birth to

Faulkner's grandson, Paul D. Summers III, in 1956 (and two more sons in 1958 and 1961), and Faulkner took a position as writer-in-residence at the University of Virginia, in part to be closer to his daughter and her growing family. During the next two years Faulkner would appear before classes to talk about his fiction and various other topics. The record of these meetings, published as *Faulkner in the University*, shows that the classroom suited Faulkner. He settled into a routine of speaking and writing, and these years saw the publication of a volume of hunting stories, *Big Woods* (1955), and the second and third volumes of the Snopes trilogy, *The Town* (1957) and *The Mansion* (1959). Faulkner's planned move to Virginia, interrupted only by his death, is a testament to the happiness that he found there. That sentiment even permeated Faulkner's final work of fiction; *The Reivers* (1962), published only a month before Faulkner's death, is a remarkably hopeful coming-of-age story that features Lucius Priest's "reiving" or "stealing" of knowledge beyond his years. The novel won Faulkner's second (posthumous) Pulitzer Prize.

In Virginia, Faulkner fueled his lifelong passion for horses by joining the Farmington Hunt Club, and in Mississippi, he continued to ride and train his own horses until just before his death. In January of 1962, he was thrown from a horse and never fully recovered from the injuries he sustained. He was thrown again on June 17 and drank increasingly as the pain worsened. Faulkner returned to Wright's Sanatorium on July 5 and suffered a massive heart attack at 1:30 a.m. on July 6. He was buried in St. Peter's Cemetery in Oxford the next day. Today, a sign on the street marking the easiest access to Faulkner's grave reads, "William Faulkner, The creator of Yoknapatawpha County." As Faulkner always insisted that the work was more important than the artist, he would have found the deceptively simple title quite fitting.

Works Cited

Blotner, *Joseph. Faulkner: A Biography*. 2 vols. New York: Random, 1974. Print.
Duclos, Donald Philip. *Son of Sorrow: The Life, Works, and Influence of Colonel William C. Falkner, 1825-1889*. San Francisco: International Scholars, 1998. Print.

Faulkner, William. *Faulkner in the University: Class Conferences at the University of Virginia, 1957-1958*. Ed. Frederick L. Gwynn and Joseph L. Blotner. Charlottesville: U of Virginia P, 1959.

___. *Lion in the Garden: Interviews with William Faulkner, 1926-1962*. Ed. James B. Meriwether and Michael Millgate. New York: Random, 1968. Print.

Hamblin, Robert W., and Charles A. Peek, eds. *A William Faulkner Encyclopedia*. Westport, CT: Greenwood, 1999. Print.

Padgett, John B. "William Faulkner Chronology." *William Faulkner on the Web*. William Faulkner on the Web, University of Mississippi, 17 Aug. 2006. Web. 25 January 2013.

CRITICAL
CONTEXTS

"The Past Is Never Dead": Faulkner's Relationship to Southern Culture and History_____

Karen M. Andrews

"There is no such thing really as was because the past is."
—*Faulkner in the University*, 84

Decades after his death, William Faulkner, one of the greatest American writers, deserves a reappraisal of his work and his relevance to contemporary readers and scholars. Faulkner is a southern writer who told particular tales about the South, which are also stories about the United States. Faulkner's fiction stages the conflicts of his era—between different castes, classes, and races and between different genders and sexual mores. While rooted in a particular place, Faulkner's fiction sheds light on the historical dimensions of human conflicts, prejudices, and divisions that speak to readers across regional and national boundaries. The struggles, grief, despair, resiliency, and aspirations of the people in Faulkner's South resonate with readers globally.

Faulkner's fiction creatively engages the voices of his particular culture to tell a bigger story. Faulkner is relevant to modern readers because his writing challenges the myths of self-sufficiency, of independent, individual identities severed from the past. Faulkner's characters are represented as communal, connected to others, the past, and a larger story.[1] Faulkner shows how individual lives are ultimately connected to both the web of history and other lives. At the same time, Faulkner's characters often experience various forms of alienation and conflict in relation to their families, communities, and these repetitive stories. For example, in *Absalom, Absalom!* (1936), Quentin Compson thinks to himself, as his Harvard roommate Shreve joins in the telling of the story about Sutpen and the South, "I am listening to it all over again I shall have to never listen to anything but this again forever so apparently not only a man never outlives his father but not even his friends and acquaintances do" (277).

Modern readers share many of the same tensions and conflicts to which Faulkner gives voice in his writing. They continue to wrestle with the legacy of white privilege and patriarchy and sexual double standards. Americans still deal with the painful legacy of racial slavery. Moreover, despite the 150 years since the Emancipation Proclamation and the end of legalized slavery, modern society is still confronted with the tragic reality of the human trafficking of men, women, and children.[2]

As much as people would like to pretend that they live in a postracial society,[3] and as much as they would like to believe that slavery—human trafficking—is part of history only and that sexism, gender violence, rapaciousness, economic exploitation, and imperialism are also things of the past, people continue to wrestle with these threatening realities. Faulkner's treatment of these "pasts" that are still "present" may help readers better recognize ways in which the land and fellow human lives are still vulnerable to exploitation, commodification, and defilement.

A significant cultural and historical thread in the tapestry of Faulkner's cultural context is the dominating concept of "the color line." W. E. B. Du Bois claimed that the problem of the twentieth century was the problem of the color line.[4] Later, after visiting the Warsaw ghetto, Du Bois expanded his definition of the color line to include other exclusionary practices: the color line "was a matter of cultural patterns, perverted teaching and human hate and prejudice, which reached all sorts of people and caused endless evil to all men."[5] Faulkner's works matter because society still wrestles with the reality of "the color line."[6]

Critics have long commented on Faulkner's ambivalence, the ways in which his texts communicate mixed messages about southern culture, particularly about race relations, the color line, female sexuality, and both the literal and figurative kinship between blacks and whites.[7] Ralph Ellison acknowledged that Faulkner's attitude is "mixed," that his narratives often encode racist ideology, or what Ellison termed

Faulkner's "personal vision of southern myth" even as he "fights out the moral problem" of the socially divisive color line (Ellison).

Indeed, Faulkner scholars and readers have wrestled with where Faulkner stands on modern expressions of gender and sexuality, and especially what his stance is on the race issues of his day. Readers have particularly struggled with the oftentimes gratuitous use of the "N-word" and other blatantly racist and derogatory discourse.[8] Most critics are cautious about applying labels to Faulkner as they acknowledge his complexity as a writer and his troubled relationships with his fellow southerners and his region's history.[9] Even New Critics—who were known for exclusively focusing on the text and not engaging historical or cultural contexts in their close readings—needed to find ways to talk about Faulkner's relationship to southern culture. For example, Cleanth Brooks, the preeminent New Critic, could not resist implicitly evaluating the relationship between Faulkner's texts and the cultural context, by acknowledging, however unwittingly, Faulkner's ambivalence in places: Brooks said that Faulkner's stance "is a mixture of deep affection and furious disapproval, of abiding loyalties and sharp specific disagreements" (370).[10]

Faulkner's fictional world of Yoknapatawpha draws upon his experiences of the South, and at the same time is distinctly his own mythical world, his "apocrypha."[11] Readers may question what Faulkner's fictional world reveals about how he envisions the relationship between the actual—or historical—and the fictional. His version of the South's flaws and the human conflicts he reflects in his fiction are his "reading" of not only his particular location, his little "postage stamp of native soil," but also of the larger myths of American culture, including the American Dream.[12]

The literary theorist Mikhail Bakhtin offers valuable interpretive tools and vocabulary for describing Faulkner's relationship to his cultural context. Bakhtin's concept of "multivocality" (heteroglossia) applies to Faulkner's richly textured novels, which include layers of different voices that are related to multiple perspectives from his social world. Bakhtin contends that the "real" and "represented" worlds are "indissolubly tied up with each other and find themselves in continual mutual interaction" (*Dialogic Imagination* 254). Novelistic discourse is social, and the relations between the author, the narrative, and the socioideological context are "dialogic" (426). In other words, novels participate in the social discourse of the author's world, and they register many of the tensions and conflicts of the social world. Thus, Faulkner's novels stage the conflicts that erupt when these different voices and competing ways of life bump up against each other. Bakhtin's theory of dialogic discourse helps readers glimpse how Faulkner's fiction serves as "a record of the novelist's era—in particular, the tensions, conflicts, and struggles that divided (and sometimes united) that era's various social groups" (Hannon 2).

In his fiction, Faulkner included voices from his culture that he did not always agree with or particularly like.[13] Because of the "dialogized nature" of novelistic discourse, even when Faulkner's fiction includes misogynistic perspectives or white caste propaganda, Faulkner also included other voices from his culture—not entirely suppressed—that contradict or indict the dominant point of view (Hannon 8). Faulkner's words are borrowed from the cultural discourses available to him, while at the same time he is creatively transforming these "borrowings" in his fiction.

Although readers may find a variety of voices in Faulkner's fiction, readers must also ask which voices are privileged, which are marginalized, and which are silenced. In other words, readers may query both the text and the appropriate social contexts to explore how Faulkner's narratives enter into conversation with the dominant ideologies and practices of his cultural context. Readers may also ask how, or in what ways, his fiction critiques the conflicts and tensions of his era, and how his fiction seems to reinforce these dominant ideologies and practices. Edouard Glissant has argued that Faulkner challenged "the supreme institution of this southern community," questioning "its very legitimacy" (21). Faulkner's fiction raises the question of the source of the

South's malediction: Could this "primordial sin" be "the South's dark entanglement with slavery, inextricable from its roots and its tormented history?" (22).

A defining feature of Faulkner's region of northern Mississippi, and of the entire Deep South, was that it was steeped in the past—in both romantic legends and painful humiliations. The dominant white caste had the shared experience of losing a war, losing power, and becoming economically dependent on the North. The Jim Crow laws and exclusionary practices enforcing the "color line" were the white caste's attempt to regain the control and power that they had previously held during the antebellum slavery era.

The "myth" of the Old South, and the New South's romanticized version of the Old South's slaveholding days, was that slavery "was paternalistic and marvelously good for its time," and that "the Confederacy, Robert E. Lee, and even common soldiers acting intuitively . . . had stood for such ideals as freedom, honor, duty, courage, and loyalty." Faulkner's biographers, Joel Williamson among them, point out that this idealization of the past was standard fare in Oxford's public schools and in Faulkner's social life growing up in northern Mississippi. Thus, readers must ask crucial questions as they explore Faulkner's relationship to his southern culture and wider cultural influences: What is Faulkner's view of the South's preoccupation with the past, with the legacy and the shame of slavery? In what ways does Faulkner's fiction engage the conflicts of the South's past, the South's preoccupation with the past, and his own family's past? In what ways does Faulkner's fiction critique that past? How does Faulkner's fiction contribute to the desire of the white South to keep blacks in their subjugated "place," and to romanticize white paternalism? To what extent did Faulkner's narratives participate in the romanticization of the antebellum and Civil War South, and/or of the more recent past? In what ways does Faulkner critique the past, historiography, and nostalgia? What is the significance of Faulkner imagining the past as 'is' not as 'was'? Is the past fixed, separate, and frozen in time, or is it fluid, continuous with now, continually being revised, and refashioned for the present moment? Faulkner argued for fluidity, and modern and postmodern readers would agree with him that there is a connection with the past because "then" is still interacting with "now."[14]

What do readers need to know about racial slavery and the South in order to understand Faulkner, especially his staging of conflicts and raising of questions about the meaning of the "color line"? Miscegenation is a motif in Faulkner's fiction that illustrates these tensions around maintaining the color line. Faulkner was aware of the "shadow" families—the black children and siblings—of many prominent southern families. Perhaps he was aware of his own ancestor's unacknowledged family?[15]

Southerners felt the need for strong boundaries between the slave and the free person. The racially mixed child, dwelling in the land "in-between," blurred these boundaries, which was not tolerable in a rigidly divided culture. There was much tension and anxiety over the blurring of boundaries. As Williamson has said, "Where slavery was strongest and getting stronger, it was also becoming whiter" (*New People* 58). Another way to look at it is that whites were "enslaving themselves" through having mixed children, and children of mixed unions took their mother's status.[16]

One significant example of how Faulkner creatively used the materials of his historical and cultural context, and how they are related to the color line, has emerged since the 2010 discovery of the diary of Francis Terry Leak, written in the mid-1800s. Faulkner read the diary several times and "was always taking copious notes" when visiting his friend's homestead in Holly Springs, Mississippi.[17] This original manuscript appears to have been the model for the old ledger in the pivotal scene in "The Bear" in *Go Down, Moses* (1942) when Ike McCaslin discovers the dark secrets of his family's slave-owning past: his grandfather McCaslin's miscegenation and incest.[18]

Not only was the diary a source for that climactic scene with the farm ledger in *Go Down, Moses*, but also Faulkner used many of the slave names listed in the diary in his fictional Yoknapatawpha County. Significantly, many of these black slave names became names of white fictional characters, which perhaps was a subversive ploy on Faulkner's part, crossing the color line with his characters. Additionally, the homestead in Holly Springs that Faulkner frequently visited featured a girl's name etched on a glass windowpane during the Civil War, a scene that occurs in some of Faulkner's works. What does this discovery say about Faulkner's relationship to the past, the meaning and significance of history? Readers can imagine Faulkner listening to the voices of his culture, paying attention, actively researching, borrowing, collaborating, and re-creating historical narratives in his fiction.

Faulkner's contemporary southern culture was shaped by the color line. Social etiquette and cultural mores were dictated by the system of white patriarchy. Readers need to understand the pervasiveness of the system of racial segregation and how the rigid caste system under "Jim Crow" was enforced in order to interpret some of the more perplexing depictions of race, and relationships, across the color line in Faulkner's fiction. Faulkner's lifetime encompasses most of the Jim Crow era (1890–1940) and also includes the beginning of the civil rights movement. The years of Faulkner's life (1897–1961) roughly coincide with the "critical period of disfranchisement, segregation, and exclusion" in the lives of black Mississippians—that is, the Jim Crow era (McMillen xiii). These years were repressive for blacks in the South, especially in Mississippi, which had the worst reputation regarding race relations in the late nineteenth and early twentieth century. Indeed, Mississippi ranked first among the states in "lynch-law."[19]

The Jim Crow regime is the most significant context for the majority of Faulkner's fiction. The introduction of the word "miscegenation" accompanied the abolition of slavery, heightening white fears of interracial mixing between newly freed black men and white women. "Miscegenation" came to be associated with the ultimate violation of the color line. The term encoded the white caste's pejorative judgment toward racial mixing, and it served as a social and political weapon to "conjure a threat to the continuation of white supremacy" (Edelstein 178). The white caste's obsession with racial "purity" was about maintaining power and white privilege. The central irony of this furor over black men crossing the color line and secretly or openly infiltrating the white "family" is that miscegenation was minimal after 1865; nevertheless, the white caste became ever more vigilant and violent toward any perceived infractions.[20]

The hierarchical caste system regulated the behavior of women and men of both "races"; and in this system, blacks generally had to acquiesce to white rule. John Dollard purported that the main function of "caste" is regulating "legitimate descent": "A union of members of the two castes may not have a legitimate child" because intermarriages between the castes implies social equality (Dollard 62). In 1920, Mississippi actually "outlawed advocacy of social equality" (McMillen 8). The caste system also regulated sexual relations outside of marriage and this domain had a definite gender bias: the sexual double standard.

The prevalence of lynching and corresponding "rape complex" was evidenced in Faulkner's own community. A prominent lynching, the Nelse Patton incident, occurred in September 1908, when Faulkner was a youth, and the local newspaper claimed that "the murder of a white woman had been avenged—the public had done their duty."[21] US senator W. V. Sullivan gave a fiery speech to work up the mob and boasted afterward: "'Cut a white woman's throat? And a negro? Of course I wanted him lynched. . . . I wouldn't mind standing the consequences any time for lynching a man who cut a white woman's throat'" (qtd. in Cullen 97–98). This rhetoric recalls similar justifications for lynching and disregard for the Constitution, especially in honor of a "white woman," and Faulkner employs similar rhetoric in both "Dry September," with white supremacist John McLendon, and in *Light in August* (1932), with the crowd's responses to the castration and lynching of Joe Christmas.

In Faulkner's early adult life, the May 1917 lynching of Eell C. Persons was advertised in many newspapers as a social event, "an execution probably without parallel in the history of the South," as he was burned at the stake (Blotner 189). Biographer Joseph Blotner indicates that there were at least three more lynchings in Mississippi. World War I brought about more tension and more savage and sadistic lynchings. Public burnings and castration became part of the lynching spectacle, especially if the man was a rape suspect. As a symbol, castration declared "that the evil was abolished permanently from the earth" and that white men were the "masters" (Williamson, *Crucible* 309). What all these lynchings have in common is the alleged transgression against a white woman by a black man. Whites who spoke out against lynching were accused of encouraging black male rape of white women, much as McLendon questions Hawkshaw's race loyalty and gender identity in "Dry September." Likewise, questioning racial segregation was inevitably linked with advocating social equality, which was equated with taboo miscegenation.

White male dominance and the prohibition of miscegenation, particularly interracial marriage, mutually reinforced each other and together composed the prevailing worldview of white southerners in Faulkner's era. Thus, Faulkner's fiction includes voices that justify segregation to hold onto power and the supremacy of the white caste. At the same time, his fiction exposes the ways in which the taboo against miscegenation camouflaged socioeconomic and gender issues. Faulkner wrote his fiction in dialogue within the historical and cultural context of racism. Faulkner's multivocal narratives, while including some of the rabidly racist voices of his culture, critique the white caste's racism and the working of white supremacist ideology on all relationships.

The miscegenation motif comes up in many of Faulkner's narratives. Faulkner's depiction of this subject shows how it connects to many other troubling tensions in his culture. Faulkner's South is a place that is averse to mixtures—what Glissant refers to as "creolization."[22]

Williamson maintains that "Southern culture is deeply purist and intolerant of mixtures . . . racial, sexual, or moral" (*Crucible* 497).

The sexual dimension of racism, emblematized by miscegenation and "its consequences,"[23] is woven throughout much of Faulkner's fiction, including the short stories "Peter," "Evangeline," "Yo Ho and Two Bottles of Rum," "Red Leaves," "Dry September," "That Evening Sun," "A Justice," "Mountain Victory," "There Was a Queen," and "Elly." It also appears in the novels *Sartoris/Flags in the Dust* (1929/1973); *Light in August*; *Absalom, Absalom!*; *Go Down, Moses*; and *Intruder in the Dust* (1948).

Intruder in the Dust includes no actual or rumored miscegenation; rather, Lucas Beauchamp is a mixed-race character, the result of his white ancestor L. Q. C. McCaslin's "crossing the color line" with a black female slave who was actually his daughter, Tomey. Lucas's "mulatto" status contributes to the plot; most of the whites resent his mixed-race identity, his claimed connection to his white ancestor McCaslin, and the fact that he does not fulfill the town's expectations to "act like a nigger."[24] Philip Weinstein sees Faulkner's last race-focused novel as "paternalistic," given "the novel's strategy for liberating Lucas": he is "saved" by white people cooperating to help him.[25] Faulkner's last novel, *The Reivers* (1962), alludes to miscegenation through two characters: Boon Hogganbeck, the part-Chickasaw, part-white central character in this comedy.[26] Interestingly, Boon ends up marrying a white woman, Everbe Corinthia (Miss Corrie), and they have a baby together at the conclusion of the novel. Everbe reforms her ways after years of working as a prostitute in a Memphis brothel; because of her marginal status she is perhaps not worthy of the white community's protection. The other significant mixed-race character in *The Reivers* is the coachman of "Boss" Lucius Priest, Ned McCaslin (called "Uncle Ned"), who proudly claims his kinship to his white grandfather, old Lucius Quintus Carothers McCaslin.

Sexual relations and the politics of gender are embedded within the South's dominant culture of racism. Some of the more radically racist theories and popular views of the mid- to late nineteenth century were waning by the 1920s, although many of these views remained popular among defenders of Jim Crow. The white caste's obsessive focus on maintaining the color line and concern over the perceived threat posed by black man–white woman miscegenation, the "taboo" form of crossing the color line, masked the obverse reality of "tolerated" miscegenation, which James Baldwin cleverly exposed in a televised debate with a white male southerner: "You're not worried about me marrying your daughter. . . . You're worried about me marrying your wife's daughter. I've been marrying your daughter ever since the days of slavery" (qtd. in Genovese 414)

Race, class, gender, and sexuality are interconnected in Faulkner's South. They influence and contribute to the South's "miscegenation complex"—the white caste's real or imagined fears of the taboo, and the conspiracy of silence about the tolerated, exploitative form of crossing the color line. The South's fear of the miscegenation "taboo"—the perceived threat of interracial sexual relationships—is linked to the dominant caste's desire to control white privilege and power, especially white patriarchy's desire to hold on to its threatened place of privilege by keeping everyone else in their socially defined "place." Thus, references to "miscegenation"—in Faulkner's social geography and in his fiction—become a nexus, a complex site where many streams of Faulkner's segregated culture come together.

Considering how Faulkner's fiction engages the South's obsession with history and stages the conflicts surrounding interracial relationships, Clytie Sutpen in *Absalom, Absalom!* embodies the Old South's paradox: she is the biracial (mulatto) slave-daughter of her master-father. Despite the official view that the races were not to mix, white men repeatedly crossed the color line to have sex with black slave women. In the chronology appended at the end of *Absalom, Absalom!*, Sutpen appears in Yoknapatawpha County in 1833, where he "takes up land, builds his house." In 1834, Clytemnestra (Clytie) was "born to a slave woman." In 1838, "Sutpen married Ellen Coldfield" (*Absalom,*

Absalom! 473). Sutpen's relationship with Clytie's mother apparently avoids the stigma of adultery, as Clytie was born four years before Sutpen married the white Ellen and seven years before Sutpen's first legitimate white child was born.

Although Sutpen is not identified as Clytie's father in *Absalom, Absalom!*'s chronology, Sutpen's paternity is clearly acknowledged in the genealogy: "CLYTEMNESTRA SUTPEN. Daughter of Thomas Sutpen and a negro slave. Born Sutpen's Hundred, 1834. Died Sutpen's Hundred, 1909" (*Absalom, Absalom!* 476). Clytie is granted the patronym, the recognition that she was sired by the white master. However, in the different narratives, Thomas Sutpen never openly acknowledges Clytie as his daughter. For instance, Rosa recalls when Sutpen returned home from the war, he greeted his white daughter Judith by physically acknowledging her, "Well daughter" (198). Sutpen then looked at Clytie, still standing with his hands on Judith's shoulders, as if indicating her privileged status, and merely said, "Ah, Clytie" (199). While his recognition of his mulatto daughter resembles that of master to slave or faithful servant, Sutpen here grants her more acknowledgment than he ever gives to his firstborn and abandoned son, Charles Bon. Clytie is permitted to live with her white family, ostensibly as domestic servant, because she observes the importance of place, and the other racial distinctions of the era.[27]

While Clytie is identified many times as a mulatto, her status as a member of Sutpen's family often is elided in Rosa's and Quentin's versions of Sutpen's story. For example, while narrating the Sutpen saga to (and with) his Harvard roommate Shreve, Quentin catches himself overlooking Clytie's status as a Sutpen: "[Sutpen] was all settled, with a wife and two children—no, three—" (323). At other times he refers to just the "two children" (326): "Yes, the two children, the son and the daughter by sex and age so glib to the design that he might have planned that too" (327). Quentin's narrative omission erases Clytie's family relationship to her half siblings Judith and Henry and to her father, Thomas Sutpen.

Rosa Coldfield's narrative includes the legend of Sutpen arriving with his Haitian "wild negros," whom she refers to as a "herd of wild beasts that he had hunted down single handedly" (14). Mr. Compson, who many times preempts Rosa's narrative, tells Quentin what Rosa neglected to tell him, that two of the twenty-odd slaves "in the wagon that day were women" (73). According to Compson, Sutpen "brought those two women deliberately; he probably chose them with the same care and shrewdness with which he chose the other livestock" (73). The ratio of male slaves to female slaves seems to support Compson's judgment. Compson's rendering of Sutpen's careful choice—due to neither "chance or oversight"—suggests that in addition to breeding slaves to increase property, miscegenation between white male slave owners and black female slaves was implicitly part of the white slave-holding South's design.

Rather than implying that Sutpen had two children only, Quentin may be commenting on the two children who were "necessary" to Sutpen's plan of establishing a legitimate dynasty. Even so, Clytie may be seen as playing a significant role in Sutpen's design. The "tolerated" miscegenational relationship she represents is built into the same design that privileges white males of the landowning class and mythologizes white females of that same class. That is, the connection between the interracial union she represents and the patrilineal design that requires chastity of white women is not openly acknowledged by the narrators. Clytie's identity as a domestic servant is always acknowledged, but the narrators' erasure of Clytie's status as sister and daughter suggests that Clytie's presence potentially threatens the status quo. Clytie's identity as Sutpen daughter and sibling, if openly acknowledged, would threaten the racial hierarchy and the South's obsession with "purity" and resistance to mixtures. The Clytie narrative sheds light on the white South's conditional acceptance of white man–black woman miscegenation. Historically, these interracial relationships were tolerated as long as they were not openly acknowledged, as long as the offspring remained "illegitimate" and were excluded from the privileges of the white family. Clytie's story in *Absalom, Absalom!* points to the asymmetries of power and the contradictions of the double standard.

What Faulkner does not include in *Absalom, Absalom!* is the perspective of Clytie's slave mother. She remains a nameless and unvoiced absence, made visible only through Clytie's "coffee-colored" skin. In Faulkner's fiction, readers primarily hear stories from the white side of the family. In other Faulkner texts, the black family's point of view is sometimes represented by the black woman's partner or husband. For example, in Faulkner's earlier story, "A Justice," in which an American Indian man violates the wife of a black male slave, the black husband's plight is sympathetically portrayed as he tries to fight for the sexual integrity of his marriage. In "The Fire and the Hearth" in *Go Down, Moses*, which takes place after emancipation, the racially mixed Lucas Beauchamp confronts white Zack Edmonds, who has taken his wife Molly into his home, presumably to nurse his baby after his white wife has died. Faulkner gives voice to Lucas's dilemma: How to God . . . can a black man ask a white man to please not lay down with his black wife? And even if he could ask it, how to God can the white man promise he wont? (*Go Down, Moses* 59)

Alternatively, Faulkner offers a glimpse of the black woman's perspective regarding the role of white power and miscegenation in his story, "That Evening Sun." The story is set during Faulkner's contemporary Jim Crow era, and Nancy, who is not given a last name, is the Compson family's washerwoman, who also does their cooking when Dilsey is ill. Nancy, who has resorted to prostitution during difficult economic times, publicly demands her pay from the white man, Mr. Stovall, "the cashier in the bank and a deacon in the Baptist church" (*Collected Stories* 291). Her accusing question, "'When you going to pay me, white man? It's been three times now since you paid me a cent'" elicits a violent response. After knocking her down, Stovall attempts to silence Nancy by kicking her in the mouth (ibid. 291).[28]

In *Go Down, Moses*, especially in part four of "The Bear," Faulkner offers another glimpse into these silenced and virtually erased members of the southern "family." Ike McCaslin's eye-opening discovery of the ledgers in the old commissary invites him to imagine what is not said directly: incest and miscegenation were part of the institution of slavery and existed within his own family. Reading between the lines, Ike as a child brings the mother and daughter back into the story, if only briefly, and exposes the white patriarch L. Q. C. McCaslin's transgressions against his black former concubine and their mulatto daughter (254–315). However, Ike's imagination is limited, as revealed in an alternative take on miscegenation in another story in *Go Down, Moses*, "Delta Autumn." When an elderly Ike McCaslin discovers that Roth Edmonds's white-looking mistress, who has been abandoned by Roth after bearing his child, is part black, he tells her to "go back North" and marry a man of her own "kind" (363). The unnamed woman then "blazed silently down at" the aging Isaac in his "huddle of blankets" in the woods. Faulkner depicts her with dignity as she reproaches Ike: "'Old man . . . have you lived so long and forgotten so much that you dont remember anything you ever knew or felt or even heard about love?'" (363).

On one hand, to old Isaac everything about this woman's relationship with Roth Edmonds seems to replicate the heritage of incest and miscegenation that he believed he had repudiated by not marrying and giving up his inheritance. She is the granddaughter of Tennie's Jim, who is a grandson of Tomasina, or "Tomey"—the daughter of the slave Eunice and the white progenitor, L. Q. C. McCaslin, who committed incest with his mulatto daughter Tomey. Consequently, Roth's mistress is also distantly related to him, as well as to Ike, through their shared ancestor Old Carothers. Roth's mistress, however, is not a replication of the slave women of the past. Although Roth has mistreated and abandoned her, she is a free woman, neither a slave nor a concubine against her will. Moreover, she initiates this conversation; she seeks out and confronts Ike, and she rejects Roth's guilt money. She suggests the possibility of mutuality, that two people may love each other across socially constructed boundaries of ethnicity and race. While her relationship with Roth hints at an alternative interracial romantic relationship, their union ultimately is asymmetrical, given the patriarchal, racist society and Roth's belief that he could buy his own freedom and relieve his guilt by "paying" her off. Even so, her voiced question about "love" remains in the narrative discourse, as does Joe Christmas's haunting question in *Light in August*: "Just when do men that have different blood in them stop hating one another?" (274).

Faulkner was writing at a crucial juncture of the South's ending of the "old order" and the beginning of the new. Faulkner's complex relationship to the cultural discourse of the "color line" points to the ongoing presence of the past in the "modern" South. There are many cultural and historical contexts of Faulkner's work that could be explored in addition to the "color line," but this conclusion offers a brief glance at Faulkner's wider contemporary culture and contexts.

Faulkner's fiction stages the struggles of the South's transition from an agrarian, traditional society to a more urban, modern society. No discussion of Faulkner's culture would be complete without reference to the Snopes clan and their role in the New South economy. Historian C. Vann Woodward referred to the New South as "the age of the Snopeses" (qtd. in Doyle 4). According to historian Don Doyle, the New South was "a period of urban growth, railway expansion, industrial development, and new fortunes for the winners." The winners were "the industrialists, bankers, merchants, and lawyers in the towns," and the losers were "the sharecroppers"—both black and white (27). The poor yeoman "competed for land and credit" with black sharecroppers (28). In recent years, scholars have delved into the cultural context of economics and politics for Faulkner's Snopes trilogy: *The Hamlet* (1940), *The Town* (1957), and *The Mansion* (1957).[29] In addition to the Snopes novels, Faulkner's short story "Barn Burning,"[30] echoed in *The Hamlet*, registers the class resentment of white yeoman farmers.

Furthermore, Faulkner's fiction reveals ways in which the South was a "colonized culture," depicting the troubled relationship between the South and the "imperial" North.[31] As Faulkner's narratives are linked to discourses on "colonial domination," his fiction resonates with those emerging into a postcolonial modern world. Williamson has argued that Faulkner speaks to the "imperialized people of the world" by writing stories about the struggles of his own "imperialized people" (363). Readers must take note of the irony, for the South was both colonizer and colonized. Because of this dual perspective, scholars such as John T. Matthews have argued that Faulkner has both a regional and a global take on US history.[32] The newer ways of looking at Faulkner's South help readers see how Faulkner's context was not merely regional, nor only "American." From a postcolonial, global perspective, the South cannot be either completely distinct from the rest of the nation or isolated from global networks of power and privilege.[33]

Faulkner came of age as a writer during a significant point in the South's transformation; his fiction chronicles his region's upheaval as it transitions to the modern world. Faulkner played a prophetic role as a writer, challenging his fellow white southerners to acknowledge the injustices of their history—which is also part of American history. Faulkner is still relevant because his fiction cautions against the commodification of the land and of our fellow human beings.[34] His fiction compels readers to listen to the different voices of his culture and their own, paying particular attention to the voices that have been marginalized or silenced.

Notes

1. Matthews, *Seeing through the South*, 3.
2. Approximately 27–30 million people are enslaved today, which means there are more slaves now than during the transatlantic slave trade. See Batstone, *Not for Sale*; Bales, *Disposable People* and *Understanding Global Slavery*; and Bales and Soldalter, *The Slave Next Door*.
3. It is easy to think that the problem of the color line has been "solved" because there is an African American president of the United States.

4. Du Bois, *Souls of Black Folk*, 23.

5. Du Bois, on his revised definition of the color line: "In the first place, the problem of slavery, emancipation and caste in the United States was no longer in
   my mind a separate and unique thing as I had so long conceived it. It was not
   even solely a matter of color and physical and racial characteristics, which was
   particularly a hard thing for me to learn, since for a lifetime the color line had
   been a real and efficient cause of misery." (DuBois, "The Negro and the Warsaw
   Ghetto," 45–46).

6. Kennedy's *The Persistence of the Color Line: Racial Politics and the Obama
   Presidency* reminds readers that "race still matters."

7. Early critics of Faulkner, such as Irving Howe, raised the question about which
   perspectives in his fiction can or should be ascribed to the author. Other early
   readers, such as Robert Penn Warren, defended Faulkner's portrayals of blacks,
   while Maxwell Geismar claimed that Faulkner was racist and sexist because
   of his disdainful portrayals of women and blacks. Charles Peavy, in *Go Slow
   Now*, also defended Faulkner's unsavory depictions of blacks and mixed race
   characters.

8. John Jeremiah Sullivan comments on the use of "nigger" as having a "taboo
   charge" in Faulkner, as well as in other writers of his era. Sullivan argues that
   "even if we were to justify Faulkner's overindulgence of the word on the grounds
   of historical context," he still finds it "unfortunate." Sullivan believes a "writer
   of Faulkner's sensitivity to verbal shading might have been better tuned to the
   ugliness of the word, and not a truth-revealing ugliness, but something more
   like gratuitousness, with an attending queasy sense of rhetorical power misused"
   ("The 'Ulysses' of Mississippi" 47).

9. Glissant claims that "Faulkner does not shrink from the harshest cruelty in his portraits. Some of the county residents exude a bestial racism, which Faulkner suggests incidentally, apart from any formal presentation, and in such a way that one
   can never tell whether he condemns this racism or accepts and applauds it" (65).

10. Burke noted that Brooks, the author of the formalist statement "no sociology,"
    could not avoid "sociology" in his treatment of Faulkner's fiction ("Formalist
    Criticism" 503).

11. Faulkner said: "Beginning with Sartoris I discovered that my own little postage
    stamp of native soil was worth writing about and that I would never live long
    enough to exhaust it, and by sublimating the actual into apocryphal I would have
    complete liberty to use whatever talent I might have to its absolute top" (*Lion in
    the Garden* 255).

12. According to Fred Hobson, "*Absalom, Absalom!* is a 'southern' novel, but it is
    much more than that—it is, indeed, a novel about the American dream just as
    fully as *The Great Gatsby* is a novel about that dream" (6).

13. Faulkner said, "I listen to the voices, and when I put down what the voices say
    it's right. Sometimes I don't like what they say, but I don't change it" (qtd. in
    Cowley 114).

14. Duck argues that Faulkner's "novels urge us to think differently about history, which becomes in Faulkner's work not a linear progression so much as a shifting set of vortices, forces and incidents which reach across periods to transform consciousness and society" (27).

15. See Williamson, *William Faulkner and Southern History*, where he argues that Faulkner's great-grandfather, William Clark Falkner, whom Faulkner referred to as the "Old Colonel," reared a "shadow family," and most likely committed incest as well as miscegenation (45).

16. Williamson, *New People*, 63.

17. Cohen.

18. As mentioned above, Faulkner had a story like this in his own family. The past is full of ghosts who haunt the present, and one of those ghosts is the biracial brother and sister, the family on the "black side" who are not acknowledged by the white family.

19. The two peak periods of mob activity were the years between 1889–1908 and 1918–22 (McMillen 230–32)

20. Cash refers to this "miscegenation complex" as the "rape complex" (117–19).

21. Lafayette County Press, Sept. 9, 1908. See Blotner, 113–14. Also see Cullen.

22. Glissant poses this question: "Is the South a society with two intertwined cultures, one dominant and the other dominated, or a society that combines two separate and distinct cultures? . . . Is cultural interaction or 'interchange' a harbinger of intermingling, miscegenation, and finally Creolization?" (69). He answers his question thusly: "Creolization is the very thing that offends Faulkner: métissage and miscegenation plus their unforeseeable consequences" (83).

23. Antebellum diarist Mary Boykin Chestnut employed this phrase as she complained about "a hideous black harem with its consequences," referring to mulatto children of white patriarchal slaveholders and black female slaves (21–22).

24. Weinstein notes that *Intruder*'s "keen (and easily decipherable) attention to contemporary racial agitation doubtless played a part in his being awarded the Nobel Prize two years later" (188).

25. "Faulkner was too honest to propose that the larger adult white South wanted anything other than to lynch this 'uppity nigger'" (Weinstein 166).

26. Boon Hogganbeck initially was introduced in "The Bear" in *Go Down, Moses* and resurfaces in *The Reivers*.

27. For example, Clytie typically sleeps on a pallet on the floor while her half-sister Judith sleeps above her in a proper bed.

28. Mr. Compson, who hires Nancy for a more respectable service, is shown to be complicit in Nancy's abuse by the Baptist deacon. He paternalistically worries about Nancy, but he does not take her plight seriously: "And if you'd just leave white men alone. . . . If you'd behave yourself, you'd have kept out of this" (*Collected Stories* 295)

29. In particular, see Matthews's chapter, "Come Up: From Red Necks to Riches," 124–71.

30. *Collected Stories*, 1950.

31. Faulkner's fiction reflects the struggles of a "people whose land had been raped and labor taken to supply raw materials for the factories of the industrial powers" (Williamson, *William Faulkner and Southern History* 363).

32. In his article "Many Mansions: Faulkner's Cold War Conflicts" Matthews argues that Faulkner's southerners "had been both perpetrators and perceived victims of colonization, creating an internal colony of slaveholding, and then later suffering subjection to federal military reconstruction and northern capitalization" (5).

33. Scholars are seeking ever "new cultural and historical maps for contextualizing Faulkner's fiction" (Duck 25).

34. According to Matthews, "Faulkner's fiction repeatedly stages moments in which the visibly invisible demand acknowledgement" (17).

Works Cited

Bakhtin, Mikhail. *The Dialogic Imagination: Four Essays*. Trans. Caryl Emerson. Trans. and ed. Michael Holquist. Austin: U of Texas P, 1981. Print.

Bales, Kevin. *Disposable People: New Slavery in the Global Economy*. Rev. ed. Berkeley: U of California P, 2004. Print.

___. *Understanding Global Slavery: A Reader*. Berkeley: U of California P, 2005. Print.

Bales, Kevin, and Ron Soldalter. *The Slave Next Door: Human Trafficking and Slavery in America Today*. Berkeley: U of California P, 2009. Print.

Batstone, David. *Not for Sale: The Return of the Global Slave Trade—And How We Can Fight It*. Rev. ed. New York: HarperCollins, 2010. Print.

Blotner, Joseph. *Faulkner: A Biography*. 2 vols. New York: Random. 1974. Print.

Brooks, Cleanth. *William Faulkner: The Yoknapatawpha Country*. 1963. Baton Rouge: Louisiana State UP, 1990. Print.

Burke, Kenneth. "Formalist Criticism: Its Principles and Limits." *Texas Quarterly* 9 (1966): 242–68. Rpt. in *Language as Symbolic Action: Essays on Life, Literature, and Method*. Berkeley: U of California P, 1966: 480–506. Print.

Cash, W. J. *The Mind of the South*. New York: Vintage, 1941. Print.

Chestnut, Mary Boykin. *A Diary from Dixie*. Ed. Ben Ames Williams. Boston: Houghton, 1949. Print.

Cohen, Patricia. "Faulkner Link to New Diary Discovered." *New York Times* 11 Feb. 2010: C1. Print.

Cowley, Malcolm. *The Faulkner-Cowley File: Letters and Memories, 1944–62*. New York: Viking, 1966. Print.

Cullen, John B., with Floyd C. Watkins. *Old Times in the Faulkner Country*. Chapel Hill: U of North Carolina P, 1961. Print.

Dollard, John. *Caste and Class in a Southern Town*. 1937. 3rd ed. Garden City, NY: Doubleday, 1957. Print.

Doyle, Don H. "Faulkner's History: Sources and Interpretation." *Faulkner in Cultural Context: Faulkner and Yoknapatawpha, 1995*. Jackson: UP of Mississippi, 1997: 3–38. Print.

Du Bois, W. E. B. *The Souls of Black Folk*. Greenwich, CT: Fawcett, 1961. Print.

___. "The Negro and the Warsaw Ghetto." 1952. *The Social Theory of W. E. B. Du-Bois*. Ed. Phil Zuckerman. Thousand Oaks, CA: Sage, 2004. 45–46.

Duck, Leigh Anne. "From Colony to Empire: Postmodern Faulkner." *Global Faulkner: Faulkner and Yoknapatawpha, 2006*. Ed. Annette Trefzer and Ann J. Abadie. Jackson: UP of Mississippi, 2009. 24–42.

Edelstein, Tilden G. "Miscegenation." *Encyclopedia of Southern Culture*. Ed. Charles Reagan Wilson and William Ferris. Chapel Hill: U of North Carolina P. 1989: 178–79. Print.

Ellison, Ralph. "Twentieth-Century Fiction and the Black Mask of Humanity." 1953. Rpt. in *Shadow and Act*. Vintage ed. New York: Random, 1972: 24–44. Print.

Faulkner, William. *Absalom, Absalom!* 1936. Corrected text. New York: Vintage, 1987. Print.

___. *Collected Stories of William Faulkner*. New York: Random, 1950. Print.

___. *Go Down, Moses*. 1942. Rpt. New York: Random House. 1990. Print.

___. *The Hamlet*. 1940. Corrected text. New York: Random, 1991. Print.

___. *Intruder in the Dust*. 1948. Corrected text in *Faulkner: Novels 1942-1953*. New York: Lib. of America. 1994. 283–470. Print.

___. *Light in August*. 1932. New York: Random, 1990. Print.

Geismar, Maxwell. *Writers in Crisis: The American Novel, 1925-1940*. Boston: Houghton, 1942. Print.

Genovese, Eugene D. *Roll, Jordan, Roll: The World the Slaves Made*. 1972. New York: Vintage, 1976. Print.

Glissant, Edouard. *Faulkner, Mississippi*. 1996. Trans. Barbara B. Lewis and Thomas C. Spear. New York: Farrar, 1999. Print.

Gwynne, Frederick L., and Joseph L. Blotner. *Faulkner in the University*. 1959. Charlotsville: U of Virginia P, 1995. Print.

Hannon, Charles. *Faulkner and the Discourses of Culture*. Baton Rouge: Louisiana State UP, 2005. Print.

Hobson, Fred. "Introduction." *William Faulkner's* Absalom, Absalom! *A Casebook*. New York: Oxford UP, 2003. 3–16. Print.

Howe, Irving. *William Faulkner: A Critical Study*. 1951. 3rd rev. ed. Chicago: U of Chicago P. 1975. Print.

Jordan, Winthrop D. *White over Black: American Attitudes toward the Negro, 1550-1812*. Chapel Hill: U of North Carolina P, 1968. Print.

Kennedy, Randall. *The Persistence of the Color Line: Racial Politics and the Obama Presidency*. Pantheon Books, 2011. Print.

Matthews, John T. "Many Mansions: Faulkner's Cold War Conflicts." *Global Faulkner: Faulkner and Yoknapatawpha, 2006*. Ed. Annette Trefzer and Ann J. Abadie. Jackson: UP of Mississippi, 2009: 3–23.

___. William Faulkner: *Seeing through the South*. Paperback ed. Wiley-Blackwell, 2012.

McMillen, Neil R. *Dark Journey: Black Mississippians in the Age of Jim Crow*. Urbana: U of Illinois P, 1989. Print.

Meriwether, James B., and Michael Millgate, eds. *Lion in the Garden: Interviews with William Faulkner 1926-1962*. New York: Random, 1968. Print.

Peavy, Charles D. *Go Slow Now: Faulkner and the Race Question*. Eugene: U of Oregon P, 1971. Print.

Sullivan, John Jeremiah. "The 'Ulysses' of Mississippi." *The New York Times Sunday Magazine* 1 July 2012: MM45–47. Print.

Warren, Robert Penn. "Faulkner: The South, the Negro, and Time." *Faulkner: A Collection of Critical Essays*. Ed. Robert Penn Warren. Englewood Cliffs, NJ: Prentice-Hall, 1966: 251–71. Print.

Weinstein, Philip. *Becoming Faulkner: The Art and Life of William Faulkner*. New York: Oxford UP, 2010. Print.

Williamson, Joel. *New People: Miscegenation and Mulattoes in the United States*. New York: Free, 1980. Print.

___. *The Crucible of Race: Black/White Relations in the American South since Emancipation*. New York: Oxford UP, 1984. Print.

___. *William Faulkner and Southern History*. New York: Oxford UP, 1993. Print.

William Faulkner's Critical Reception_____

Taylor Hagood

After the hard work of producing a novel or short story, an author wants people not only to read the work but also to talk about it. If readers like the piece, the conversation that ensues can take multiple forms. A formal, published conversation carried on by professionally trained scholars and literary critics is referred to as the "critical reception." No matter how complex people's comments in this conversation can be, they are like any other conversation in that they talk about why the text is important, either to themselves as individuals or to the world in general, and they respond to what has been said by others.

The critical reception of the writing of William Faulkner has been long and complex. Faulkner is one of the most written-about authors in the English language, and this writing has taken many different forms, from biography to the most erudite criticism. Each year, multiple books and massive numbers of articles are published, making it difficult for even the most ardent and diligent Faulknerians to keep up. Given the daunting nature of this body of work to someone new to the field, the effort here will be to help orient the reader, not only in knowing what has been published, but also to acquaint him or her with the general movements that have developed during the six decades in which a recognizable community of Faulkner scholars emerged and during the eight decades since people have been commenting on Faulkner and his work.

This introductory essay is structured to accommodate—as much as is possible—both the chronological and thematic development of this critical reception. Like any field of scholarship, there is a recursive quality about it, a returning to topics: Just as families retell the same stories or sports fans debate controversial referee decisions years later, scholarly discussions often return to certain points even as new interests arise. Because of this cyclical aspect of critical discussion, the various topics of criticism and methods of critical approach will be presented in the order in which they appear and some sense of their individual development presented at that point.

Limitations of space unfortunately prevent a detailed treatment of even a small selection of critical texts; explanation and evaluation of all of them (including literally thousands of articles) is impossible. This essay will confine itself primarily to scholarship originally written and published in English, although there is a tremendous body of material in other languages. In going to any library with significant scholarly holdings, the reader will undoubtedly encounter books and articles not mentioned in this essay, and the author apologizes to all scholars who must necessarily be left out and means it as no reflection on them or the quality or importance of their work. However, with a sense of the overall movements in the Faulkner scholarly conversation, the reader encountering scholarship not mentioned here can enjoy the lovely experience of both discovering something new for him or herself and understanding how it relates to the larger picture of the Faulkner critical conversation.

The Early Responses: Reviews, Catalogues, and Biography

The initial response to any writing appears in the form of book reviews written by professional critics who read and evaluate books and publish their comments in journals such as the *New York Times Book Review* or the *Times Literary Supplement*. The reviews of Faulkner's work offer important insights into what was on the minds of Faulkner's first readers and how they represented his works to the rest of the reading population. Many of these are buried in old journals that are often inaccessible to the general public, but happily a compendium of them is available in the form of *William Faulkner: The Contemporary Reviews*, edited by M. Thomas Inge. By reading Inge's book one can get a strong sense of which reviewers admired Faulkner's difficult writing and which found it more trouble than it was worth.

Concurrent with the reviews, and so also during Faulkner's lifetime and just after his death, there sprung up another type of scholarship that may be described as a cataloguing of the characters, places (including discussion of the connection between real-life Oxford, Mississippi, and fictional Jefferson), and perhaps most helpfully the often obscure and colloquial sayings, mannerisms, and other details that could well baffle a reader not from Mississippi or familiar with Faulkner's moment. G. T. Buckley, Robert W. Kirk, and Elmo Howell are a few of many scholars who provided this type of response, although their writing is generally in short form and requires some searching. This impulse has continued and can take on interesting aspects, an example being Robert Harrison's *Aviation Lore in Faulkner* (1985), which orients readers in everything from Faulkner's use of the history of flight to the details of aerodynamics. Also in this cataloguing vein is Bruce F. Kawin's *Faulkner and Film* (1977), which addresses Faulkner's own screenwriting along with adaptations of his work (including a very useful filmography). Two of the most important figures in this mode of criticism have been Robert W. Hamblin and Charles A. Peek, who have published both individually and together on such projects as *A William Faulkner Encyclopedia* (1999) and *A Companion to Faulkner Studies* (2004). The cataloguing strain of scholarship ultimately gave birth to the University Press of Mississippi's *Reading Faulkner* series, edited by Noel Polk. The books in this series offer literally page-by-page guidance on the difficult and at times otherwise inaccessible details of Faulkner's writing. Polk's name, incidentally, is an important one in Faulkner studies, not only because of this series and his own critical writing, but also because he edited the standard editions of Faulkner's writing.

There is an obvious biographical aspect to this cataloguing scholarship, and in fact outright biography was another important branch of the early response to Faulkner's writing. At times this work featured comment by Faulkner's friends, associates, and family, examples being *Old Times in the Faulkner Country* (1961), by John B. Cullen;

Talking about William Faulkner: Interviews with Jimmy Faulkner and Others (1996), edited by Sally Wolff with Floyd C. Watkins; and perhaps most notably *My Brother Bill* (1963), by Faulkner's writer-artist brother John. Proper biography began with Robert Coughlan's 1953 short biography, *The Private World of William Faulkner*. The most important biographical work is the massive two-volume *Faulkner: A Biography* (1974), by Joseph Blotner. The only major biographer who actually knew Faulkner, Blotner is profoundly significant to the world of Faulkner scholarship. Although largely available now only in the compressed and updated single volume edition, this biography nevertheless offers an ocean of information and is the source from which all subsequent biographers have drawn and with which all Faulkner scholars must be familiar. As for those subsequent biographers, a few of their names are Frederick Karl, Richard Gray, and Jay Parini. In their works and others can be found interesting new interpretations of Faulkner's life and its relation to his writing.

The First Wave: New Critical and Structuralist Responses

Although reviews are important, they are often not enough to lift a literary author above the pack to the point of justifying the kind of cataloguing and biographical work just described. Prizes such as the Pulitzer and the Nobel helped immensely in creating such visibility. But even their awarding arguably came with the help of promotion by critics. While a few efforts were made early in Faulkner's career, such as George Marion O'Donnell's 1939 essay "Faulkner's Mythology," the most influential of this kind of work was Malcolm Cowley's introduction to *The Portable Faulkner* (1946).

The importance of Cowley's essay and of *The Portable Faulkner* cannot be overestimated. Cowley saw Faulkner's body of work as a unified whole that developed a mythology about the fictional Yoknapatawpha County. While Faulkner's writing was actually a bit more expansive and not necessarily so unified, Cowley presented a compelling argument, and he arranged stories and excerpts of longer works to create a volume that presented a consistent and chronological story of the history of Yoknapatawpha. The degree of artificiality in so doing was and is finally less important than the fact that the book and its introduction framed Faulkner and his work for later literary critics. *The Portable Faulkner* and Cowley's introduction played a major role in casting Faulkner as a major and important writer, and Lawrence Schwartz argues in *Creating Faulkner's Reputation* that Cowley's introduction portrayed Faulkner's work as being in line with conservative Cold War politics and so helped induce the decision to award him the 1949 Nobel Prize in Literature.

Cowley's work also ushered in the response of the mid-twentieth century figures involved in what is called "New Criticism" who minutely engaged with texts and searched for the kinds of unifying strains (often paradoxically achieved through contradictory elements in the text) that Cowley had sniffed out. Between 1952–54, there ran three volumes of a journal entitled *Faulkner Studies*, which is now available in a single reprinted volume and offers a glimpse at the Faulknerian scholarly climate of the moment. The fact is that there was a remarkably large body of work (several books and hundreds of articles) produced in the 1950s and 1960s. The most remembered are a handful of books that took on the bulk of Faulkner's work in elegant explication: Olga Vickery's *The Novels of William Faulkner* (1959), Edmund Volpe's *A Reader's Guide to William Faulkner* (1964), and Michael Millgate's *The Achievement of William Faulkner* (1966). The most important single critic of this period was Cleanth Brooks, who wrote three highly regarded volumes: *William Faulkner: The Yoknapatawpha Country* (1963), *William Faulkner: Toward Yoknapatawpha and Beyond* (1978), and *William Faulkner: First Encounters* (1983).

Equally notable were structuralist approaches. A number of these examined the architecture of the texts, others focused on the spaces and places of Yoknapatawpha, and still others dealt with the role of myths and archetypes in Faulkner's writing. Many combined all three.

Examples of this work abound in the journals of the 1960s and 1970s, one memorable instance being Calvin S. Brown's "Faulkner's Geography and Topography." Standout books include Richard P. Adams's *Faulkner: Myth and Motion* (1968), Walter Brylowsky's *Faulkner's Olympian Laugh: Myth in the Novels* (1968), and Lynn Gatrell Levins's *Faulkner's Heroic Design: The Yoknapatawpha Novels* (1976).

Many of the viewpoints of New Criticism and structuralism have since been absorbed and some even discounted because they tend to proceed from a white-southern-aristocratic sympathetic viewpoint, typically rendering a vision of Faulkner that leaves race, gender, sexuality, and Confederate and neo-Confederate ideals and policies unproblematized. They and their underlying cultural assumptions therefore should not be taken as indicative of current critical opinion. On the other hand, even now these books, with their eloquent prose, can offer pleasurable reading for anyone new to Faulkner, providing orientation in what can at times seem an overwhelming fictional world.

Faulkner and Theory: The Great Flowering of Faulkner Scholarship

Cleanth Brooks's career extended into the 1980s, but by the time he had finished his final volume, the trends in the critical response to Faulkner had changed dramatically. The 1980s and 1990s saw the growth of theory-driven criticism, when the conservative and markedly antitheoretical values of New Criticism gave way to approaches to literature that took into account theories provided by psychoanalysis, structuralism, and ultimately poststructuralism, which questioned not only language but also the constructs of race, gender, class, and many other aspects of society.

The change began in the 1970s, when writers started to move away from the assumptions of New Criticism, opening up Faulkner's texts to multiple discourses rather than focusing exclusively on them as closed systems. A critic who undertook such an approach was André Bleikasten. French interest in Faulkner had long been strong, and Bleikasten continued this work in *Faulkner's "As I Lay Dying"* (1973); *The Most Splendid Failure: Faulkner's "The Sound and the Fury"* (1976); and, later, the immense work, *The Ink of Melancholy: Faulkner's Novels from "The Sound and the Fury" to "Light in August"* (1990). At first glance, these volumes might look like New Criticism in their patient spinning out of close readings, but Bleikasten's work is informed by the subtle textual engagements of his French contemporaries, perhaps most recognizably Roland Barthes, whose notions of intertextuality and the almost erotic "pleasures" of the text were influential in helping scholars navigate the nuances of creative writing. Textured by the realizations of reader-response criticism as well as structuralist and poststructuralist developments in critical theory, these works offered provocative readings much less concerned with boxing Faulkner's work into a Cowley-like totalizing vision but rather focused on parsing difficult questions about Faulkner's writing and even criticism itself and its own limitations and constructedness. These early volumes also marked a move toward book-length studies of single Faulkner texts, a practice that would continue throughout this period. Such single-text studies overwhelmingly favored certain canonized books that were considered "great"—*The Sound and the Fury* (1929); *As I Lay Dying* (1930); *Light in August* (1932); *Absalom, Absalom!* (1936); and *Go Down, Moses* (1942)—although there were scholars who continued to follow in the vein of Brooks and Vickery, engaging all of Faulkner's work. Examples of these would be Gary Lee Stonum in *Faulkner's Career: An Internal Literary History* (1979), which argued that in each novel lay the seeds of the next, and Doreen Fowler in *Faulkner's Changing Vision: From Outrage to Affirmation* (1983), which also focused on Faulkner's development by arguing that instead of his writing diminishing in power (as many scholars argue), it can be seen to strengthen over the course of his career in certain respects.

On the heels of Bleikasten's first book came one of the most unique and enthralling publications of Faulkner criticism ever written—John T. Irwin's *Doubling and Incest/Repetition and Revenge* (1975). Written in a single extended essay, the book pushes the conventions of critical writing in both form and content. It is the first Faulkner book to take the approach of applying a theoretical framework to Faulkner's writing: Irwin employs Freudian psychoanalysis in a deep investigation of Quentin Compson and his motives. Moreover, Irwin's approach also nodded to Barthes in its intertextuality, as it considered Sigmund Freud and Friedrich Nietzsche alongside Faulkner. The result is an innovative volume that continues to impress, and it stands as the conceptual prototype for the kinds of criticism to follow.

For not only Freud and Barthes but Jacques Lacan, Michel Foucault, Jacques Derrida, Julia Kristeva, Luce Irigaray, and many other theorists had by now become the pillars upon which literary criticism was being built. It was a time when scholars could be found who self-identified as Freudian or Lacanian or Derridean—scholars who were expert in the contributions of one of these theorists and were part of a school of critics that applied those theories to primary texts. William Shakespeare received perhaps the most attention, but Faulkner became one of the other figures upon whose work the latest theories were tried because the scope, detail, and philosophical depth of his oeuvre provided ample testing ground. This work poured out in hundreds of articles, including those in the main journal of the field, the *Faulkner Journal*. The University Press of Mississippi also began to publish the plenary lectures of the *Annual Faulkner and Yoknapatawpha Conference* held in Oxford, Mississippi. For over twenty-five years, these volumes have served as a barometer for following developments in the field, with titles such as *Faulkner and Race*, *Faulkner and Ideology*, *Faulkner and Psychology*, and *Faulkner and Material Culture*—titles that signal not only theoretical underpinnings of these approaches but also highly politicized critical approaches that dealt with the positions of the traditionally unempowered in US society and hence in Faulkner's writing.

As for books using these new approaches, they appeared quickly and in great variety. Just a year after the appearance of Irwin's book, Myra Jehlen published *Class and Character in Faulkner's South*, a Marxist reading sensitive to social hierarchies in ways previous scholarship was not. The end of the decade saw Donald M. Kartiganer's *The Fragile Thread: The Meaning of Form in Faulkner's Novels* (1979), which takes a subtle structuralist and psychoanalytic approach. In 1982, John T. Matthews published *The Play of Faulkner's Language*, an overtly Derridean approach to the "major novels" listed above that read the absence of conceptual and narrative "centers" in Faulkner as part of a general machinery of deferring of meaning as delineated by Derrida. Two books that both dealt with race were published the next year. The first, *Faulkner: The House Divided*, by Eric Sundquist, argued that miscegenation formed the central tension of Faulkner's works. The second book was *Faulkner's "Negro": Art and the Southern Context*, in which Thadious M. Davis explained that Faulkner spent most of his efforts grappling with the white southern construction of the "Negro" to the point that he was often unable to explore the characters of actual people of color. The end of the decade saw Karl Zender's distinctly materialist approach to Faulkner's work, *The Crossing of the Ways* (1989), which examined how everything from money to education shaped and affected Faulkner's career and vision, especially in his later novels. Joseph R. Urgo also broke with the trend of focusing on the "major works" by dealing with the later novels in his recuperative reading of the Snopeses, particularly Flem, as figures able to throw off the old yoke of aristocratic rule in *Faulkner's Apocrypha: "A Fable," Snopes, and the Spirit of Human Rebellion* (1989).

The next decade saw these theoretical and cultural approaches carried forward. One of the things that occupied the attention of critics as the decade turned was the way so many voices competed with one another for cultural attention in Faulkner's writing. Stephen M. Ross's *Fiction's Inexhaustible Voice: Speech and Writing in Faulkner* (1989) undertakes a Mikhail Bakhtin–informed consideration of the polyvocalic nature of Faulkner's writing, with sensitivity to Bakhtin's attention to the undertones and overtones of culturally embedded utterances. Robert Dale Parker, in *"Absalom, Absalom!"*

The Questioning of Fiction (1991) and Judith Lockyer, in *Ordered by Words: Language and Narration in the Novels of William Faulkner* (1991), also explore Faulkner's work according to Bakhtinian principles. John N. Duvall's *Faulkner's Marginal Couple: Invisible, Outlaw, and Unspeakable Communities* (1990) examines the ways cultural outsiders in Faulkner form couples who together maintain the strength to resist cultural norms. Doreen Fowler's *Faulkner: The Return of the Repressed* (1997) uses an openly Lacanian approach with its relentless furthering of Freud's principles to show the ways characters negotiate language and cultural status in the formation of identity. And Philip Weinstein, in *Faulkner's Subject: A Cosmos No One Owns* (1992), shows the ways minority voices threaten to crowd out and overpower Faulkner himself as the white empowered owner of his own cosmos. Certain books honed in specifically on women in Faulkner. Although an early work on Faulkner's women had appeared in David Williams's *Faulkner's Woman: The Myth and the Muse* (1977), it was in the 1990s that feminist criticism of Faulkner really took off. Minrose C. Gwin's *The Feminine and Faulkner* (1990) considers the ways women characters in Faulkner are agents of disruption and subversion, and Diane Roberts pressures female stereotypes in *Faulkner and Southern Womanhood* (1994). Deborah Clarke also focuses on the disruptive power of women, employing specifically Kristeva's challenge of Lacan's phallocentrism—or privileging as well as recognizing culture's tendency to gender power as masculine—to examine the function of mothers in *Robbing the Mother: Women in Faulkner* (1994).

The foregoing list is dizzying to say the least, making it appropriate to sum up the strands of criticism extant by the end of the 1990s. Essentially, the kinds of questions to be asked about Faulkner had been opened up to a much broader spectrum. Where most scholars before had been concerned with delving into the secrets of the text to address southern conventions, aspects of myth, or the functions of place, these new scholars prodded the role of women and people of color, the ways Faulkner's writing exemplified linguistic and psychoanalytic theory, and so forth. Where most of the New Critical efforts were content to maintain a focus on the workings of the text, these scholarly treatments sought either to understand something about society through Faulkner's writing or to hold his writing up against society. There remained much admiring of Faulkner, but there could also be found mild and at times even severe criticism of his blind spots, although generally there was a sense, again, that his work was rich enough to warrant extensive and broad treatment.

The Twenty-First Century: Global Faulkner

From the mid-1990s into the twenty-first century, many of the theoretical trends continued—Karl Zender's second volume *Faulkner and the Politics of Reading* (2002) being an example—but there also began to spring up scholarly examinations of Faulkner that contextualized him in relation to literature and culture across the globe.

One new strain of Faulkner criticism that developed was the move of comparing him to other writers. Margaret Donovan Bauer's *William Faulkner's Legacy: "What Shadow, What Stain, What Mark"* (2005) is an interesting example of such work, finding the influence of Faulkner in the works of Larry McMurtry, Lee Smith, Pat Conroy, and others, while Joseph Fruscione's *Faulkner and Hemingway: Biography of a Literary Rivalry* (2012) examines the actual and intertextual relationship of the two famous contemporaries. The prime candidate for comparison, however, was Toni Morrison. Bauer discusses Morrison in relation to Faulkner, and three books on this topic particularly stand out: *What Else but Love? The Ordeal of Race in Faulkner and Morrison* (1996), by Philip Weinstein; *Subversive Voices: Eroticizing the Other in William Faulkner and Toni Morrison* (2001), by Evelyn Jaffe Schrieber; and *Unflinching Gaze: Morrison and Faulkner Re-Envisioned* (1997), a collection of essays edited by Carol A. Kolmerten, Stephen M. Ross, and Judith Bryant Wittenberg.

The biggest change in critical focus, however, was that of considering Faulkner in the context of slave-plantation culture, which was part of the larger New Southernist movement that sought to understand the US South hemispherically as part of the global south. Richard Godden's first book *Fictions of Labor: William Faulkner and the South's Long Revolution* (1997) anticipates this work by examining the real history of the Haitian Revolution alongside that in Faulkner's novel *Absalom, Absalom!*, but the global south approach to Faulkner was essentially a postcolonial one kick-started by the Martinican writer Edouard Glissant in his work entitled *Faulkner, Mississippi* (1999). In the book, Glissant shows that his home resembles Mississippi, and his vision, much like other Caribbean writers, echoes Faulkner's own. This work stimulated much scholarship, with articles by both new and established Faulkner scholars—a nice repository being *Look Away! The U.S. South in New World Studies* (2004), edited by Jon Smith and Deborah Cohn. Other works include Charles Baker's *William Faulkner's Postcolonial South* (2000), Hosam Aboul-Ela's *Other South: Faulkner, Coloniality, and the Mariátegui Tradition* (2007), and Valérie Loichot's *Orphan Narratives: The Postplantation Literature of Faulkner, Glissant, Morrison, and Saint-John Perse* (2007). Significantly, the topic of the 2009 *Faulkner and Yoknapatawpha Conference* was "Global Faulkner."

While the global Faulkner change dominated much of the first decade of the twenty-first century, there were other significant developments. One of these was a return to certain earlier concerns in Faulkner criticism, often done with the advantage of an awareness of contemporary theory-based criticism. Blair Labatt's *Faulkner the Storyteller* (2005) marks a semireturn to New Criticism and structuralism in its focus on the mechanics of plotting in Faulkner's writing, mostly in the Snopes novels. Charles Aiken's *William Faulkner and the Southern Landscape* (2009) reexamined the literal grounds of Faulkner's work from a geographer's perspective. Owen Robinson's *Creating Yoknapatawpha: Readers and Writers in Faulkner's Fiction* (2006) revisited reader-response criticism of a few decades earlier. Charles Hannon's *Faulkner and the Discourses of Culture* (2005) examined the competing voices in culture in a manner reminiscent of Duvall and Weinstein. Taylor Hagood's *Faulkner's Imperialism: Space, Place, and the Materiality of Myth* (2008) also discussed competing voices by returning to a global-south and postcolonial-theory conditioned reading of the staples of myth and place. The biographical and cataloguing strains reemerged too, examples being Judith L. Sensibar's *Faulkner and Love: The Woman Who Shaped His Art* (2009), John Matthews's *William Faulkner: Seeing through the South* (2009), and one of the most sensational volumes to appear in a long time—*Ledgers of History: William Faulkner, an Almost Forgotten Friendship, and an Antebellum Diary* (2010), in which Sally Wolff discovered a diary from which Faulkner apparently drew many ideas for his writing.

Another interesting trend that developed in the past decade was that of a kind of Faulkner-informed scholarly/creative nonfiction hybrid essay in which scholars reflect on their own lives, experiences, and situations as they develop critical readings of Faulkner's work. The first of these was Houston A. Baker's, *I Don't Hate the South: Reflections on Faulkner, Family, and the South* (2007) in which he talks about growing up as an African American in Louisville, Kentucky, and the reciprocities of that place and experience with Faulkner's Mississippi. In 2010, Polk published his collection of essays, *Faulkner and Welty and the Southern Literary Tradition*, which achieves high essay form, and in the same year, Philip Weinstein's *Becoming Faulkner: The Art and Life of William Faulkner* undertakes a biography tinged by the author's personal experiences.

It should be added that during this time and throughout the history of the Faulkner critical discussion, certain fine books and articles appeared that did not necessarily follow the trends but nevertheless had an important impact on the field and are definitely ones for developing Faulkner scholars to know. Jay Watson's *Forensic Fictions: The Lawyer Figure in Faulkner* (1993) is such an example. In the 2000s, some of these efforts include Ted Atkinson's prodding of the proletariat side of Faulkner in *Faulkner and the Great Depression* (2006) and Peter

Lurie's brilliant investigation of the role of vision, including vision and film, in *Vision's Immanence: Faulkner, Film, and the Popular Imagination* (2004).

The latest thing to have happened to Faulkner studies is the Internet. The 2000s saw multiple websites dedicated to Faulkner, most notably the highly influential *William Faulkner on the Web*, published by University of Mississippi English professor John B. Padgett. The hypertext resource edition of *The Sound and the Fury*, edited by University of Saskatchewan professor Peter Stoicheff and others, is an important website that offers a plethora of ways into that difficult text, from graphic presentations of its timeline to a chronology of its events. At the time of this writing, the website *The Digital Yoknapatawpha Project*, initiated by University of Virginia professor Stephen Railton, is being developed by a team of scholars. As the second decade of the twenty-first century deepens, digital platforms will be ones to follow as Faulkner critics look forward to what new aspects will be discussed in the texts.

Works Cited

Aboul-Ela, Hosam. *Other South: Faulkner, Coloniality, and the Mariátegui Tradition.* Pittsburgh: U of Pittsburgh P, 2007. Print.

Adams, Richard P. *Faulkner: Myth and Motion.* Princeton: Princeton UP, 1968. Print.

Aiken, Charles S. *William Faulkner and the Southern Landscape.* Athens: U of Georgia P, 2009. Print.

Atkinson, Ted. *Faulkner and the Great Depression: Aesthetics, Ideology, and Cultural Politics.* Athens: U of Georgia P, 2006. Print.

Baker, Charles. *William Faulkner's Postcolonial South.* New York: Peter Lang, 2000. Print.

Baker, Houston A., Jr. *I Don't Hate the South: Reflections on Faulkner, Family, and the South.* Oxford: Oxford UP, 2007. Print.

Bauer, Margaret Donovan. *William Faulkner's Legacy: "What Shadow, What Stain, What Mark."* Gainesville: UP of Florida, 2005. Print.

Bleikasten, André. *Faulkner's As I Lay Dying.* Trans. Roger Little. Bloomington: Indiana UP, 1973. Print.

___. *The Ink of Melancholy: Faulkner's Novels from* The Sound and the Fury *to* Light in August. Bloomington: Indiana UP, 1990. Print.

___. *The Most Splendid Failure: Faulkner's* The Sound and the Fury. Bloomington: Indiana UP, 1976. Print.

Blotner, Joseph. *Faulkner: A Biography*. 2 vols. New York: Random, 1984. Print.

Brown, Calvin S. "Faulkner's Geography and Topography." PMLA 77 (1962): 652–59. Print.

Brylowski, Walter. *Faulkner's Olympian Laugh: Myth in the Novels*. Detroit: Wayne State UP, 1968. Print.

Buckley, G. T. "Is Oxford the Original of Jefferson in William Faulkner's Novels?" PMLA 76 (1961): 447–54. Print.

Clarke, Deborah. *Robbing the Mother: Women in Faulkner*. Jackson: UP of Mississippi, 1994. Print.

Coughlan, Robert. *The Private World of William Faulkner*. New York: Avon, 1953. Print.

Cowley, Malcolm. Introduction. *The Portable Faulkner*. By William Faulkner. 1946. New York: Penguin, 2003. vii–xxxi. Print.

Cullen, John B. *Old Times in the Faulkner Country*. Chapel Hill: U of North Carolina P, 1961. Print.

Davis, Thadious M. *Faulkner's "Negro": Art and the Southern Context*. Baton Rouge: Louisiana State UP, 1983. Print.

Duvall, John N. *Faulkner's Marginal Couple: Invisible, Outlaw, and Unspeakable Communities*. Austin: U of Texas P, 1990. Print.

Faulkner, John. *My Brother Bill: An Affectionate Reminiscence*. New York: Trident P, 1963. Print.

Faulkner Studies. Vols. 1–3. New York: Kraus, 1966. Print.

Fowler, Doreen. *Faulkner: The Return of the Repressed*. Charlottesville: UP of Virginia, 1997. Print.

___. *Faulkner's Changing Vision: From Outrage to Affirmation*. Ann Arbor: UMI Research P, 1983. Print.

Fruscione, Joseph. *Faulkner and Hemingway: Biography of a Literary Rivalry*. Columbus: Ohio State UP, 2012. Print.

Glissant, Edouard. *Faulkner, Mississippi*. Trans. Barbara Lewis and Thomas C. Spear. Chicago: U of Chicago P, 1999. Print.

Godden, Richard. *Fictions of Labor: William Faulkner and the South's Long Revolution*. Cambridge: Cambridge UP, 1997. Print.

Gray, Richard. *The Life of William Faulkner: A Critical Biography*. Oxford: Blackwell, 1994. Print.

Gwin, Minrose C. *The Feminine and Faulkner: Reading (Beyond) Sexual Difference*. Knoxville: U of Tennessee P, 1990. Print.

Hamblin, Robert W., and Charles A. Peek, eds. *A William Faulkner Encyclopedia*. Westport: Greenwood P, 1999. Print.

Hannon, Charles. *Faulkner and the Discourses of Culture*. Baton Rouge: Louisiana State UP, 2005. Print.

Harrison, Robert. *Aviation Lore in Faulkner*. Amsterdam, Neth.: John Benjamins, 1985. Print.

Howell, Elmo. "Faulkner and Tennessee." *Tennessee Historical Quarterly* 21 (1963): 251–62. Print.

Inge, M. Thomas. *William Faulkner: The Contemporary Reviews*. Cambridge: Cambridge UP, 1995. Print.

Irwin, John T. *Doubling and Incest/Repetition and Revenge: A Speculative Reading of Faulkner*. Baltimore: Johns Hopkins UP, 1975. Print.

Jehlen, Myra. *Class and Character in Faulkner's South*. New York: Columbia UP, 1976. Print.

Karl, Frederick. *William Faulkner, American Author: A Biography*. New York: Weidenfeld, 1989. Print.

Kartiganer, Donald M. *The Fragile Thread: The Meaning of Form in Faulkner's Novels*. Amherst: U of Massachusetts P, 1979. Print.

Kawin, Bruce F. *Faulkner and Film*. New York: Frederick Ungar, 1977. Print.

Kirk, Robert W. *Faulkner's People: A Complete Guide and Index to Characters in the Fiction of William Faulkner*. Berkeley: U of California P, 1963. Print.

Kolmerten, Carol A., Stephen M. Ross, and Judith Bryant Wittenberg, eds. *Unflinching Gaze: Faulkner and Morrison Re-Envisioned*. Jackson: UP of Mississippi, 1997. Print.

Labatt, Blair. *Faulkner the Storyteller*. Tuscaloosa: U of Alabama P, 2005. Print.

Levins, Lynn Gatrell. *Faulkner's Heroic Design: The Yoknapatawpha Novels*. Athens: U of Georgia P, 1976. Print.

Loichot, Valérie. *Orphan Narratives: The Postplantation Literature of Faulkner, Glissant, Morrison, and Saint-John Perse*. Charlottesville: U of Virginia P, 2007. Print.

Lurie, Peter. *Vision's Immanence: Faulkner, Film, and the Popular Imagination*. Baltimore: Johns Hopkins UP, 2004. Print.

Matthews, John T. *The Play of Faulkner's Language*. Ithaca: Cornell UP, 1982. Print.

___. *William Faulkner: Seeing through the South*. Oxford: Wiley-Blackwell, 2009. Print.

O'Donnell, George Marion. "Faulkner's Mythology." 1939. *William Faulkner: Three Decades of Criticism*. Ed. Frederick J. Hoffman and Olga W. Vickery. East Lansing: Michigan State UP, 1960. 82–93. Print.

Padgett, John B. *William Faulkner on the Web*. U of Mississippi, 12 July 2012. Web. 24 Jan. 2013.

Parini, Jay. *One Matchless Time: A Life of William Faulkner*. New York: Harper, 2004. Print.

Peek, Charles A., and Robert W. Hamblin, eds. *A Companion to Faulkner Studies*. Westport, CT: Greenwood P, 2004. Print.

Polk, Noel. *Faulkner and Welty and the Southern Literary Tradition*. Jackson: UP of Mississippi, 2008. Print.

Railton, Stephen. *Digital Yoknapatawpha Project, The*. n.p., 31 Jan. 2012. Web. 24 Jan. 2013.

Roberts, Diane. *Faulkner and Southern Womanhood*. Athens: U of Georgia P, 1994.

Robinson, Owen. *Creating Yoknapatawpha: Readers and Writers in Faulkner's Fiction*. New York: Routledge, 2006. Print.

Ross, Stephen M. *Fiction's Inexhaustible Voice: Speech and Writing in Faulkner*. Athens: U of Georgia P, 1989. Print.

Schwartz, Lawrence H. *Creating Faulkner's Reputation: The Politics of Modern Literary Criticism*. Knoxville: U of Tennessee P, 1988. Print.

Sensibar, Judith L. *Faulkner and Love: The Women Who Shaped His Art*. New Haven: Yale UP, 2009.

Smith, Jon, and Deborah Cohn, eds. *Look Away! The U.S. South in New World Studies*. Durham: Duke UP, 2004. Print.

Stoicheff, Peter, et al. *The Sound and the Fury: A Hypertext Edition*. U of Saskatchewan, Feb. 2011. Web. 24 Jan. 2013.

Sundquist, Eric. *Faulkner: The House Divided*. Baltimore: Johns Hopkins UP, 1983. Print.

Urgo, Joseph R. *Faulkner's Apocrypha: A Fable, Snopes, and the Spirit of Human Rebellion*. Jackson: UP of Mississippi, 1989. Print.

Weinstein, Philip. *Becoming Faulkner: The Arts and Life of William Faulkner*. Oxford: Oxford UP, 2010. Print.

___. *Faulkner's Subject: A Cosmos No One Owns*. New York: Cambridge UP, 1992. Print.

___. *What Else but Love? The Ordeal of Race in Faulkner and Morrison*. New York: Columbia UP, 1996. Print.

Williams, David. *Faulkner's Women: The Myth and the Muse*. Montreal: McGill-Queen's UP, 1977. Print.

Wolff, Sally. *Ledgers of History: William Faulkner, an Almost Forgotten Friendship, and an Antebellum Diary*. Baton Rouge: Louisiana State UP, 2010. Print.

Wolff, Sally, and Floyd C. Watkins, eds. *Talking about William Faulkner: Interviews with Jimmy Faulkner and Others*. Baton Rouge: Louisiana State UP, 1996. Print.

Zender, Karl. *Faulkner and the Politics of Reading*. Baton Rouge: Louisiana State UP, 2002. Print.

___. *The Crossing of the Ways: William Faulkner, the South, and the Modern World*. New Brunswick, NJ: Rutgers UP, 1989. Print.

Reading Faulkner through Morrison_____

Doreen Fowler

Readers of the fiction of Toni Morrison sometimes hear eerie echoes of Faulkner. Both Faulkner and Morrison employ themes of the Old South—slavery, incest, miscegenation, Jim Crow, and reconstruction and its aftermath; and both are preoccupied with issues of identity, autonomy, and history.[1] At the same time, as an African American writer whose literary work develops out of an African American folk and oral tradition, Morrison is also decidedly different from Faulkner. Scholars have puzzled over the intertextual relationship between the two writers: one, the great-grandson of a Confederate colonel and slaveholder, the other, a descendant of southern slaves. Some scholars have suggested that Faulkner, who preceded Morrison by a generation, influences her writing; others have argued that Morrison corrects Faulkner; and still others have suggested that Morrison, to use Henry Louis Gates's term, "signifies on," (i.e., creatively improvises beyond) Faulkner's literary works.

Morrison's own comments about a literary relationship with Faulkner have been contradictory. On the one hand, she has emphatically denied a Faulknerian influence. "I am not like Faulkner," she said forcefully in an interview with Nellie McKay (Morrison, Interview 152). However, in response to a question following a reading at the 1985 Faulkner and Yoknapatawpha Conference, she admitted that all writers tend to deny any writerly influence: "I am typical, I think, of all writers who are convinced that they are wholly original" ("Faulkner" 296–97); she also acknowledged that, as a reader, she was indebted to Faulkner: "There was for me not only an academic interest in Faulkner but in a very, very personal way, in a very personal way as a reader, William Faulkner had an enormous effect on me, an enormous effect" (296).

How then is one to read the recurring Faulknerian motifs in Morrison's fiction? Morrison is not Faulkner's disciple; neither is she critiquing or revising his fiction. Rather, Morrison is teaching how to read Faulkner; in particular, she is teaching whites how to read race in Faulkner's fiction. My position is that Morrison's fiction uncovers a submerged perspective on race informing Faulkner's novels. She teases out racial meanings in his fiction that have eluded readers for whom black and white are discrete, dichotomous categories.[2]

A Faulkner novel to which Morrison repeatedly returns in her own fictions is *Absalom, Absalom!* Most often, critics have examined parallels between *Absalom* and Morrison's *Beloved* (1987) because both are novels about the wreckage caused by racial slavery and racial division in the pre- and post-Civil War period.[3] However, Philip Weinstein, Roberta Rubenstein, and John Duvall have noted that Morrison's *Jazz* also reprises many of the central motifs of *Absalom*. More specifically and to extend that notion, it is through the character Golden Gray in *Jazz* that Morrison offers readers another way to read the enigmatic character Charles Bon, in Faulkner's novel.

Absalom, Absalom! is often considered to be Faulkner's greatest and least readable novel. In 1936, when Faulkner had just finished writing *Absalom*, he offered the opinion that his latest novel "is the best novel yet written by an American" (Bezzerides 83). But most contemporary reviewers did not share Faulkner's assessment. Reviewing the novel for the *New Yorker*, Clifton Fadiman said the publication of *Absalom* marks "the final blowup of what was once a remarkable, if minor talent" (64). The reviewer for *Time* offered a more nuanced opinion that anticipates the view of many beleaguered twenty-first-century readers of the novel. He wrote that *Absalom* is "the strangest, longest, least readable, most infuriating and yet in some respects the most impressive novel that William Faulkner has written" ("Southern" 67). Certainly many students would agree that the novel is infuriating and unreadable. Indeed, some have volunteered the opinion that the book is only nominally in the English language.

The difficulty of *Absalom, Absalom!* is its opaque, modernist form. Simply put, *Absalom* is the story of a southern plantation owner and slaveholder, Thomas Sutpen, and his (black and white) descendants.

Faulkner chooses to tell the story of the rise and fall of the House of Sutpen through a series of character-narrators who tell fragmentary, variant, and sometimes contradictory versions and who often seem to not know the story they tell. More maddening still, these character-narrators tell the story in sentences overburdened with qualifying phrases added to qualifying phrases and clauses heaped upon clauses (with repeated turns to negative constructions that seem to not tell) in narrations that seem to dance around the subject and take two steps backward for every one step forward.

What is most puzzling about this opaque formal structure is that the novel appears to be a search for meaning even as the waves of dense prose work to conceal meaning.[4] The novel begins with a mystery that the character-narrators ostensibly are trying to solve: After fighting side by side for four years during the Civil War, why did Henry Sutpen draw his gun at the gate of the Sutpen mansion and shoot and kill Charles Bon, a man who was his beloved friend and the fiancé of his sister? Four character-narrators seem to weave endless circles of words around this mysterious murder: Miss Rosa Coldfield, the sister of Sutpen's wife and herself the fiancée of Thomas Sutpen for a short time; Mr. Compson, the son of General Compson, Thomas Sutpen's only friend; Quentin Compson, Mr. Compson's son; and Shreve McCannon, a Canadian who is Quentin's roommate at Harvard. Curiously, a motive for the murder is only proposed in the final pages of the novel by the two character-narrators who are the furthest removed from the events they narrate, Quentin and Shreve. Prior to this long deferred denouement, the character-narrators seem stymied. Mr. Compson, for example, plainly states that his telling fails to tell:

It's just incredible. It just does not explain. Or perhaps that's it: they don't explain and we are not supposed to know. . . . Yes, Judith, Bon, Henry, Sutpen: all of them. They are there, yet something is missing: they are like a chemical formula . . . ; you bring them together in the proportions called for, but nothing happens; you re-read, tedious and intent, poring, making sure that you have forgotten nothing, made no miscalculations; you bring them together again and again nothing happens: just the words, the symbols, the shapes themselves, shadowy, inscrutable and serene, against that turgid background of a horrible and bloody mischancing of human affairs. (80)

On the surface, Mr. Compson seems to be merely expressing frustration, the same frustration that the reader feels, who has slogged through pages of aimlessly meandering sentences only to be told that Mr. Compson's account "does not explain." Read for coded meanings, however, Mr. Compson's words contain clues that point to the reason why his narration fails. His account "does not explain" because "something is missing." If one turns to Toni Morrison, she points out that race is what "you can't find" ("Art" 101) in the character-narrators' telling of the fall of the southern planter class.

In a 1993 interview in the *Paris Review*, Morrison describes putting together for her students a lecture where she traced the absence of race in *Absalom, Absalom!*:

Faulkner in *Absalom, Absalom!* spends the entire book tracing race, and you can't find it. No one can see it, even the character who *is* black can't see it. I did this lecture for my students that took me forever, which was tracking all the moments of withheld, partial or disinformation, when a racial fact or clue *sort* of comes out but doesn't quite arrive. I just wanted to chart it. I listed its appearance, disguise and disappearance on every page, I mean every phrase! . . . Do you know how hard it is to withhold that kind of information but hinting, pointing all of the time? And then to reveal it in order to say that is *not* the point anyway? It is technically just astonishing. As a reader you have been forced to hunt for a drop of black blood that means everything and nothing. The insanity of racism. So the structure is the argument. . . . No one has done anything quite like that ever. So, when I critique, what I am saying is, I don't care if Faulkner was a racist or not; I don't personally care, but I am fascinated by what it means to write like this. ("Art" 101)

As Morrison perceptively observes, *Absalom* is such a technically demanding novel because the white southern character-narrators censor their narratives of any "racial fact or clue." Race is "withheld" or "disguise[d]"; or it appears as "disinformation." In particular, the character-narrators erase signs of racial intermixture that threaten white dominance. Miss Rosa's narration is a case in point. Purportedly she is telling the Sutpen story to Quentin to explain "why Heaven saw fit to let us lose [the war]" (13), but her explanation fails to explain because she omits any reference to people of color save as a slave underclass. For example, she never mentions the octoroon wife of Charles Bon, who visits Sutpen's Hundred and whom Mr. Compson saw; nor does she ever mention Charles Bon's son by the octoroon wife, whom Judith and Clytie raised at Sutpen's Hundred. Charles Bon's mulatto race son is absent from Miss Rosa's narration even when she buries Judith in a grave next to him. This kind of racial omission, as Morrison points out, is "on every page, I mean every phrase" of the novel, and it is driven by a white refusal to acknowledge any black-white interfacing.

The critical "racial fact" that is "withheld" by the narrators until the final pages of the novel is Charles Bon's racial identity. Charles Bon is "shadowy," "curious," "enigmatic," and "impenetrable" (74) in their telling because they refuse to acknowledge the merging of white and black that he embodies. Bon's long-withheld identity is the solution to the mystery of why Henry killed Bon; and this "missing" racial factor is only restored when Quentin and Shreve, far removed from the South in a dorm room in Cambridge, surmise that Charles Bon was Thomas Sutpen's unacknowledged son by a woman of mixed race, whom Henry killed to prevent a black man from marrying his sister. In the novel's closing sentences, the Canadian Shreve says what the other character-narrators have evaded or disguised with language: Charles Bon—Charles Good—whom Rosa, Henry, and Judith love, is a "nigger Sutpen" (302). The long-deferred revelation that Charles Bon embodies the threat of racial mixing explains why Henry killed his beloved friend. But there remains still another mystery in the novel: Why is Charles Bon so determined to defy Henry's interdiction even in the face of death?

In their reconstructions of events, Mr. Compson, Quentin, and Shreve all insist that Charles leaves Henry no option but to kill him. Henry kills Charles at the last possible moment, on the eve of the wedding, at the gate of the Sutpen mansion to which the two had ridden side by side. Before that, Henry had repeatedly asked Charles: "*Do you renounce?* and the other saying *I do not renounce*" (105). As Quentin and Shreve observe, at any time, Bon could have backed down: "'He could have, but he never even tried" (286). Rather Bon chooses to ride forward "calm and undeviating, . . . fatalist to the last" (105) right into Henry's bullets. It is Bon who forces Henry's hand; it is Bon who knows from the beginning what he will do; it is Bon, calm, smiling, and unwavering, who delivers the ultimatum to Henry:

"You are my brother."

"No, I'm not. I'm the nigger that's going to sleep with your sister. Unless you stop me, Henry." (286)

Reading these events, Philip Weinstein has interpreted Bon as "openly suicidal when confronting the insult embodied in [his] black blood" (*What Else* 149). Is Bon suicidal because of his mixed race? If not, why does he insist on the marriage to Judith, knowing that Henry will kill him if he persists? Why does he ride into Henry's bullets?

By the end of *Absalom, Absalom!*, the reader understands that Miss Rosa, Mr. Compson, Quentin, and Shreve are not writing the story of Thomas Sutpen, but the story of Charles Bon. Ultimately, the character-narrators fail to write this story, because, to them, Charles Bon is always a cipher. However, Morrison also has taken up the story of Charles Bon, and her telling penetrates the seemingly "impenetrable" Charles Bon. As a number of scholars have observed, Morrison's

Golden Gray in *Jazz* is an avatar of Charles Bon, and an intertextual reading of *Jazz* with *Absalom* suggests an answer to the haunting question: why does Charles demand recognition? Why does he refuse to obey the southern interdiction against racial merging?

As Weinstein, Duvall, and Rubenstein have observed, Golden Gray and Charles Bon seem to be doubles—alike and different. Both Charles Bon and Golden Gray are raised as privileged white men who discover when they reach manhood that one of their parents is black. Both are raised by women who lie to them; both are fatherless and feel this loss as an aching absence; and both are driven to find the absent father. A critical difference between the two men is that Bon, whose "black blood" derives from his mother, goes in search of his white father, Thomas Sutpen, while Golden Gray is determined to find his black father. The truly signifying difference between the two stories is the way the white father, Thomas Sutpen, and the black father, Hunter's Hunter or Henry LesTroy, respond (or do not respond) to the return of a long-lost son.[5]

As Quentin and Shreve reconstruct Bon's story, Bon is a son in search of "indisputable recognition" from his missing father (255). He needs "the physical touch even though in secret, hidden—the living touch of that flesh warmed before he was born by the same blood which it had bequeathed him to warm his own flesh with" (255). Whereas Golden Gray's black father welcomes him into his home (172), when Sutpen sees Charles, there is "no flicker, nothing, [in] the face in which he saw his own features" (278). In the Quentin-Shreve narration, Charles thinks to himself: *"He would just have to write 'I am your father. Burn this' and I would do it. Or if not that, a sheet a scrap of paper with the one word 'Charles' in his hand, and I would know what he meant and he would not even have to ask me to burn it"* (261). But Sutpen gives Charles "no word" (285), "no sign" (256). When his father, Thomas Sutpen, refuses to acknowledge him, he resolves to marry Judith so as to be recognized as a member of the family.

Sutpen refuses to acknowledge Charles because Charles embodies a blurring of black and white that threatens white racial purity. Sutpen is not alone in this denial of racial intermixture. He is representative of all the southern planters who refused to recognize their own black progeny. Morrison's *Jazz* records this same southern refusal to see or to know what was plainly before them—black and white interrelatedness. The slaveholder, Colonel Gray, in *Jazz*, has "seven mulatto children on his land" (141), none of whom are acknowledged. To cite another instance, when Vera Louise, the white daughter of the slaveholder Colonel Gray, becomes pregnant by a black boy, her family refuses to recognize her and "no word, then or ever, passed between them" (141). Vera Louise's family acts as if she and her mulatto son, Golden Gray, do not exist in the same way that Sutpen refuses to recognize the existence of his mulatto son, Charles Bon. The narrative form of *Absalom, Absalom!* seems to repeat Thomas Sutpen's act of disowning by withholding until the last pages of the novel Charles Bon's identity as Sutpen's black son.

Both Golden Gray and Charles Bon embody an interplay of black and white that the white southern characters in the two novels insist does not exist. In *Jazz*, through the narrative of Golden Gray and Wild, Morrison explores that border zone in a way that explains why Charles Bon dies to defend it. Gray starts out as a man who clings to white privilege and who seeks out his black father to kill him; but eventually he changes and comes to embrace his mixed racial identity. Wild, the wild black woman he meets on the way to find his father, incarnates the blackness that whites in the novel are determined to segregate and contain. The unexpected idyllic union of Gray and Wild symbolizes Gray's complete owning of the interdependence of black and white, an owning that makes Gray whole.

Golden Gray changes in *Jazz*. Reared as a privileged white, he assumes that white privilege is natural and immutable. For him, the color line is uncrossable until his eighteenth birthday when he is told that his father is a black man, and everything changes: "He had always thought there was only one kind [of black person]—True Belle's kind. Black and nothing. Like Henry LesTroy. Like the filthy woman snoring on the cot. But there was another kind—like himself" (149). Before he learns of his own black ancestry, blacks are "nothing." This equation of blacks with "nothing" resonates with *Absalom, Absalom!* where blacks are also seen as "nothing" or ciphers, and they are erased from the narrative.

At first, faced with his own black heritage, Gray wants to erase it, and he searches for his father so as to kill the source of this black blood. On the way, he encounters Wild, who, fleeing him, runs headlong into a tree and is knocked unconscious. Wild, as her name suggests, exists outside of the dominant white culture. "[N]aked, berry-black," "covered with mud," "leaves . . . in her hair" (144), she is "an armful of black, liquid female" (145). Gray's spontaneous reaction to her echoes the word "nothing": "He wants nothing to do with what he has seen" (144). She embodies exactly what Gray and the whites in both *Jazz* and *Absalom* are trying to expel, and, bending to examine her, Gray "hold[s] his breath against infection or odor or something. Something that might touch or penetrate him" (144). Even when Gray decides to lift the girl into his carriage and carry her with him to his father's house, his motive for taking her with him is to distance himself from blackness: "the awful-looking thing lying in wet weeds was everything he was not as well as a proper protection against and anodyne to what he believed his father to be, and therefore (if it could just be contained, identified)—himself" (149). Gray's word choice here is significant. The wild, naked, black girl is "everything he was not"; that is, she is the opposite black pole that imbues a white identity with meaning, and, juxtaposed with this naked, wild black girl, Golden Gray feels intensely his white difference. She is the black "not me" in relation to which a white identity signifies.

At this juncture in Golden Gray's story, something unexpected happens. Looking at the "savage" woman, he wonders if "the figure" was "a thing that touched him" (149); that is, he wonders if they are continuous; does he contain within himself what she is? Even "at the moment when his scare was sharpest" she "looked also like home comfortable enough to wallow in" (150). The word "home" here points to Freud's definition of the uncanny double. For Freud, the uncanny double is the *unheimlich*, or unhomelike, that which is our own but which we have estranged by denial, as signified by the prefix "un." Gray's first reaction to this eerie sense of kinship is to again deny it: "But who could live in that leafy hair? That unfathomable skin?" (150). Then he recalls that "he already had lived in and with it: True Belle had been his first and major love, which may be why two gallops beyond that hair, that skin, their absence was unthinkable" (150). Formerly he had defined True Belle as "black and nothing," but he now perceives that she is "home," and her absence would leave him lacking.

Golden Gray's black kin includes not only True Belle, who mothered him, but also the black father he never knew and whom he now realizes he needs. When Gray arrives at Henry LesTroy's cabin, he brings with him the unconscious wild woman. Waiting for his father to arrive, Gray changes into the "formal, elegant" (157) clothes he brought for the occasion. When he lays them on the bed and looks at the arrangement, it looks like "an empty man with one arm folded under" and he feels an aching, insupportable loss:

> Only now, he thought, now that I know I have a father, do I feel his absence: the place where he should have been and was not. Before, I thought everybody was one-armed, like me. Now I feel the surgery. The crunch of bone when it is sundered, the sliced flesh and the tubes of blood cut through, shocking the bloodrun and disturbing the nerves. They dangle and writhe. Singing pain. Waking me with the sound of itself, thrumming when I sleep so deeply it strangles my dreams away. There is nothing for it but to go away from where he is not to where he used to be and might be still. Let the dangle and the writhe see what it is missing; let the pain sing to the dirt where he stepped in the place where he used to be and might be

still. I don't need the arm. But I do need to know what it could have been like to have had it. . . . This part of me that does not know me, has never touched me or lingered at my side. When I find it, will it wave to me: Gesture, beckon to me to come along? . . . . It doesn't matter. I will locate it so the severed part can remember the snatch, the slice of is disfigurement. Perhaps then the arm will no longer be a phantom, but will take its own shape, grow its own muscle and bone, and its blood will pump from the loud singing that has found the purpose of its serenade. (158–59)

Morrison's prose here hammers home how essential a father is to a son's development of self-identity. The absence of a father is compared to the amputation of an arm. Without his black father, Gray is "an empty man." Gray, who had started out with the objective of killing his black father, now sees that there is an emptiness in him that only his father's presence can fill:

What do I care what the color of his skin is, or his contact with my mother? When I see him, or what is left of him, I will tell him all about the missing part of me and listen for his crying shame. I will exchange then; let him have mine and take his as my own and we will both be free, arm-tangled and whole. (158–59)

The freedom and autonomy he seeks, he understands now, is not to be found in distancing and denying what is his own, as his arm is his own, but by embracing it. He can be "whole" and "free" only if "arm-tangled" with his black father. The denial of kinship that characterizes *Absalom, Absalom!* in *Jazz* leaves Golden Gray "amputated" because he is insisting on imposing divisions on what is fluid and inmixed. By accepting his black father and being accepted by his father, Gray comes "home"; that is, he achieves "that longed for authenticity, . . . a right to be in this place" (160).

Like his black father, Wild is also necessary to Golden Gray. The text of *Jazz* aligns Henry LesTroy and Wild. To Gray, Wild seems both "savage" (155) and like the very embodiment of blackness; similarly, Gray envisions his missing father as "the blackest man in the world" (157) and as "the black and savage man who bothered him and abused his arm" (160). Whereas Henry LesTroy is the returned absent father, Wild is a substitute for a lost emotional attachment to his first mother, True Belle; and, unlike Charles Bon's story, Golden Gray's ends with a reconciliation of cultural oppositions like mother and father and black and white. Morrison conjures this space outside of culture's exclusive, either-or ordering with the image of Gray's "young man's head of yellow hair long as a dog's tail next to [Wild's] skein of black wool" (167) and with a glimpse of Wild and Golden Gray's rock home. Some seventeen years after the reader last sees Gray and the pregnant Wild, Wild's son, Joe Trace, tracks his mother to a natural burrow in a rock formation. Joe Trace had been seeking his lost mother; what he finds is the union of mother and father, nature and culture, self and other, a union that the social order forbids, but, inside this "private place," Joe feels "at peace" (183).

That peace is denied to Charles Bon in *Absalom, Absalom!*, but he dies to affirm it. Whereas Golden Gray in *Jazz* finds "home," Charles Bon is always a "forlorn nameless and homeless lost child" (215) who comes to the door of his father's house and is turned away. Philip Weinstein characterizes Bon's homelessness this way: "In the patri-archal poetics of *Absalom*, black is an uninhabitable subject position for a mulatto son" (*What Else* 149). To modify somewhat Weinstein's reading, it is not that the mulatto son cannot assume subjectivity, it is that whites in the novel refuse to permit a mulatto son to inhabit the subject position. Charles Bon can be a subject as long as he is interpret-ed as a white man. However, if he insists on having a trace of African ancestry acknowledged, then whites dictate that he must be "a nigger," who does not signify. Bon is killed precisely because he will be both black and a subject, and this is what he means when he says to Henry: "I'm the nigger that's going to sleep with your sister. Unless you stop me, Henry" (286). Bon does not die because "the insult embodied in [his own] black blood" (*What Else* 149) makes him "suicidal," but because he will not "renounce"(105) the racial intermixing that he embodies and that a marriage to Judith threatens; and, when Henry shoots Bon, the murder is the last of the novel's many attempts to erase Bon's meaning.

Bon refuses to collude with a white-dominant culture that denies racial elision so as to foster the myth that cultural designations such as black and white are separate, unbridgeable categories. Read for latent meanings, his last dying gesture is to affirm what white southerners would deny—that black and white are continuous with one another. Bon's last gesture is to switch Judith's photograph with a photograph of his octoroon wife and child so that, after his death, Judith finds on his body a metal case that had contained a picture of her but that now frames an image of the octoroon wife and child. The reason for Bon's switching of the pictures is the subject of much speculation in the novel.[6] It is also of note that Charles Bon is censored throughout the novel. The switching of the pictures is a coded message; it is a way for him to speak in his own voice. What does he say? The picture substitution—replacing Judith's photograph with a photograph of the other woman and child—suggests an equation of two women and two families: just as he loves and is related to Judith so also he loves and is tied to this woman and their child, who are culturally defined by "a drop of black blood."[7] As Morrison astutely notes of *Absalom, Absalom!*, "a drop of black blood . . . means everything and nothing." Bon's drop of black blood is made "nothing," or erased, by whites in the novel, but without it, Charles Bon, like Golden Gray, is incomplete: it is "everything" to him. The picture of the octoroon wife and child that Bon carries to his death is a concrete way for Bon to acknowledge his tie to people of color. The picture says: "they are mine and I am theirs," and, if we read Faulkner through Morrison, we can decipher Bon's message.

Notes

1. Morrison is thoroughly versed in Faulkner's fiction. Her MA thesis at Howard University was a study of alienation in the fiction of Faulkner and Virginia Woolf. During interviews and in her critical work *Playing in the Dark*, Morrison has talked about teaching and reading Faulkner.

2. Duvall writes that Morrison "causes us to rethink Faulkner" (5). Kolmerten, Ross, and Wittenberg write that "our reading of Faulkner has been—must be—profoundly changed by our reading of Morrison" (xv), O'Donnell writes that one should read Faulkner "through Morrison" (226).

3. See essays by Hogan, Kodat, and Novak in Kolmerten, et al., *Unflinching Gaze*.

4. Critics have offered a number of explanations of this off-putting form. Among other interpretations, some have suggested that Faulkner's form approximates his meaning that all representation is misrepresentation because words never get the meaning right. See O'Donnell; Matthews; Kartiganer; Watkins; Irwin; Brooks; Weinstein, *Faulkner's Subject*; Moreland; and Fowler, "Reading the Absences" and *Faulkner: The Return of the Repressed*.

5. As Rubenstein notes, both Gray and Bon are "defined by the radical absence of the father," and both are "haunted" by a need to be "legitimized by that father" (157).

6. For her part, Miss Rosa refuses to recognize the existence of the octoroon wife or her child, and, accordingly, in her account she omits the switch. As she sees the scene, the picture in the frame is of Judith. The substitution of the photograph of the octoroon wife and child for Judith's picture is Mr. Compson's contribution to the story of Charles Bon, and, for Mr. Compson, by switching the pictures, Bon proves himself to be "at least an intending bigamist even if not an out and out blackguard" (71). Later, in the course of his joint narration with Quentin, Shreve revises Mr. Compson's hard judgment. Shreve speculates that Bon replaced Judith's photograph with the picture of the other woman and child so as to earn Judith's contempt and release her: "It was because he said to himself, 'If Henry don't mean what he said, it will be all right; I can take it out and destroy it. But if he does mean what he said, it will be the only way I will have to say to her, I was no good, do not grieve for me'"(287).

7. Muhlenfeld astutely argues that Judith's actions of racial inclusion following Bon's death are driven by the switched pictures. After Bon's murder, Judith invites Bon's octoroon wife and their child to mourn at Bon's grave, and, when Bon's son is orphaned, she brings him to live with her and Clytie at Sutpen's Hundred. In Muhlenfeld's reading, Judith interprets the switched pictures as meaning that Bon loved his octoroon wife and son, and, because he cared for them, she welcomes them into the Sutpen home.

Works Cited

Bezzerides, A. I. *William Faulkner: A Life on Paper*. Ed. Ann Abadie. Jackson: UP of Mississippi, 1980. Print.

Brooks, Peter. *Reading for the Plot*. New York: Knopf, 1984. Print.

Duvall, John N. "Toni Morrison and the Anxiety of Faulknerian Influence." *Unflinching Gaze: Morrison and Faulkner Re-envisioned*. Eds. Carol A. Kolmerten, Stephen M. Ross, and Judith Bryant Wittenberg. Jackson: UP of Mississippi, 1997. 3–16. Print.

Fadiman, Clifton. "Faulkner, Extra-Special, Double-Distilled." *New Yorker* 31 Oct. 1936: 62–64. Print.

Faulkner, William. *Absalom, Absalom!* 1936. New York: Vintage, 1990. Print.

Fowler, Doreen. *Faulkner: The Return of the Repressed*. Charlottesville: U of Virginia P, 1997. Print.

___. "Reading the Absences: Race and Narration in Faulkner's *Absalom, Absalom!*" *Faulkner at One Hundred: Retrospect and Prospect*. Ed. Donald M. Kartiganer and Ann J. Abadie. Jackson: UP of Mississippi, 2000. 132–39. Print.

Fowler, Doreen, and Ann J. Abadie, eds. *Faulkner and Women: Faulkner and Yoknapatawpha, 1985*. Jackson: UP of Mississippi, 1986. Print.

Hogan, Michael. "Built on the Ashes: The Fall of the House of Sutpen and the Rise of the House of Sethe." *Unflinching Gaze: Morrison and Faulkner Re-envisioned*. Eds. Kolmerten, Ross, and Wittenberg. Jackson: UP of Mississippi, 1997. 167–80. Print.

Irwin, John T. *Doubling and Incest/Repetition and Revenge*. Baltimore: Johns Hopkins UP, 1975. Print.

Kartiganer, Donald. *The Fragile Thread: The Meaning of Form in Faulkner's Novels*. Amherst: U of Massachusetts P, 1979. Print.

Kodat, Catherine Gunther. "A Postmodern *Absalom, Absalom!*, a Modern *Beloved*: The Dialectic of Form." *Unflinching Gaze: Morrison and Faulkner Re-envisioned*. Eds. Kolmerten, Ross, and Wittenberg. Jackson: UP of Mississippi, 1997. 181–98. Print.

Kolmerten, Carol, Stephen M. Ross, and Judith Bryant Wittenberg. "Introduction." *Unflinching Gaze: Morrison and Faulkner Re-envisioned*. Eds. Kolmerten, Ross, and Wittenberg. Jackson: UP of Mississippi, 1997. ix–xv. Print.

___, eds. *Unflinching Gaze: Morrison and Faulkner Re-envisioned*. Jackson: UP of Mississippi, 1997. Print.

Matthews, John T. *The Play of Faulkner's Language*. Ithaca: Cornell UP, 1982. Print.

Moreland, Richard C. *Faulkner and Modernism: Rereading and Rewriting*. Madison: U of Wisconsin P, 1989. Print.

Morrison, Toni. "The Art of Fiction CXXXIV." Interview with Elissa Schappell. *Paris Review* 129 (1993): 83–125. Print.

___. "Faulkner and Women." *Faulkner and Women: Faulkner and Yoknapatawpha, 1985*. Eds. Doreen Fowler and Ann J. Abadie. Jackson: UP of Mississippi, 1986. 295–302. Print.

___. Interview by Nellie McKay. *Contemporary Literature* 24.4 (1983): 413–29. Print.

___. *Jazz*. New York: Knopf, 1992. Print.

___. *Playing in the Dark: Whiteness and the Literary Imagination*. Cambridge: Harvard UP, 1992. Print.

___. *Virginia Woolf's and William Faulkner's Treatment of the Alienated*. Ithaca: Cornell U Libraries, 1955. Print.

Muhlenfeld, Elisabeth. "'We Have Waited Long Enough': Judith Sutpen and Charles Bon." *Southern Review* 14 (1978): 66–80. Print.

Novak, Phillip. "Signifying Silences: Morrison's Soundings in the Faulknerian Void." *Unflinching Gaze: Morrison and Faulkner Re-envisioned*. Eds. Kolmerten, Ross, and Wittenberg. Jackson: UP of Mississippi, 1997. 199–216. Print.

O'Donnell, Patrick. "Faulkner in Light of Morrison." *Unflinching Gaze: Morrison and Faulkner Re-envisioned*. Eds. Kolmerten, Ross, and Wittenberg. Jackson: UP of Mississippi, 1997. 219–27. Print.

Rubenstein, Roberta. "History and Story: Sign and Design: Faulknerian and Postmodern Voices in *Jazz*." *Unflinching Gaze: Morrison and Faulkner Re-envisioned*. Eds. Kolmerten, Ross, and Wittenberg. Jackson: UP of Mississippi, 1997. 152–64. Print.

"Southern Cypher." *Time* 2 Nov. 1936: 67. Print.

Watkins, Floyd C. "What Happens in *Absalom, Absalom!*?" *Modern Fiction Studies* 13.1 (1967): 79–88. Print.

Weinstein, Philip M. *Faulkner's Subject: A Cosmos No One Owns*. New York: Cambridge UP, 1992. Print.

___. *What Else but Love? The Ordeal of Race in Faulkner and Morrison*. New York: Columbia UP, 1996. Print.

Misreading "the Other" as a Strategy of Narrative Empathy in *Go Down, Moses*

Patrick E. Horn

William Faulkner's fiction frequently depicts the limits and failures of human empathy, which can be defined as imaginative identification with the minds of others through both cognitive and affective domains.[1] In particular, *Go Down, Moses* (1942) may be read as an extended meditation on the limits of interracial empathy in nineteenth- and twentieth-century US southern culture. In the first chapter, titled "Was," slave owner Hubert Beauchamp is so blinded by racial categorization that he fails to recognize that the very slave whose future hangs in the balance of a high-stakes hand of poker is the one dealing the cards. In "The Fire and the Hearth," two distant cousins fail to imaginatively identify with each other's mental state—one unable to manage single parenthood following his wife's death, the other deprived of his wife's company without request, permission, or explanation—because, according to the logic of Jim Crow, one is "white" and the other "black." In "Pantaloon in Black," a sheriff's deputy fundamentally misreads the actions of a grieving man who has recently lost his wife as a sign of the man's *in*humanity. In "The Old People," Walter Ewell derides Boon Hogganbeck's powers of perception, quipping that what the large buck Boon claimed to see was probably just "somebody's stray cow" (178). In "The Bear," the (white) authors of an antebellum plantation ledger are unable to comprehend why a (black) mother would commit suicide after her daughter is seduced by her own (white) father and then dies in childbirth. In "Delta Autumn," an old white man cannot imagine why a southern black woman might willingly enter into a sexual relationship with a young white lover, and in "Go Down, Moses," a "progressive" but sanctimonious white lawyer characterizes an old black woman's desire for justice after her grandson is executed as a penchant for pageantry. Each story turns around a failure to empathize with some figure of categorical difference.

Empathy, an imaginative interpersonal relation, can enable individuals to transcend categorical differences, such as race, gender, class, culture, and sexuality—converting perceptions of "Others" into recognition of fellow humans.[2] Empathy relies upon "theory of mind" cognitive processes in which humans intuit the mental states of others by interpreting facial expressions, postures, gestures, and other forms of nonverbal communication, as well as all the nuances of language. These "mindreading" functions begin to develop at an early age and become a common part of daily life for most humans, although some studies have found that autistic subjects have trouble performing them.[3] Unlike its close cousin sympathy, empathy involves a "feeling into" that comes close to embodying the other—hence its popular connotations of "walking a mile in someone else's shoes" and "feeling one's pain"—as opposed to merely describing pity or compassion or feeling *for* others.

Empathy is also central to the experience of reading fiction, which both requires and promotes various forms of identification with unfamiliar narrators and characters. Melanie Green and other social scientists have researched the cognitive phenomenon of "narrative transport"—the process by which readers enter into narrative worlds and experience forms of disconnection or "escape" from their actual, embodied surroundings. Transportation theory helps to explain the "phenomenological experience of enjoyment through immersion in a narrative world" as well as the "persuasive effects of narratives" (Green et al. 312). Becoming transported by or absorbed in a work of literature can also bring about less pleasant emotions such as fear, grief, or anger. Imaginative immersion in fictional worlds predisposes readers to experience narrative empathy. Fritz Breithaupt writes that "fiction exists by inviting, channeling, and managing empathy" (402), and the same might be said more broadly of narratives in general. While human responses to narratives seem to rely upon empathy, the experience of empathy is also grounded in the practices of constructing, telling, and repeating narratives—practices that human children of various (if not all) cultures learn at a very young age (Prince 58). Lisa Zunshine explains that "literature pervasively capitalizes on and stimulates theory of mind mechanisms that had evolved to deal with real people. . . . As a sustained representation of numerous interacting minds, the novel feeds the representation-hungry complex of cognitive adaptations whose very condition of being is a constant social stimulation" (10). For these reasons, a narratological approach to literature—one that attends closely to narrative structures and relationships—may allow readers to better understand the complex cognitive dynamics that produce the varied responses to literary texts.

Narrative empathy emerges along multiple axes or planes of relation. First, we can analyze the *diegetic empathy* of certain narrators or characters for other narrators or characters. This term harks back to the ancient Greeks' distinction between *diegesis*, or narrated content, and *mimesis*, or represented content. For Plato, poets who narrated historical events engaged in diegesis: "the poet is speaking in his own person; he never leads us to suppose that he is any one else." But when they spoke in the voice of historical figures, they engaged in mimesis, as when Homer "does all that he can to make us believe that the speaker is not Homer, but the aged priest [Chryses] himself" (III.86). In more contemporary terms, film scholars distinguish between diegetic sounds and musical scores: dialogue and other "sound issuing from the story space" are considered an organic component of the film's auditory "narrative," while a score is generally considered to be piped in from "outside" the film's ostensible "reality" (Bordwell 332). Following this logic, one might say that diegetic empathy is the empathy that emerges (or fails to emerge) within the narrative "world" of the fictional text.

Imagine a simple scene in which one character narrates the experience of some other character: In addition to the narrator's diegetic empathy for the character described (or lack thereof), the reader may empathize (to varying degrees) with the narrator as well as the other character.[4] However, this *readerly empathy* is rarely experienced as a perfect mirroring of the narrator's own mindset. While readers may be inclined to identify more closely with the positions and attitudes of the narrator than those of other characters in the text, readers also consider the narrator's interests and motives, as well as the appropriateness of his or her characterizations and responses to events, as the plot of a narrative unfolds. James Phelan emphasizes the role of "narrative progression" in readers' formulations of narrative judgments. The experience of reading entails a "synthesis of both the textual dynamics that govern the movement of narrative from beginning through middle to end" as well as the readers' responses to those events (3). Therefore, although readers may not identify perfectly with the attitudes and beliefs of the narrator, they do tend to experience a given fictional text similarly. "Texts are designed by authors in order to affect readers in particular ways," although the "efficacy" of their designs varies from reader to reader (4). Phelan proposes that narratives can be best understood as rhetorical acts through which meaning is produced as an exchange between author, text, and reader.

Suzanne Keen envisions narrative empathy as a form of communication that originates with the author imagining some intended audience. She argues that authors employ various modes of *strategic empathy*, "attempt[ing] to direct an emotional transaction through a fictional work aimed at a particular audience, not necessarily including every reader who happens upon the text" (142).[5] Keen describes the reader's experience of narrative empathy in terms of accuracy: Targeted readers receive the author's "transmission" either accurately or inaccurately. While authors such as Faulkner may very well write with some intended message or motive in mind, Keen's model seems to trivialize the complexity of fictional texts; it reduces the narrative form to a communiqué, and it potentially excludes those readers not intended as "recipients." This essay proposes a more open-ended and text-centered notion of narrative empathy wherein authors craft their literary works in order to structure readers' responses, with varying degrees of efficacy. These responses may not be reducible to "accurate" or "inaccurate" receptions; they may include internal conflict and dissonance as well as simple identifications, and they are likely to shift and change as the narrative progresses. As Fritz Breithaupt and others have noted, the *absence* of diegetic empathy may elicit readerly empathy more strongly than the most empathetic narrator. Faulkner's fiction often functions in this manner: Some of his most powerful statements or messages are indirect, unspoken, or even disavowed. Who can read, for example, Jason Compson's characterization of his niece Quentin in *The Sound and the Fury* (1929)—"Once a bitch always a bitch, what I say" (173)—without experiencing a visceral negative reaction to his words? Reading this passage, one is more likely to identify with the niece's misfortune of having Jason as a guardian than to accept his statement at face value. But who can determine the extent to which readers' sentiments or conclusions "accurately" reflect Faulkner's own? We might more profitably examine the ways in which literary texts structure and elicit certain responses: the technologies of narrative empathy.

Not only do the stories that comprise *Go Down, Moses* culminate in dramatic misperceptions and mischaracterizations; they are structured in a manner that encourages readers to recognize and respond to these failures. By revealing the actual attitudes and beliefs of the "Othered" characters before they are then seemingly misjudged, the stories highlight the errors of those who pass judgment in advance, or lacking full knowledge: In other words, they implicitly critique the logic of prejudice. The text therefore informs the reader about the *diegetic truth* of each situation within the ordered, contained world of the narrative before depicting *mis*perceptions on the part of narrators or characters, which are often premised on racialized logic.[6] These crucial failures of empathy often occur at or near the end of the story, when the reader will be best informed about the mental states of the characters in question and therefore most able to recognize the errors—a psychological version of dramatic irony. Through this construction, Faulkner's stories in *Go Down, Moses* prepare readers to identify and reject the failed empathy of certain narrators and characters by first enabling readers to empathize with those characters who are later misjudged as "Others."

Scholars have long discussed and debated how much credit and/or blame Faulkner merits for his fictional depictions of difficult cultural material. Racism, sexism, classism, violence, and simple human cruelty all feature prominently in his work. Therefore, critics often question the extent to which readers should consider the author guilty of, or at least embroiled in, his own characters' "sins." When does a literary text move from portraying, say, racist behavior to actually becoming a racist text? Philip Weinstein argues that Faulkner's black characters are "largely deprived by the narrative of interior voice, of point of view, of a sense of their own past and future (their memories and desires)—blacks as represented by Faulkner are truncated figures" (44). In a similar vein, Thadious M. Davis writes that "Faulkner seems able to acknowledge the tyranny of the cultural stereotype, especially in his portraits of Lucas and Rider. . . . He transforms it more fully into an underlying imaginative conception which serves his art, though he still cannot escape it" (243).

Although there will be no attempt to offer any definitive answer to the age-old questions of authorial intention or responsibility, it will be argued that Faulkner's novel, *Go Down Moses*, presents some of its most offensive material in such a fashion as to guide the reader's response to it in particular ways.[7] Characters who malign "Others" most egregiously in the novel do so in ways that contradict information to which readers have previously been privy, or they appear to misrepresent the nature of those characters' actions. Typically in these situations (though not always), white male characters misrepresent the thoughts and actions of black characters, both male and female. But Faulkner's novel is structured such that it prompts readers to note and respond to these misrepresentations. Therefore, one might consider *Go Down, Moses* as a psychology experiment designed to elicit readers' empathy and disapproval or even outrage through the offensive attitudes and behaviors of certain characters. Considering the text in this way should not necessarily excuse Faulkner for all of the misconceptions that inhabit his fictional world, but it does seem to reveal his (at least partial) awareness of them as such. Although the novel does reproduce the ideology of Jim Crow in many of its representations, it seems to do so in order to undermine that logic, inviting readers to critique its own characters' stated conclusions. Instances of conspicuous misjudgment abound in the novel, but this essay will focus on three particular failures of diegetic empathy and the reader responses that these failures seem designed to provoke. First, the scene from "Was" in which Terrel (or "Turl") deals a fateful hand of poker will be analyzed; then, the deputy sheriff's concluding statement in "Pantaloon in Black" will be examined; and finally, Gavin Stevens's erroneous characterization of Mollie Beauchamp in the novel's final chapter will be addressed.[8]

Despite opening with a chase scene involving a fugitive slave, *Go Down, Moses*'s first chapter sets a comic (or perhaps tragicomic) tone for the novel. Tomey's Turl, as readers later learn, is both half brother and nephew to Buck and Buddy McCaslin, the unorthodox southern planters who have allowed their slaves to take over the "big house" and built themselves a log cabin instead (250–51). The chase is sporadic and convoluted: Turl initially eludes his pursuers, and he ultimately helps determine his own fate through a poker game that results from a confusing series of wagers between Buck, Buddy, and Hubert Beauchamp.

The sordid subtext of this story is that human lives are treated as currency, as wagers to be "raised" and "called" or "passed." Not only the lives of slaves are gambled: In the final game, Buddy offers "Buck McCaslin against Sibbey's dowry" (26). Hence, if Buddy loses, his brother will have to marry Hubert's sister Sophonsiba "without any dowry" (25). This "dowry" is itself measured in human lives, for Hubert had initially offered Sibbey's reluctant suitor his female slave Tennie, Turl's love interest and eventual wife (259). The "pot" becomes more complicated when Buddy raises "them two niggers," meaning that Hubert would have to pay $300 to purchase Turl if he loses. Ironically, the *loser* of the hand would pay to keep the enslaved couple together. This twisted wager therefore subverts both the ideal of white southern womanhood—Buddy is desperately trying to free Buck from having to marry Sophonsiba—and the usual conventions of American slavery, in which enslaved couples were more often separated to suit their white owners' whims than united at the masters' inconvenience.

Before the hand of poker began, Hubert had instructed Buddy's young cousin "Cass" McCaslin to "Go to the back door and holler. Bring the first creature that answers, animal mule or human, that can deal ten cards" (25). This meant, of course, a slave, though Hubert's instructions reveal his lack of conviction regarding the slaves' humanity. After Buddy's raise, and at the climactic point of the narrative, the identity of the card dealer is revealed. Hubert glances up in the dark room and shines a lamp on "Tomey's Turl's arms that were supposed to be black but were not quite white" (28) and then up to reveal his face, the face of a mixed-race relative whose life Buddy had just wagered. The strategic positioning of this revelation renders it simultaneously the story's dramatic climax and a sort of anticlimax. Hubert merely turns his cards "face-down" and says, "I pass, Amodeus" (28).

Hubert folds rather than calling Buddy's bet because he realizes (too late) that this "creature" who had dealt the cards might actually have some interest and agency in the situation at hand. The outcome is later recorded in the McCaslin plantation ledgers: *"Tennie Beauchamp 21 yrs Won by Amodeus McCaslin from Hubert Beauchamp Esqre Possible Strait against three Treys in sigt Not called 1859 Marrid to Tomys Turl 1859"* (259). But it is Hubert's initial failure to identify Turl (or Terrel) as fully human, as an individual with vested interests and a poker player like himself, that causes him to fold and therefore to lose the bet: The story turns upon his dramatic failure of empathy. In the same moment that Hubert realizes his folly—right after he asks "Who dealt these cards, Amodeus?" (28)—readers can imagine the cleverness of Turl, who *may* (the novel never reveals the final card) have intentionally dealt his half brother a straight. The failure, or belated appearance, of diegetic empathy elicits readerly empathy for the "Other": readers recognize Hubert's folly, just as he does. As a result, Turl remains part of the McCaslin family and gains a wife—and as it turns out, Buck goes on to marry Sophonsiba anyway.[9] This conclusion sets the tone for the novel as a whole, and scenes of strategic misreading recur in every subsequent story.

Critics have often questioned why Faulkner included the chapter titled "Pantaloon in Black" in the novel. This story does not directly include any members of the McCaslin and Beauchamp families that the other stories focus on; its central character, Rider, simply rents a house on Roth Edmonds's land. As Linda Wagner-Martin points out, many early reviewers of the novel wondered "how . . . to relate that story to the rest of the book" (3). However, its pivotal scene, toward the end of the chapter, reveals a startling failure of empathy caused by racist ideology, and this failure places the story at the thematic heart of the novel.

The chapter opens with the scene of Rider, a young black man of enormous strength who works at the nearby sawmill, burying his young wife Mannie. The unidentified narrator relates their brief romance and marriage: Rider's life of hard work, weekend whiskey and dice games, and "nameless" women had changed six months ago "when he saw Mannie, whom he had known all his life, for the first time" (134). Since then the couple had lived a life of quiet routine: their savings steadily growing; he working weekends to rebuild, reroof, and refloor the house; and she preparing for him "the sidemeat, the greens, the cornbread, the buttermilk from the well-house, the cake which she baked every Saturday now that she had a stove to bake in" (135). Their brief life together is described in terms of newlywed commitment, contentment, and prosperity—although the narrator's commodification of their relationship into soul food and home improvement calls up the previous critiques by Davis and Weinstein. After her death, Rider sees a vision of Mannie and begs her, "Wait. . . . Den lemme go wid you, honey" (136). But the specter fades, and he descends into a terrible state of agitation and duress, working maniacally, walking aimlessly and furiously through the woods, and eating without being able to taste his food. When Rider's uncle urges him to put his "faith and trust" in the Lord, Rider rejects his advice: "Whut faith and trust? . . . Whut Mannie ever done ter Him?" (140). Likewise, his aunt begs him to pray, calling after Rider, "'Spoot! Spoot!' . . . the name he had gone by in his childhood and adolescence, before the men he worked with and the bright dark nameless women he had taken in course and forgotten until he saw Mannie that day and said, 'Ah'm thu wid all dat,' began to call him Rider" (146). Through this narration, Rider emerges as an individual with a family history and a complex psyche who has undergone two life-changing experiences: He fell in love, and then his beloved was inexplicably taken away. After Mannie's death, neither religion nor "white-mule" corn whiskey can assuage his mental anguish; he laments that "Hit look lack Ah just cant quit thinking" (154). Rider's grief and anger at God are made evident to the reader and at least partly explain his sudden and violent action: Without warning, he kills Birdsong, the white night watchman who had been cheating him and the other mill workers at dice for fifteen years.

After Rider has been arrested, thrown in jail, taken out of the jail, and lynched, the sheriff's deputy relates the story to his wife:

They ain't human. They look like a man and they walk on their hind legs like a man, and they can talk and you can understand them and you think they are understanding you, at least now and then. But when it comes to the normal human feelings and sentiments of human beings, they might just as well be a damn herd of wild buffaloes. (149–50)

This startling racist diatribe demonstrates the deputy's utter lack of empathy for a man so deeply bereaved at his wife's death that he seemingly sought out and ensured his own destruction. One might argue that the entire story of "Pantaloon in Black" is engineered to exhibit the humanity of Rider; by the time readers encounter the deputy's comment, it has become patently clear that his judgment is erroneous. This scene of failed empathy seems designed to abrade and offend the reader—not only because the comment is racist, but also because it contradicts the emotional "facts" of the story that readers have already witnessed. If the phenomenological experience of reading a story is, as James Phelan explains, a process of forming judgments in progression with the developing plot, this statement is placed precisely at the point where the readers' judgments regarding Rider have become fully formed. This placement makes it evident that the deputy has fundamentally *misread* Rider and his story.

"Pantaloon in Black" also includes what Phelan calls an internal "narratee," or an audience embedded within the narrative: the deputy's wife, to whom he relates his version of the story's events. Her reaction to the deputy's narrative serves as a ready model for the reader's own response. When he begins his account—"Now you take this one today"—she cuts him off before he can even begin, with the retort "I wish you would" (150). Later, after he has recounted the entire series of events, she upbraids him again: "I think if you eat any supper in this house you'll do it in the next five minutes" (154). The deputy's wife's apparent lack of interest or credence in his account further undermines his misreading of the story and inclines the reader to reject it as well. Readers' previously formed empathy for Rider (and perhaps also pre-existing attitudes toward racist ideology) precludes the possibility of readerly empathy for the sheriff's deputy.

The introduction of Gavin Stevens as the mouthpiece for the novel's conclusion—and its final strategic misreading—is confounding and double-voiced. The ostensibly progressive white lawyer is introduced as "Gavin Stevens, Phi Beta Kappa, Harvard, Ph.D., Heidelberg" (353), and he proves to be an intriguingly contradictory figure. Does the unidentified narrator revere Stevens or mock him? Is this introduction homage or ridicule? At different points throughout the story, the answer seems to be one or the other, or both simultaneously. Stevens's figure even seems at times to serve as an avatar for the flesh-and-blood figure of Faulkner himself, perhaps with a modicum or even a heaping portion of self-satire. Like the author, he is a writer and a scholar of sorts: His "serious vocation was a twenty-two-year-old unfinished translation of the Old Testament back into classic Greek" (353). The nature of this pursuit suggests both a passionate attention to detail and a lack of regard for pragmatic applications of one's work.

In the final chapter, "Go Down, Moses," readers learn that Mollie Beauchamp's grandson, Samuel Beauchamp (aka "Butch"), is scheduled to be executed in Chicago for allegedly killing a policeman (a charge that he denies). Mollie comes to Stevens's office and tells him, "I come to find my boy. . . . And you the law" (353–54). Mollie explains that Roth Edmonds "sold him in Egypt. . . . I just knows Pharoah got him" (353–54), and Stevens remembers that Edmonds "had caught the boy breaking into his commissary store and had ordered him off the place and had forbidden him ever to return" (355). Like those in many of Faulkner's works, this scene reveals multiple perspectives from which to understand a historical event. Here, even the semantic registers of Gavin and Mollie's language are different: She speaks in an Old Testament–infused African American vernacular, and his is the legalistic language of prominent white landowners in the postbellum South.

Gavin Stevens's initial response to Mollie's request seems admirable, especially given the racial codes and politics of their time (the story is set in or around 1940). He consults the local newspaper editor; he meets with Miss Worsham, an old white woman with whom Mollie lives; he arranges a proper casket for the young man; and he solicits donations in town to pay for Samuel's burial. Yet while visiting Miss Worsham and Mollie, Stevens seems troubled by Mollie's accusation that Edmonds "sold my Benjamin . . . Sold him in Egypt . . . Sold him to Pharoah and now he dead" (362). His immediate response is "I'd better go," and the narration suggests that he feels unable to breathe during this interchange. The reason for Stevens's sudden shortness of breath is unclear. Does he take offense at the charges that Mollie levels at Roth Edmonds? Does he feel somehow complicit in the young man's death? Does he disagree that whites are responsible for Butch's death? Or is he merely uncomfortable in Mollie's presence and with her incantatory song?

Stevens's characterizations of Mollie Beauchamp mark her as "Other"; Stevens focuses on her age, gender, and race, and he refers to her throughout the story in the coded language of Jim Crow. Stevens's first address to Mollie—"Beauchamp? . . . You live on Mr Carothers Edmonds' place" (353)—identifies her as a dependent and a member of the racially stratified plantation society in which she was denied the full rights of citizenship. Stevens's deferential (full) naming of "Mr Carothers Edmonds" contrasts with the terse "Beauchamp," as he greets her, devoid of courtesies or honorifics. When Mollie begins to explain her situation, Stevens cuts her off with the dismissive phrase "Wait, Aunty" (353), and he goes on to refer to her repeatedly, both in his narration and his subsequent conversation with the newspaper editor, as "the old Negress" (354–55).

When Stevens learns that Mollie is the sister of a black man whom Stevens has known all his life, he muses, "They were like that. You could know two of them for years. . . . Then suddenly you learn by pure chance that they are brothers or sisters" (354). Not only does Stevens's rhetoric of "you" and "them" establish Mollie Beauchamp as a racialized Other, but his narration presumes an audience (or narratee) who, like him, is white and accepts the racial hierarchies of the Jim Crow South. In short, Stevens is unable or unwilling to imaginatively identify with Mollie, and rather than attempting to perceive their common humanity, he emphasizes the inscrutability of blacks—an unknowable, unpredictable "them"—with "their" ability to surprise people like "us."

After Stevens has arranged a ceremonial burial for the young man, he drives behind the hearse with the newspaper editor, Mr. Wilmoth. Wilmoth tells Stevens that Mollie had instructed him, "I wants hit all in de paper. All of hit" (365). This prompts Stevens to think, in what are nearly the final words of the novel, "*She doesn't care how he died. She just wanted him home, but she wanted him to come home right. She wanted that casket and those flowers and the hearse and she wanted to ride through town behind it in a car*" (365). In this final rationalization, which Stevens feels compelled to make for perhaps the same reasons that he previously "had to leave" the grieving grandmother, he dismisses the nature of Samuel Beauchamp's death, telling himself that "she doesn't care how he died," that Samuel was executed for a crime that he may not have committed. The story opens with a scene in which Samuel tells a census taker that his occupation is "getting rich too fast" (352)—with the double connotation of robbery and of a newfound prosperity that whites might not appreciate. Moreover, Mollie's injunction to put the story of Samuel's death and burial in the paper—"all of hit"—belies Stevens's conclusion that she didn't care how he died. His description of Mollie's desire for a proper burial for her grandson as a childish or ostentatious demand to be humored by tolerant whites such as himself—"that casket and those flowers and the hearse"—and his description of the ceremony itself—"she wanted to ride through town behind it in a car"—are dismissive and bereft of empathy. Stevens, the self-appointed figure of white liberal tolerance, absolves himself of any guilt in the matter by arranging the pageant that he believes Mollie is really after.

Stevens's neat resolution to the events in "Go Down, Moses" also misjudges the importance of Samuel's death. Over the course of *Go Down, Moses*, the McCaslin and Beauchamp lines falter and fail, in both their white and black lineages. Ike McCaslin is childless and nearing eighty at the beginning of the novel. Samuel's mother Nat dies in childbirth, and his father abandons him. Roth Edmonds's child with the unnamed woman in "Delta Autumn" is unlikely to grow up with any intimate knowledge of his ancestral land or family relations; he may never return. This final death represents the culmination of a long series of failures to thrive; the McCaslin and Beauchamp descendents are few and scattered; the dissolution of two once-proud southern families is almost complete. Therefore, Stevens's complacent summary seems especially inappropriate to this final, tragic turn of events.

Stevens misreads Mollie and her story: Despite his good intentions and his attempts to appease the old woman, he fails to empathize with her or her family on a fundamental human level. Readers are likely to find his conclusion unsettling and inappropriate, incommensurate with the scope of the novel's dramatic subject. Gavin Stevens's failure of diegetic empathy is Faulkner's finishing touch: one final misjudgment designed to elicit the reader's uncomfortable or dissatisfied response.

As discussed earlier in this essay, scholars disagree about the extent to which Faulkner's fiction should be considered guilty of the same problems and shortcomings it highlights. Lee Jenkins acknowledges that black characters are often treated unfairly by white characters in Faulkner's fiction, but insists that they are ultimately allowed a degree of autonomy and dignity. "Faulkner's [black characters] . . . may still be the obverse reflection of the whites they live among, but they are at least recognized as entities who cannot be easily known, whose reality must be grasped with some effort, and who may conceivably have some hard-earned and honorable conception of themselves that may belie the mockery, contempt, and amusement of paternalistic whites" (223). The reader is left to cipher the attempts of African American characters at "some . . . honorable conception of themselves" (223), and it is often only through the conspicuous absence of (white) empathy that Faulkner gestures toward the dignity or shared humanity of the (black) Other.

A narratological approach to Faulkner's fiction that accounts for the text's role in guiding and eliciting readerly empathy for "the Other" might help to contextualize the literary sins of which the author is sometimes accused. The notion that his black characters "cannot be easily known" does not always hold true in this novel; Lucas Beauchamp and Rider are two examples of black characters who emerge with psychological depth and individual identity.[10] But Faulkner's fiction often features white characters who fail to "know" their black counterparts—and even their black relatives—because of dramatic failures of diegetic empathy. These failures are strategically placed to highlight their errors and misjudgments. David Wyatt argues that "when it comes to race, we are all readers, or misreaders; race is not a fact, but America's most complex and damaging figuration. And Faulkner makes it clear [in *Go Down, Moses*] that any take on race will be a reading" (281). Perhaps the way twenty-first-century readers, approach that reading can shed new light on Faulkner's art.

Go Down, Moses demonstrates that the absence of diegetic empathy may function as a powerful technology for eliciting readerly empathy, especially when its absence is strategically placed in conspicuous locations. The failures by many of Faulkner's narrators or characters to empathize with figures of difference may provoke a strong sense of empathy on the part of the reader toward these abused textual "Others"—not merely because of the reader's own political leanings or ideological identifications, but because the text leads readers to witness and respond to the perceptual shortcomings of those who prejudge fellow humans as "Others."

Notes

The author gratefully acknowledges the invaluable feedback of Minrose Gwin, Rebecka Rutledge Fisher, Jessica Martell, and Zackary Vernon, without whom this essay would not have been possible.

1. The *Oxford English Dictionary* defines "empathy" as "the power of projecting one's personality into (and so fully comprehending) the object of contemplation," noting that the word entered the English language as a translation of the German term *Einfühlung*, which originally referred to aesthetic appreciation of a work of art. *Merriam-Webster Collegiate Dictionary* offers a psychological definition more common in contemporary usage: "the action of understanding, being aware of, being sensitive to, and vicariously experiencing the feelings, thoughts, and experience of another," as well as the "capacity" for such a relation. *Empathy*, as used in this essay, draws on both senses of the term.

2. The term "Others" will be used in this essay as a floating signifier to refer to the perception of radical alterity or categorical difference. Thus, it refers to those perceived as belonging to some group of which the observer is not a member. The "Other" category exists in the mind of the beholder, and it varies based on cultural and historical context. As Edward Said has observed, "The construction

of identity . . . involves the construction of opposites and 'others' whose actuality is always subject to the continuous interpretation and re-interpretation of their differences from 'us.' Each age and society re-creates its 'Others'" (332).

3. For more detailed discussions of theory of mind or "mindreading" practices, see Simon Baron-Cohen, *Mindblindness: An Essay on Autism and Theory of Mind* (Cambridge: MIT P, 1995); Sanjida O'Connell, *Mindreading: An Investigation into How We Learn to Love and Lie* (New York: Doubleday, 1998); Shaun Nichols and Stephen P. Stich, *Mindreading: An Integrated Account of Pretence, Self-Awareness, and Understanding Other Minds* (New York: Oxford UP, 2003); and Lisa Zunshine, *Why We Read Fiction: Theory of Mind and the Novel* (Columbus: Ohio State UP, 2006).

4. Passages or entire texts in which the narrator's identity is unclear present obvious challenges to this simple explanation, as does the practice of free indirect discourse, which is common in modernist fiction. However, even when the narrator is unclear or unidentified, diegetic empathy can be said to exist to the extent that the narrative imaginatively identifies with the character described. The third person omniscient perspective might therefore be said to rely upon diegetic empathy. This term, broadly defined, can refer to the empathy of a narrator for another character or the empathy of one character for another character, within the world of the narrative.

5. Keen identifies three categories of strategic empathy: *bounded strategic empathy*, which "occurs within an in-group, stemming from experiences of mutuality, and leading to feeling with familiar others"; *ambassadorial strategic empathy*, which "addresses chosen others with the aim of cultivating their empathy for the in-group, often to a specific end"; and *broadcast strategic empathy*, which "calls upon every reader to feel with members of a group, by empathizing our common vulnerabilities and hopes" (142). Because this essay's analysis is more focused upon the functions of the literary text than the author's intended audience, these categories have been eschewed in favor of a "strategic empathy" that does not presuppose or imply specific readers.

6. Post-structuralist philosophers and theorists are quick to note that no absolute or essential truth is ever obtainable within the realms of language or narrative. However, diegetic truth may be understood as the apparent state of being as revealed by narrators and characters within the finite and imaginary world of a fictional narrative. Faulkner's fiction repeatedly points out and probes at the ineffability of certain knowledge; nevertheless, within the worlds he creates, some sense of trustworthy narration generally emerges. When Faulkner's narratives are rendered suspect (as in *Absalom, Absalom!* when Quentin and Shreve speculate about the antics and motives of historical figures), they generally do so openly and self-consciously. Nevertheless, diegetic truth should never be characterized as absolute or essential.

7. Although it was originally published as *Go Down, Moses and Other Stories*, Faulkner always insisted that the book was a novel rather than a short-story collection. During one question-and-answer session at the University of Virginia,

the author explained that he added extra material to "The Bear" because the novel centers around how "the Negro and the white phase of the [McCaslin] family" were the "same people," and "the rest of the book was a part of [Isaac's] past too" (qtd. in Gwynn and Blotner 4).

8. Though Faulkner spells this character's name as "Molly" in "The Fire and the Hearth," the spelling "Mollie," as the narrator refers to her throughout the final chapter, will be used.

9. The novel does not fully explain how Buck comes to marry Sophonsiba, though she is clearly working hard to win his affections during the first story, set in 1859. By 1867, the couple has married, they have moved back into the "big house" that Buck and Buddy had previously forfeited to their slaves, and Sophonsiba has given birth to their only son, Isaac (287–88).

10. In "The Fire and the Hearth," Lucas expresses moral outrage: "How to God . . . can a black man ask a white man to please not lay down with his black wife?" (58). He plans to upbraid the disrespectful young man who has married his daughter: "*it will be a lesson to him about whose daughter to fool with next time*" (61, 70). He experiences a change of heart about the treasure he had resolved to find with his metal detector: "I reckon to find that money aint for me" (127). These passages demonstrate that Faulkner was perfectly "able" to write black characters who escape the "tyranny of the cultural stereotype"; indeed, that aim is precisely what animates the character of Lucas Beauchamp. His ability to create compelling female characters or to provide them with original, individual voices is another question.

Works Cited

Bordwell, David. *Film Art: An Introduction.* 9th ed. New York: McGraw-Hill, 2010. Print.

Breithaupt, Fritz. "How I Feel Your Pain: Lessing's Mitleid, Goethe's Anagnorisis, and Fontane's Quiet Sadism." *Deutsche Vierteljahrsschrift für Literaturwissenschaft und Geistes-Geschichte* (Mar. 2008): 400–23. Print.

Davis, Thadious M. *Faulkner's "Negro": Art and the Southern Context.* Baton Rouge: Louisiana State UP, 1983. Print.

Faulkner, William. *Go Down, Moses.* 1942. New York: Vintage, 1990. Print.

___. *The Sound and the Fury.* 1929. New York: Vintage, 1992. Print.

Glissant, Edouard. *Faulkner, Mississippi.* Trans. Barbara Lewis and Thomas C. Spear. New York: Farrar, 1996. Print.

Green, Melanie C., Timothy C. Brock, and Geoff F. Kaufman. "Understanding Media Enjoyment: The Role of Transportation into Narrative Worlds." *Communication Theory* 14.4 (Nov. 2004): 311–27. Print.

Gwynn, Frederick L., and Joseph L. Blotner. *Faulkner in the University.* 1959. Charlottesville: UP of Virginia, 1995. Print.

Jenkins, Lee. *Faulkner and Black-White Relations: A Psychoanalytic Approach.* New York: Columbia UP, 1981. Print.

Keen, Suzanne. *Empathy and the Novel.* New York: Oxford UP, 2007. Print.

Matthews, John T. "Touching Race in *Go Down, Moses.*" *New Essays on* Go Down, Moses. Ed. Linda Wagner-Martin. New York: Cambridge UP, 1996. 21–47. Print.

Phelan, James. *Experiencing Fiction: Judgments, Progressions, and the Rhetorical Theory of Narrative.* Columbus: Ohio State UP, 2007. Print.

Plato. *The Republic.* New York: Penguin, 2003. Print.

Prince, Gerald. *A Dictionary of Narratology.* Lincoln: U of Nebraska P, 1987. Print.

Said, Edward W. *Orientalism.* New York: Vintage, 1994. Print.

Wagner-Martin, Linda. Introduction. *New Essays on* Go Down, Moses. Ed. Linda Wagner-Martin. New York: Cambridge UP, 1996. 1–20. Print.

Weinstein, Philip. *Faulkner's Subject: A Cosmos No One Owns.* New York: Cambridge UP, 1992. Print.

Wyatt, David. "Faulkner and the Reading Self." *Faulkner and Psychology: Faulkner and Yoknapatawpha,* 1991. Jackson: UP of Mississippi, 1994. Print.

Zunshine, Lisa. *Why We Read Fiction: Theory of Mind and the Novel.* Columbus: Ohio State UP, 2006. Print.

CRITICAL
READINGS

Faulkner the Cannibal: Digesting Conrad_____

Jacques Pothier

One of William Faulkner's rare elaborate statements on his art of fiction appears in two unpublished drafts for an introduction to *The Sound and the Fury* (1929), his first masterpiece. They were probably written in 1933 for a new edition, but were only published posthumously and are now easy to find, for instance in the Norton edition of the novel. Faulkner explained how with this book he learned what writing was about:

> When I finished *The Sound and the Fury* . . . I discovered then that I had gone through all that I had ever read, from Henry James through Henty to newspaper murders, without making any distinction or digesting any of it, as a moth or a goat might. After *The Sound and the Fury* and without heeding to open another book and in a series of delayed repercussions like summer thunder, I discovered the Flauberts and Dostoeveskys and Conrads whose books I had read ten years ago. ("Introduction" 226)

The metaphor of digesting that Faulkner uses is also that of Brazilian author Oswald de Andrade who, in his *Manifesto Antropófago* (1928) outlined how postcolonial writers could digest with profit the influences of mainstream literature rather than be weighed down by them. The *Manifesto Antropófago* drew on the reputation of the natives from the Brazilian forest: as a cannibal knew the best pieces of his enemy's body, cannibalism consisted in ingesting the virtues of one's enemy without surrendering one's identity, in a kind of homage. A healthy diet implied a good digestion. In the postcolonial situation of modernist Brazil, cultural cannibalism, or anthopophagy, meant a critical assimilation of global Western culture as it was sifted by the colonial center in Europe. The Brazilian "cannibal" was not alienated by the dominant culture, but as an astute dietician, he was in a position to select the morsels of his enemy that could reinforce his cultural constitution. The inspiration for this essay derives from a study by Scott G. Williams entitled "Eating Faulkner Eating Baudelaire: Multiple Rewritings and Cultural Cannibalism," in which Williams also draws on the concept of anthropophagy. It is a modernist idea: one can relate it to T. S. Eliot's famous review essay on James Joyce's *Ulysses* (1922), in which he praised the author's "mythical method," the way in which a modernist writer recycles the classics and the myths inherited from them.

In his comment on writing *The Sound and the Fury*, Faulkner traces his influence to a variety of texts, ranging widely from the great novelists of the Western tradition to forgotten authors of pulp fiction as well as the everyday rubble of newspaper stories. He ends up specifically mentioning three major literary influences: Gustave Flaubert, Fyodor Dostoevsky, and Joseph Conrad, none of whom, by the way, are American authors. In comments he made at the University of Virginia in 1957, while claiming that one could find similarities between his writing and that of any one of his great predecessors, Faulkner went into specific detail about Conrad's influence. In response to a question about the influence of Conrad's narrative technique of looking at an event by throwing light on it from the past and the future as well as the present and from the point of view of various characters, Faulkner replied that he thought all writers did that. Because Conrad was writing in a foreign language and he had not had much schooling, Faulkner thought they were both "a little more obvious than the others" (Gwynn and Blotner 142). With tongue-in-cheek modesty, Faulkner points to the rugged quality of the style he shares with Conrad. Later in the same session, when pressed to be specific, he mentioned a few titles: *The Nigger of the "Narcissus"* (1897), "Falk," "The End of the Tether," and "Youth." When asked if he read *Nostromo* (1904), Faulkner said, "Haven't read that in years" (Gwynn and Blotner 144–45).

However, many years before, there is evidence that Faulkner did read *Nostromo*. "Carcassonne," a very short story first published in 1931, is an excellent example to approach the distillation of Conradian influence in Faulkner. "Carcassonne" has a privileged place in

Faulkner's short pieces if only because it concludes the selection of his *Collected Stories* (1950), which were carefully chosen and ordered under the direction of the author. In the wake of T. S. Eliot's "Love Song of J. Alfred Prufrock" and *The Waste Land* (1922), the piece is rich in literary allusions. The practically plotless piece is a surrealistic prose-poem in which the narrator, an aspiring poet, daydreams of escaping on the Pegasus-like horse of his imagination from the weight of his "skeleton" (echoed by the "carcass" in "Carcassonne"). He is so destitute that he has to live in a rat-infested garret, with only "an unrolled strip of tarred roofing" as bed clothing. The bones, rats, and garret seem to stem from Eliot's *Waste Land*:

> But at my back in a cold blast I hear
> The rattle of the bones, and chuckle spread from ear to ear.
> A rat crept softly through the vegetation . . .
> White bodies naked on the low damp ground
> And bones cast in a little low dry garret,
> Rattled by the rat's foot only, year to year. (III, lines 185–87, 193–95)

The Waste Land conjured up a rootless, cosmopolitan experience. "Carcassonne" refers to foreign locations too—not just in the title, that uses the name of the famous French medieval town, but also in the location of the exile's garret:

> Beneath him Rincon followed its fatal, secret, nightly pursuits, where upon the rich and inert darkness of the streets lighted windows and doors lay like oily strokes of broad and overladen brushes. . . .

> Luis, who ran the cantina downstairs, allowed him to sleep in the garret. But the Standard Oil Company, who owned the garret and the roofing paper, owned the darkness too; it was Mrs Widdrington's, the Standard Oil Company's wife's, darkness he was using to sleep in. (*Collected* 895, 897)

For many years readers and critics (if they noticed) wondered what Latin American country Faulkner or his protagonist might have visited—not too far from the South perhaps? In one of the best essays on "Carcassonne," Noel Polk suggests comparing this Rincon with the destination of the characters in "Divorce in Naples," a story set just before "Carcassonne" in the collection, which drifts from Naples through the strait of Gibraltar, along the Gulf Stream "to Tortugas, and into the general region of Puerto Rico," where there really happens to be one Rincon, which goes unmentioned in that story (Polk 33).

The reference to the art of painting in the sentence where "Rincon" is named hints to another lead, as it points to an artistic connection: In *Nostromo*, Conrad's novel set in South America, there is a Rincón near his imaginary Sulaco, with a posada if not a cantina. The colonial dominance of the Standard Oil Company executives in Faulkner's short story provides a parallel with the power of Mr. Gould, the *inglès* who runs the San Tomé mine in Conrad's novel. Most likely the Latin America that Faulkner had visited for "Carcassonne" was bookish. The discreet allusion to Rincon appears to be an all but private homage to Conrad, but the Spanish undertone introduces the figure of the quixotic character, whose horse becomes the vehicle for an escape into the world of the imagination. Quixote is also an important figure in what Faulkner owed his forerunners: The sense of honor pushes numerous Faulkner characters to an absurd and foolish denial of reality, from Quentin Compson to the tall convict in *The Wild Palms* (1939), and from Gavin Stevens to Lucius Priest in the later novels. In one of the two plots that make up *The Wild Palms*, two characters are reminiscent of the famous twosome of the tall thin knight with the sad face and his plump short servant Sancho Panza. An idealist like Don Quixote, the tall convict in "Old Man" believed that he could be a successful train robber by scrupulously imitating the procedures described in the *Detective Gazette* he read. The tall convict is in a state of uncomprehending outrage against the deceptions of fiction: The pulp fiction he read betrayed him by suggesting methods that proved completely impractical, and he cannot get over the offense he suffered from fiction writers. This theme may find its earlier illustration in Cervantes, but Faulkner could also have found it in another of his favorite novels, Flaubert's *Madame Bovary* (1857; English translation, 1886).

As John T. Matthews has suggested, "to be white and a poet of the South in the New World also means to inhabit quarters haunted by skeletons in the corners" (242). Through Conrad, Faulkner seems to play in "Carcassonne" with the figures of the American gothic—the skeletons in the closet of a colonial rule marked by the special South American dilemma of a freedom from the colonial power obtained by the fight of the ruling class, who themselves never checked or questioned their exploitation of the indigenous workers.

Another story by Faulkner, designed as a kind of companion piece to "Carcassonne," is also set in Rincon, but the local color is stronger. "Black Music" has exactly the same setting as "Carcassonne," as the protagonist explains: "I sleep in the attic over the cantina yonder. The house belongs to the Company, and Mrs. Widrington, Mr. Widrington's wife, the manager's wife, she lets me sleep in the attic. It's high and quiet, except for a few rats" (*Collected* 803). The failed poet in "Black Music" is identified as one Wilfred Midgleston, who could be a representative of the colonial power out of Conrad if his speech did not sound so southern. The narrator learns that he is actually from New York, but twenty-five years in Rincon have caused him to take up the dialect of the South because of the humid Latin American climate—or, one could suggest, through the unwanted, contaminating legacy of a system of labor common to the whole Caribbean basin? The displacement to another South allows a fresh approach to issues that have been too stifling at home—the kind of uneasiness with the English language that Faulkner strangely claimed as the main common point between Conrad and himself.

Beyond these rather anecdotal homages to Conrad's exploration of the colonial experience, Faulkner adopted the structural device of the frame narrative for which Conrad is known. Although "Black Music" is not a very effective short story, it is one of the early attempts in which the narrator is someone who tells the story of someone else he met in a colorful exotic outpost and who had a curious story to tell. This is a technique that Faulkner adopted and refined, and one of the best examples of it is the novel that may compete with *The Sound and the Fury* for the title of his masterwork: *Absalom, Absalom!* (1936).

It can be said that *Absalom, Absalom!* revolves around the figure of Thomas Sutpen, but that would be misleading: Rather, it is about how this character from the past haunts characters in the present, who take turns elaborating their vision of the former planter, that all but one have only heard about through the local legend. In *Absalom, Absalom!* there are two distinctly different successive paradigms: Through the first six chapters the characters try to *know* about Sutpen, guided by evidence or their own prejudice and frustrations; in the later chapters Shreve and Quentin leave off their attempts to remember and reconstruct and begin self-consciously to invent. Quentin attempts to make sense of the obscurities of Sutpen's destiny with the interested involvement of his roommate at Harvard, a figure from a different world (he is Canadian) in a completely different setting (a snowy winter night). They forgo the need to recover an unattainable factual reality, and the story of Sutpen as they reinvent it strives toward consistency because it so strongly affects the young men they are: worried about love, identity, and recognition from the older generations.

Conrad's *Heart of Darkness* (1902) provided a comparable narrative situation, though less complex—but it is a much shorter narrative. In a prologue, five friends are waiting for the turn of the tide on a cruising yawl in the mouth of the Thames River. The expanse of the estuary prompts memories of the great sailors who issued from there to explore the world and settled empires. The turn of the tide suggests a reversal of focus: from outward to inward, from forward to backward looking. Among the group, Marlow launches on a meditation: "'And this also,' said Marlow suddenly, 'has been one of the dark places of the earth'" (493). The theme of darkness is thus introduced, drawing a parallel between what might have been the approach of savage Britain by Roman colonists nineteen centuries before and the contemporary colonial situation—Marlow goes on to tell of his journey to the African heart of darkness, and of his fascination with Kurtz. The story is therefore framed by a sense of how it matters at the time and place where is it told. Such is also the decentering movement that makes it possible for Quentin Compson, the central perceiving subject in *The Sound and the Fury*, to attempt to negotiate the heritage of the South. As Faulkner puts it in the first pages of the novel, "Quentin had grown up with that; the mere names were interchangeable and almost myriad. . . . his very body was an empty hall echoing with sonorous defeated names; he was not a being, an entity, he was a commonwealth. He was a barracks filled with stubborn back-looking ghosts still recovering, even forty-three years afterward, from the fever which had cured the disease" (*Absalom* 9).

Absalom, Absalom! is Faulkner's most notable work on the Old South, the antebellum period that is at the core of the region's identity, but it is also famously about the ambiguous love-and-hate relationship of the southerner with his region, about the power of the myth and the process of mythmaking. Thomas Sutpen is not just the mysterious planter re-created more than half a century after his death by Quentin Compson, a southern student exiled in wintery Harvard, and his Canadian roommate, but he is a fascinating myth of the South, such an appealing story that Shreve keeps asking for more. The novel is rooted in the South but seems to imply that this southern identity implies deterritorialization—and this northern detour is repeated in the diegesis of Sutpen's story by another deterritorialization—the Haitian interlude, a few pages into chapter seven of the novel.[1]

Absalom, Absalom! is a fable about desire and how it informs, conditions, shapes but also whets our curiosity of the past, a country as exotic as far-away places, as Victor Segalen remarked when he defined exoticism as the enjoyable experience of "all that is foreign to our present, daily awareness, all that is not our customary mental tone."[2]

Segalen underlines that this is a satisfying aesthetic pleasure: As they patch together the story of the old planter out of partial and contradictory clues, the two students project themselves onto this character out of the past, who becomes fictional, but also more closely actual. Years later in *A Fable* (1954), Faulkner was to comment on this paradox, upholding the relevance of history as desire-driven narrative against the cold truth of facts. He described the great mythical narratives as "the firmament of man's history instead of the mere rubble of his past" (*Fable* 814). In *Absalom, Absalom!* Quentin's father is shown to draw an aesthetic pleasure from the almost tragic elusiveness of historic truth:

> Or perhaps that's it: they don't explain and we are not supposed to know. We have a few old mouth-to-mouth tales; we exhume from old trunks and boxes and drawers letters without salutation or signature, in which men and women who once lived and breathed are now merely initials or nicknames out of some now incomprehensible affection which sound to us like Sanskrit or Chocktaw. . . . They are there, yet something is missing; they are like a chemical formula exhumed along with the letters from that forgotten chest, carefully, the paper old and faded and falling to pieces, the writing faded, almost indecipherable, yet meaningful, familiar in shape and sense, the name and presence of volatile and sentient forces, you bring them together in the proportions called for, but nothing happens; you re-read, tedious and intent, poring, making sure that you have forgotten nothing, made no miscalculation; you bring them together again and again and nothing happens: just the words, the symbols, the shapes themselves, shadowy inscrutable and serene, against the turgid background of a horrible and bloody mischancing of human affairs. (*Absalom* 83–84)

While foregrounding the aesthetic and emotional value of the work of memory, Faulkner is actually completely aware of the historical background. The character of Thomas Sutpen is fictitious, but Faulkner is aware of the history of northern Mississippi where he situates Sutpen's

Hundred, as Don H. Doyle has shown.[3] At the beginning of the nineteenth century, while Haiti became independent, Mississippi was Indian territory except for a strip of land along the Gulf of Mexico, which was at the hands of the Chickasaw tribe who had agreed to interbreeding and trading with the whites.[4] Gradually during the first third of the nineteenth century, the Chickasaw people integrated their economy with the white plantation system, granted land to enterprising white settlers, then finally yielded the area to a consortium of white settlers to walk the Trail of Tears to exile in Oklahoma. The Chickasaw era was over in 1836; the old southern plantation system in which Sutpen carved out his estate had no more than twenty-five years to thrive on this "frontier" before the Civil War broke out. The situation was not typical, but there will have been a few cases like his.

The recollected memories of Rosa Coldfield in the novel's first chapter find Sutpen turning up out of nowhere with his gang of wild black slaves, with whom he talks a foreign language, and with a French architect commissioned to build his stately house. It has been noted that Sutpen's importation of slaves occurs at a time when this had become illegal.[5] This erroneous timing may stem from the intertextual interference with a fictional source—a transposition from another narrative Faulkner read when he was starting his work on what was to become *Absalom, Absalom!*—and this will be another instance of the writer digesting any kind of material.

In 1934, Howard Hawks had asked Faulkner to work on a screen adaptation of Blaise Cendrars's 1925 novella *L'Or*, which had then almost immediately been translated into English as *Sutter's Gold* (Blotner 851). Cendrars had written the story of a fellow countryman, German Swiss emigrant Johann August Suter (he became John Sutter in the United States), who abandoned his family and started scouring the Pacific in search of fruitful businesses. In Honolulu, Sutter had the idea of recruiting Kanak workers to labor on the plantation he was planning to start in California, just as in *Absalom, Absalom!* Sutpen brought in Haitian slaves to work on his plantation. In 1839, Sutter arrived in what was still Spanish California and received a grant for a stretch of land in the Sacramento valley. He developed his project methodically, increasing his estate through astute negotiations with Mexicans and Americans, and became very rich. But in 1848 gold was found on his grounds, and it was overrun by forty-niners during the California gold rush. His carefully designed plan was shattered, just as Sutpen's plan was wrecked by the onset of the Civil War. Sutter ended his career in endless lawsuits and pleadings with the federal authorities to save some of his dream without ever receiving any compensation.

After working for a few weeks on this screenplay, which was never shot, Faulkner returned to the novel that he had been working on since the beginning of that year, but at this stage, it probably took a decisive turn and incidentally found its definite title. Originally the Haitian episode was not attached to the geographic and historic backdrop of the connection between the Caribbean francophone world and New Orleans. Whether Faulkner was inspired by Cendrars's Sutter, the pattern of Sutter's life seems to enrich the core situation of the novel as it is recollected from what his grandfather told Quentin: Sutpen's father, the local legend has it, was a poor white from the Atlantic Piedmont. Quentin learns how Sutpen would have witnessed his father's humiliation when, unable to earn a living in the Tidewater plantations, he had been sent on an errand to the big house. At the entrance door he was told by a black house servant to go around to the back, the servant having denied him the right of way. Behind the black man's body, he could see the reclining figure of the master of the house in his hammock, sipping his mint julep with his shoes off. He had sworn to himself that one day he would be this man. To become this man, he was to build on what he had heard at school:

> What I learned was that there was a place called the West Indies to which poor men went in ships and became rich, it didn't matter how, so long as that man was clever and courageous. . . . So when the time came when I realised that to accomplish my design I should need first of all and above

all things money in considerable quantity and in the quite immediate future, I remembered what he had read to us and I went to the West Indies (*Absalom* 200).

Sutpen may be seen as another quixotic figure, and in an intertextual cross-reference, the text of *Absalom, Absalom!* refers to "Carcassonne" and its Latin American Conradian atmosphere. At this stage in the novel the reader has yet to learn that Sutpen exposed himself to the "Latin culture," but like Don Quixote, he trusted the books that his teacher made him read, conveying a version of the myth of El Dorado, and "so he went to the West Indies." Long after, when his dreams of success had been thwarted repeatedly, Sutpen was to retain this quixotic bend: In a dreamlike reconstruction of Rosa Coldfield's impression of Sutpen, Quentin Compson imagines how Sutpen may have sounded on his way back from fighting in the Civil War, "*talking that which sounded like the bombast of a madman who creates within his very coffin walls his fabulous immeasurable Camelots and Carcassonnes*" (*Absalom* 132).

Unlike the American Indian context that is accurately depicted in several of Faulkner's narratives, the introduction of Haitian slaves seems to be unselfconsciously free of any concern for factual accuracy. The reason for this suspension of accuracy, one could argue, lies in the extremely complex narrative structure, a Russian doll embedding of narratives: Quentin is telling his student friend about his recollection of what his father told him about what his own father (Quentin's grandfather) would have heard from Thomas Sutpen, who was commenting on his own exposure to the myth of El Dorado. Any time the story was reframed to be embedded in another narrative, distortions could occur. It is consistent with the colonial legend that because of his skin color, Sutpen should be associated with the ruling class in the Caribbean colony, and, therefore, he should marry the planter's daughter. (Her Spanish blood is consistent with the fact that half of the island of Hispaniola is Santo Domingo, now the Dominican Republic.) His repression of a slave revolt confirms his status.

After leaving his father's home, Sutpen had gone straight to the West Indies—according to Faulkner's own chronology included at the end of the novel—in 1820, when Sutpen was fourteen. As Maritza Stanchich has argued, drawing on Edward Said, in this passage, Haiti—not identified by name yet—is regarded as it was perceived by Americans at the beginning of the nineteenth century in a clearly colonial perspective: "Americans tended to imagine it as a void into which they could pour their own ideas."[6] The island embodies the fantasy of the colonial treasure available to anyone who cares to go and pick it up. Simultaneously, Faulkner suggests the kinship between the plantation system in the American South and in the Caribbean colonial basin that preceded it. Sutpen settles in "a little island set in a smiling and fury-lurked and incredible indigo sea, which was the halfway point between what we call the jungle and what we call civilization, halfway between the dark inscrutable continent from which the black blood, the black bones and flesh and thinking and remembering and hopes and desires, was ravished by violence, and the cold known land to which it was doomed" (*Absalom* 207). An overseer on a French landlord's plantation, he marries the planter's daughter without paying much attention to the detail that his wife was a Spaniard.

Six years later, Sutpen is besieged by black insurgents in the big house. The smell of burning sugar cane, "the olfactory metaphor for the ultimately unsubduable chaos of Haiti" (Kreyling 130), pervades the air, and the narrator's imagination rides on, supplementing the missing archive. Quentin's grandfather only knows that it was necessary for Sutpen to withdraw in front of the menacing workmen. Imagination provides the rest:

A spot of earth which might have been created and set aside by Heaven itself, Grandfather said, as a theatre for violence and injustice and bloodshed and all the satanic lusts of human greed and cruelty, for the last despairing fury of all the pariah-interdict and all the doomed. . . .

And he overseeing it, riding peacefully about on his horse while he learned the language (that meagre and fragile thread, Grandfather said, by which the little surface corners and edges of men's secret and solitary lives may be joined for an instant now and then before sinking back into the darkness where the spirit cried for the first time and was not heard and will cry for the last time and will not be heard then either), not knowing that what he rode upon was a volcano, hearing the air tremble and throb at night with the drums and the chanting and not knowing that it was the heart of the earth itself he heard, who believed (Grandfather said) that earth was kind and gentle and that darkness was merely something you saw, or could not see in; overseeing what he oversaw and not knowing that he was overseeing it. (*Absalom* 207–08)

The island is described as a transitory space between the dark continent and the United States, between the wilderness and civilization, and is a vague midway point on the Middle Passage as if the sense of reality dissolved on the island where the only certainty seems to be the future foretold by a bloody Voodoo mojo. The *overseer* is guilty of *oversight*, as if meanings dissolved and melted in the sun. The island night is full of the sound of the beating drums from a recurring Western imagery of Africanism, and the double meaning of darkness echoes Conrad, but the passage, with the throbbing drums echoing the context of Marlow's nighttime encounter with Kurtz, is also reminiscent of the mutinied slaves aboard the *San Dominick* in Herman Melville's "Benito Cereno" (the name of the ship in that story, the *San Dominick*, suggests Santo Domingo). In the first pages of the novella, Melville describes the "enchantment" of boarding a ship so full of dark faces, the ship's Gothic structure, and the fascination reinforced by the rhythmic din on board that dulled the innocent American into completely missing the nature of the power dynamic aboard:

Always upon first boarding a large and populous ship at sea, especially a foreign one, with a nondescript crew such as Lascars or Manilla men, the impression varies in a peculiar way from that produced by first entering a strange house with strange inmates in a strange land. . . . The living spectacle it contains, upon its sudden and complete disclosure, has, in contrast with the blank ocean which zones it, something of the effect of enchantment. The ship seems unreal; these strange costumes, gestures, and faces, but a shadowy tableau just emerged from the deep, which directly must receive back what it gave. . . . The six hatchet-polishers neither spoke to others, nor breathed a whisper among themselves, but sat intent upon their task, except at intervals, when, with the peculiar love in Negroes of uniting industry with pastime, two-and-two they sideways clashed their hatchets together, like cymbals, with a barbarous din. All six, unlike the generality, had the raw aspect of unsophisticated Africans. (Melville 49–50)

In *Absalom, Absalom!* the barricaded white family and Sutpen end up firing off muskets into the Haitian night with the inhabitants invisible in the scenery, as they were under the fire of Conrad's gunship in *Heart of Darkness*:

Once, I remember, we came upon a man-of-war anchored off the coast. There wasn't even a shed there, and she was shelling the bush. . . . In the empty immensity of earth, sky, and water, there she was, incomprehensible, firing into a continent. Pop, would go one of the six-inch guns; a small flame would dart and vanish, a little white smoke would disappear, a tiny projectile would give a feeble screech—and nothing happened (*Portable Conrad* 506).

Memory allows inconsistencies, but Faulkner's text keeps reminding the reader that these fascinating pages are what "Grandfather said." In Haiti, we are left to surmise, Sutpen would have become this Kurtz-like figure, as evidenced when he later organized fights between his half-wild slaves on his Mississippi estate. (Slaves and their descendants organized cockfights all over Hispaniola.) The pages on the planter's family besieged in their house may bring to mind images of the Citadelle Laferrière, the formidable citadel that King Henri Christophe built in the north of the island between 1805 and 1820 against the possibility of a French attack. Built with the forced labor of twenty thousand slaves and designed by engineer Henri Barré, a mulatto, the fortress seems to foreshadow Sutpen's architectural ambition for Sutpen's Hundred.

The narrative is silent about how Sutpen managed to escape the siege and how he defeated the insurgents. For some undescribed reason, things quieted down, and Sutpen married the planter's daughter, and that was all. Sutpen and his wife found sanctuary in New Orleans, as did many white inhabitants of the former French colony of Saint-Domingue. According to Shreve's and Quentin's reconstruction of the story, only after Charles's birth does Sutpen realize that his father-in-law had withheld from him the fact that the Spanish woman was actually a mulatto. Once again, as had been the case for Popeye in *Sanctuary* (1931), the Latin outsider brings in a threatening darkness that the American South will want to keep at bay. This explains why Sutpen must have relinquished his wife and son, but it did not prevent Sutpen from finding an octoroon wife, having a son, Charles Bon, who in turn thought of himself as a black man, married a purely black woman, and had a black son, Jim Bond. This Jim Bond is the last descendant of Thomas Sutpen, proving that under a Latin hood or not, darkness not only seeps in but prevails. In the famous last page of the novel, Shreve McCannon, possibly in parody of the southern obsession with miscegenation, foresaw that "in time the Jim Bonds are going to conquer the western hemisphere. Of course it wont be in our time and of course as they spread toward the poles they will bleach out again like the rabbits and the birds do, so they wont show up so sharp against the snow. But it will still be Jim Bond; and so in a few thousand years, I who regard you will also have sprung from the loins of African kings" (*Absalom* 302–03).

As Richard Godden has noted, the Haiti episode may be regarded as mythical: The transit through Haiti allows Sutpen to appropriate the

Southern concern about slave revolt in the first half of the nineteenth century (Godden 492). But Michel Kreyling signals another context: "the 'anachronism' for which Faulkner is often faulted—misdating the slave insurrections of 1791–1804 to the 1820s—is less embarrassing if we accept Faulkner's own present moment (the end of the U.S. occupation of Haiti) as the milieu in which Sutpen is mostly imagined and drawn" (Kreyling 131).[7] The two-decade long military occupation of Haiti (1915 through 1934) could be tolerably on the consciousness of Faulkner's 1936 readers, just as the colonial situation could be the context of Conrad's 1899 readership. In any case, as Rincon was in the earlier stories, Haiti in *Absalom, Absalom!* is a cultural construction, as the Congo is in *Heart of Darkness*.

Regardless of the facts in the Haitian experience, the Haitian detour seems to free the white man's dark soul, his "heart of darkness," just as the memory of Kurtz led Marlow to meditation on the colonial experience throughout the ages. Sutpen's neighbor may be horrified by the wild fights at Sutpen's Hundred, although they but bring to light the violence inherent in the southern slave economy. Old Compson, close as he was to Sutpen, could not but think of this outrage as he heard Sutpen tell him his memories: "and he sitting on the log, Grandfather said, telling it, making the gestures to tell it with, whom Grandfather himself had seen fight naked chest to chest with one of his wild niggers by the light of the camp fire while his house was building . . . and no bones about the fighting either, no handshaking and gratulations while he washed the blood off and donned his shirt" (*Absalom* 209).

Modern American author Toni Morrison generalizes this experience as a central process in the building of white American awareness in terms that are extraordinarily consistent with Sutpen's predicament: "Africanism is the vehicle by which the American self knows itself as not enslaved, but free; not repulsive, but desirable; not helpless, but licensed and powerful; . . . not damned, but innocent; not a blind accident of evolution, but a progressive fulfilment of destiny" (Morrison 52). The Haitian experience would have been the turning point in

Sutpen's maturation after his childhood trauma, the essential episode in his narrative. Voodoo, the drums, and the Creole language of Haiti symbolize the *othering* of Thomas Sutpen, the process Toni Morrison has described as essential in the accomplishment of full American identity, which is Sutpen's concern:

> I want to suggest that these concerns—autonomy, authority, newness and difference, absolute power—not only become the major themes and presumptions of American literature, but that each one is made possible by, shaped by, activated by a complex awareness and employment of a constituted Africanism. It was this Africanism, deployed as rawness and savagery, that provided the staging ground and arena for the elaboration of the quintessential American identity. (Morrison 44)

Thus, Haiti functions as a feature of the southern gothic, a displacement in space substituted for the weight of temporality that had been an essential feature of the European or northern gothic (see Hawthorne's *House of the Seven Gables* [1851]). Morrison cites Poe's *Narrative of Arthur Gordon Pym of Nantucket* (1838) as another such spatial detour: "Through the use of Africanism, Poe meditates on place as a means of containing the fear of borderlessness and trespass, but also as a means of releasing and exploring the desire for a limitless empty frontier" (Morrison 51). As in Francis Ford Coppola's film *Apocalypse Now* (1979), which is a transposition of *Heart of Darkness*, the revelation is not situated in time—a faraway future, but now, in another country. In his novel, published in 1936—the same year as the publication of *Gone with the Wind*—Faulkner roots Sutpen's seemingly outlandish design in a hemispheric white American Dream of escape from poverty and hope for freedom that is exposed as dependent on ethnic violence against the African other. In his initial meditation in *Heart of Darkness*, Marlow imagined the personal initiation that a commission to Britain must have been for "a decent young citizen in toga": "All that mysterious life of the wilderness that stirs in the forest, in the jungles,

in the hearts of wild men. There's no initiation either into such mysteries. He has to live in the midst of the incomprehensible, which is also
detestable. And it has a fascination, too, that goes to work upon him.
The fascination of the abomination—you know. Imagine the growing
regrets, the longing to escape, the powerless disgust, the surrender, the
hate" (*Portable Conrad* 495). In *Absalom, Absalom!* Sutpen's "Haitian
detour" is not so much an adventure of Thomas Sutpen in the Caribbean Sea, but a foray into the inherited African "Orientalism" Faulkner
inherits from the figures of otherness in Conrad's *Heart of Darkness*—
a vehicle to explore the contradictions and ambiguities of the South.

Toward the end of his life, Argentine writer Jorge Luis Borges declared: "I do not write, I rewrite. . . . We are all the heirs of millions
of scribes who have already written down all that is essential a long
time before us. We are all copyists, and all the stories we invent have
already been told."[8] It is how this cultural legacy is processed that matters. Writers will pick from other literary traditions details of plots,
characters, or manners that, although firmly rooted in a cultural tradition, find echoes in the sort of human reality their fiction addresses,
possibly because they happen to express more strikingly than within
one's home culture's tropes something universal about the human experience. Anthropophagy becomes anthropology. The universe of the
foreign writer and his or her manner becomes a counterpoint, a mirror,
a rarefied metaphor, almost abstract, of the ideal home country.

Notes

1. "Diegesis," as used by Gérard Genette, refers to the fictional world created by
the narrative process in which a story is supposed to take place. A population
is said to be deterritorialized—a term possibly stemming from Gilles Deleuze
and Félix Guattari (*Anti-Oedipus*. Minneapolis: U of Minnesota P, 1972), when
they experience a weakening of the bond between culture and the sense of place.

2. Translated from the original French: "tout ce qui est en dehors de nos faits de
conscience actuels, quotidiens, tout ce qui n'est pas notre 'Tonalité mentale'
coutumière" (Segalen 33).

3. See Doyle, chapter 1.

4. The "civilized tribes" are five American Indian tribes of the American southeast whose history was intimately linked to that of the South and its migrations: Creek, Chocktaw, Chickasaw, Cherokee, and Seminole. As early as the eighteenth century, these tribes were involved in the plantation system, if only because the planters tried to enslave them (the Seminoles were largely crossbred in the process), but also because they adopted the plantation system and let white settlers join their communities. The five tribes were exiled to Oklahoma in 1830 by the American government in the well-known episode of the Trail of Tears. For an overview of the history of these populations, see Walter L. Williams, 167–68.

5. On the anachronism of this episode, see Godden 489–95.

6. Stanchich draws on Edward Said's *Culture and Imperialism* (New York: Knopf, 1993) to show that *Absalom, Absalom!* represents through Sutpen the American imperialist position.

7. Kreyling identifies the memoir of a captain of the US Marine Corps, John Craige's *Black Bagdad*, published in 1933, as reflecting an experience close to that of Thomas Sutpen, but there is no evidence that Faulkner was aware of it.

8. In Jacques Chancel, Jorge Luis Borges, *Radioscopie* (Paris: Editions du Rocher, 1999), 74, 76. Quoted in Kristal, 135.

Works Cited

Apocalypse Now. Dir. Francis Ford Coppola. Perf. Martin Sheen, Marlon Brando, and Robert Duvall. United Artists, 1979. Film.

Blotner, Joseph. *Faulkner: A Biography*. 2 vols. New York: Random, 1974. Print.

Cendrars, Blaise. *L'Or: la merveilleuse histoire du général Johann August Suter*. Paris: Grasset, 1925. Print.

___. *Sutter's Gold*. Trans. Henry Longan Stuart. New York: Harper, 1926. Print.

Conrad, Joseph. *Heart of Darkness. The Portable Conrad*. Ed. Morton Dauwen Zabel. New York: Viking, 1947. 490–603. Print.

___. *Nostromo*. 1904. London: Penguin, 2007. Print.

Doyle, Don H. *Faulkner's County: The Historical Roots of Yoknapatawphha*. Chapel Hill, NC: U of North Carolina P, 2001. Print.

Eliot, T. S. *The Waste Land and Other Poems*. London: Faber, 1940. Print.

___."Ulysses, Order and Myth." *Selected Prose of T. S. Eliot*. Ed. Frank Kermode. New York: Harcourt, 1975. Print.

Faulkner, William. *Absalom, Absalom! Novels 1936–1940*. New York: Library of America, 1990. 1–315. Print.

___."Black Music." *Collected Stories*. New York: Random, 1950. 799–821. Print.

___. "Carcassonne." *Collected Stories*. New York: Random, 1950. 895–900. Print.

___. *A Fable. Novels 1942–1954*. New York: Library of America, 1994. Print.

___. Introduction. *The Sound and the Fury*. By Faulkner. New York: Norton, 1994. 225–28. Print.

Godden, Richard. "*Absalom, Absalom!* and Faulkner's Erroneous Dating of the Haitian Revolution." *Mississippi Quarterly* 47.3 (1994): 489–95. Print.

Gwynn, Frederick L., and Joseph Blotner, eds. *Faulkner in the University: Class Conferences at the University of Virginia, 1957–1958.* Charlottesville: UP of Virginia, 1959. Print.

Kreyling, Michael. *The South That Wasn't There: Postsouthern Memory and History.* Baton Rouge: Louisiana UP, 2010. Print.

Kristal, Efrain. *Invisible Work: Borges and Translation.* Nashville: Vanderbilt UP, 2002. Print.

Matthews, John T. "Recalling the West Indies: From Yoknapatawpha to Haiti and Back." *American Literary History* 16.2 (2004): 238–62. Print.

Melville, Herman. "Benito Cereno." *The Piazza Tales.* 1856. Evanston, IL: Northwestern UP, 1998. 46–117. Print.

Morrison, Toni. *Playing in the Dark: Whiteness and the Literary Imagination.* New York: Vintage, 1992. Print.

Polk, Noel. "William Faulkner's 'Carcassonne.'" *Studies in Short Fiction* 12 (1984): 29–43. Print.

Segalen, Victor. *Essai sur l'exotisme: une esthétique du divers.* 1955. Paris: Fata Morgana, 1978. Print.

Stanchich, Maritza. "The Hidden Caribbean 'Other' in William Faulkner's *Absalom, Absalom!* An Ideological Ancestry of U. S. Imperialism." *Mississippi Quarterly* 49.3 (1996): 603–17. Print.

Williams, Scott G. "Eating Faulkner Eating Baudelaire: Multiple Rewritings and Cultural Cannibalism." *Faulkner Journal* 25.1 (2009): 65–84. Print.

Williams, Walter L. "Indians and Blacks." *Encyclopedia of Southern Culture.* Eds. Charles Reagan Wilson and William R. Ferris. Chapel Hill: U of North Carolina P, 1989. 167–68. Print.

A Furious Echo: Hearing Dublin's Joyce in Faulkner's Yoknapatawpha_____

Kieran Quinlan

It has been said that the publication of Irish novelist James Joyce's *Ulysses* in Paris in 1922 was the single most important literary event in twentieth-century writing in English, though the book's influence has permeated the works of several authors in other languages as well. It is often asserted that William Faulkner's 1929 *The Sound and the Fury* is the essential novel of the same era in the American canon. In addition, it is everywhere accepted that these two very "difficult" novels relate to one another in numerous ways, particularly with regard to the narrative techniques represented in them. In its most extreme form, the argument goes: no Joyce, no Faulkner—or at least not the Faulkner readers now know (Weinstein 346). As a consequence, even in cases in which a reader is unfamiliar with the details of Joyce's great work, some knowledge of the background to and strategies employed in *Ulysses* can serve as a guide to making one's way through Faulkner's similarly experimental—that is, modernist—creation. Moreover, both Joyce and Faulkner came from places that faced similar cultural challenges in the early decades of the twentieth century.

Joyce and Faulkner grew up in societies that, from the perspectives of London and New York, were regarded as provincial. They were also societies that had a deep but frequently sentimental view of the wrongs done to them, a view reinforced in the contemporary fiction and poetry of both areas; though Ireland had a much older tradition in Irish Gaelic and even English than was the case with Oxford, Mississippi, a small town founded just sixty years before Faulkner's birth. However, there were fresh stirrings in Ireland with the emergence of the Irish Renaissance writers in the 1890s, led by the poet W. B. Yeats and the playwright J. M. Synge. Joyce, an iconoclastic younger writer, would often parody their work, but he was also well aware that it had prepared the soil for his own artistic emergence. Twenty or more years later, seeing what had taken place in "backward" Ireland must have given encouragement to Faulkner in "backward" Mississippi, as it was to do to subsequent writers from the American South such as Robert Penn Warren and Eudora Welty. In other words, if the Irish could do it, then so could the southerners. Hence, the literary movement that was to become known as the Southern Renaissance with William Faulkner as its premier exhibit. That both Joyce and Faulkner should in time adopt and extend the experimental practices of an innovative high modernism rather than a more traditional narrative approach can be seen as either astonishing—which it was—or, as many recent critics have pointed out, a reflection of their own origins in cultures that were broken, fragmented, disordered, their pasts intruding awkwardly into their presents, and the trajectories of their repressed and repressive nationalisms uncertain and incomplete. More than the reigning imperial establishments, they became the new voices of what would turn out to be a dislocated century.

Joyce wrote a semiautobiographical account of growing up in Ireland and his eventual decision to escape the restrictions of its insular culture in order to "forge . . . the uncreated conscience of my race" in his 1916 *A Portrait of the Artist as a Young Man* (213). A seminal book—with which Faulkner was also quite familiar—*Portrait* is not, however, a highly experimental one, though its hero, Stephen Dedalus, reappears in *Ulysses*. Joyce left Ireland for good in 1904, spending the rest of his life between residences in Italy, Switzerland, and France, where he came into contact with many other innovators of the modernist age, including his champion, the American poet Ezra Pound, to whom T. S. Eliot was to dedicate the equally experimental *The Waste Land* (1922). Although Joyce had left Dublin, however, all of his subsequent writings would be about that city and its people, making its provinciality a matter of interest to cosmopolitan audiences around the globe. In this, Joyce would provide a very specific example for Faulkner in his own effort to convert rural northern Mississippi—a "postage stamp" of a place that he re-created as the fictional Yoknapatawpha County—into a setting of importance for the denizens of New York and other American cities, and even for some of Paris's best-known intellectuals (most notably, the philosopher Jean-Paul Sartre). In writing so intimately about their home territories and in treating them with a degree of what Joyce had earlier termed "scrupulous meanness" (*Selected Letters* 83), both authors were engaged in creating a "conscience" for their respective social groups. Often they revealed unpleasant truths in the process, a circumstance that frequently provoked the ire of the local inhabitants, even as it enthralled more broad-minded but less involved outsiders.

As an Irishman, Joyce inherited a centuries-old history of subjugation and foreign rule by England. In a way, then, his writings are the cry of the long-defeated, if still unvanquished, for recognition and inclusion in the larger culture and society of the Western world and, at the same time, a self-conscious despair at such never-ending preoccupation with what his character Stephen Dedalus refers to as the "nightmare" of history from which he is "trying to awake" (Joyce, *Ulysses* 34/28). In the nationalist narrative that was becoming ever more popular in early twentieth-century Ireland, there had been an "English" presence for over seven hundred years—a presence resisted from almost the very beginning in the twelfth century. Matters were exacerbated by the Protestant Reformation of the sixteenth century, during which Ireland largely remained Catholic, and by the penal laws of the eighteenth century, which restricted the rights of Catholics in terms of religious practice, ownership of property, and participation in educational and professional life. Events such as the Flight of the Earls (1607), Oliver Cromwell's siege of Drogheda (1649), the Battle of the Boyne (1690), the American- and French-inspired 1798 Rebellion, the Great Famine (1845–54), and the Fenian deportations of the late nineteenth century were part of daily lore in an Ireland still under British rule during Joyce's era. There were other narratives that stressed the mingling of Irish and English histories, and in 1900, most Irish people, Joyce included, were relatively content with the political situation since a measure of autonomy was in the offing. After all, Joyce, in the character of Stephen Dedalus, was more anxious to escape that "nightmare" of history than revel in its wrongs. The "nets" of Irish culture that Stephen lists include nationalism, Catholicism, and language (at a time when nationalists wished to revive a dying Irish Gaelic speech), rather than the petty tyrannies of British dominance (Joyce, *Portrait* 171). Still, as with Joyce's leaving Dublin but never writing about anything else, Irish history in all its elements is very much present in *Ulysses*. Faulkner would take note (Sykes 526–27). Furthermore, Sherwood Anderson, the American writer who urged Faulkner to use the material of his native place, was also a great admirer of Joyce.

Faulkner's inheritance was also fraught with the oppressions of the recent past: his ancestors' defeat in the Civil War, the occupation of the state by the Union army in its aftermath, the disenfranchisement of those who had served as Confederate officers, the humiliations of the decade of Reconstruction, and the overall decline of his once-prominent family's role in local affairs. In his 1936 *Absalom, Absalom!*, in which he reintroduces Quentin Compson (a character who bears some resemblance to a younger Faulkner) from *The Sound and the Fury*, the latter is described as "an empty hall echoing with sonorous defeated names" of dead heroes and lost battles from the nightmare of which he too sometimes wishes to awake (7). In a very Joycean turn of phrase, Faulkner describes Quentin as "not a being, an entity" but rather "a commonwealth" (*Absalom, Absalom!* 7). At the same time, Faulkner profoundly recognized the racial injustices that had led to that war and the need to free himself from the southern writer's tendency to romanticize its defeats and the Greco-Roman, slaveholding civilization that it was said to have replicated. Unlike Joyce, however, Faulkner chose to remain in his native region, which was perhaps why he decided to fictionalize its names rather than use them as they were as Joyce had provocatively done.

Ulysses took seven years to write, not an inordinate amount of time given the novel's length and complexity. Joyce meditated on the exact sequence of the words in every sentence of its almost eight hundred pages and on many other matters related to its multiple symbolic structures. The novel has eighteen chapters and follows the lives of Stephen Dedalus and Leopold Bloom, an Irish Jew living in a somewhat hostile religious environment, in meticulous detail through eighteen hours of a single day. The sequence of events is modeled on that of Homer's *Odyssey* (ca. 725 BCE; English translation, 1614), which recounts the many adventures of a canny Odysseus—Ulysses in Latin—and his crew as they return from the Trojan War, Odysseus's eventual meeting with his son Telemachus, the slaughter of his wife's suitors, and reunification with the beloved Penelope. The correspondence, however, is conducted on several different levels so that, for example, Odysseus's escape from the one-eyed Cyclops, a man-eating monster, is paralleled in Joyce's narrative by Bloom escaping from a pub where he is being threatened by a xenophobic, tunnel-visioned Irish nationalist called the Citizen. But Joyce's parallel is rarely sanguinary: the slaughter of the suitors in the original story is retold in Molly's mental dismissal of all those she suspects might at various times have been interested in her, including her current—and perhaps first—extramarital lover, in favor of her returned husband, Leopold. Yet while several of Joyce's chapters are given over, wholly or partially, to the interior monologue or stream-of-consciousness style that was to have such an influence on Faulkner, there are other techniques and linguistic flights, undertaken in creative fidelity to the original story, that Faulkner has chosen not to imitate or for which he has no need. Joyce's Telemachus figure, Stephen Dedalus—educated, introspective, preoccupied with his own inadequate father and, thematically at least, seeking a replacement in Bloom—would form a partial template for Faulkner's Quentin Compson. Even more tortured and alienated in his being than Dedalus, Compson is also painfully aware of the inadequacies of his father's fatalistic philosophy in dealing with the rage and despair smoldering within him.

In all, then, there are three main elements that Faulkner not so much acquired from Joyce as found illustrated in his life and writing: a workbook of interior monologue or stream-of-consciousness style, an example of how a provincial history could be transformed into the universal, and a model of a particular character's consciousness close to what he himself wished to write about. Less importantly, Faulkner also learned how events that were taking place at disparate times could be unified by reference to a foundational myth: the *Odyssey* for Joyce, the events of the Christian Holy Week for Faulkner, though the latter was less interested in the specific details of the original religious story.

Faulkner never explicitly acknowledged all of this, but he did frequent Joyce's favorite café in Paris in 1925 in hopes of seeing the author at a distance—Faulkner lacked the confidence to approach Joyce—and already revered him as a novelist (Blotner 452). Faulkner may have become familiar with *Ulysses*—then banned in the United States as immoral and often smuggled into the country by writers returning from Europe—as early as 1924, two years after its publication (and possibly on its first serialized appearance in the modernist *Little Review* from 1918 to 1920). Still, though Faulkner admitted this influence too when Joyce's biographer Richard Ellmann interviewed him in 1958, he was vague or evasive as to its details (297). Often he contradicted himself—either deliberately or inadvertently—as to when it had occurred. Whatever "anxiety of influence" may have weighed on Faulkner, one need not assume the worst motives for such indirection: a writer, lost in the intricacies of a difficult composition, will often forget the details of its genesis or be so aware of the uniqueness of his own accomplishment that he will rightly resent attributing it to an earlier model. In attempting to explain this complex influence, Joyce scholar Hugh Kenner doubts that Faulkner, an extremely busy author in the 1920s, ever read the whole of the novel; he also points out that when Faulkner began his own work in the Joycean vein, there was little explanatory commentary available even from Joyce himself as to its contours. Nevertheless, Kenner is equally sure that *Ulysses* served as an inspiration for Faulkner's own undertaking (22, 27, 31).

So, while there is no direct knowledge of specific "borrowings" that Faulkner may have made from Joyce—unlike Virginia Woolf, whose

1925 *Mrs. Dalloway* shows a strong Joycean influence and whose extant notebooks describe in detail how she read *Ulysses*, even using colored markers to keep track of different episodes—we can fairly easily decipher similarities and contrasts between Joyce's and Faulkner's respective methods. But most of all, we should attend to T. S. Eliot's review of *Ulysses* in November 1923, with which Faulkner was likely familiar:

> In using the myth [of Homer's *Odyssey*], in manipulating a continuous parallel between contemporaneity and antiquity, Mr. Joyce is pursuing a method which others must pursue after him. *They will not be imitators, any more than the scientist who uses the discoveries of an Einstein in pursuing his own, independent, further investigations.* It is simply a way of controlling, of ordering, of giving a shape and a significance to the immense panorama of futility and anarchy which is contemporary history. . . . Instead of narrative method, we may now use the mythical method. (177–78; emphasis added)

Indeed, while it is now accepted that Joyce's intention was to celebrate the "foul rag and bone shop" of the ordinary (to use Yeats's phrase from "The Circus Animal's Desertion," line 40), rather than castigate its "futility," Faulkner's own method in *The Sound and the Fury* would seem to better fulfill Eliot's premise of "giving a shape and a significance to the immense panorama of futility and anarchy which is contemporary history." That particular novel begins with "a tale told by an idiot, full of sound and fury," which does not perhaps so much "signif[y] nothing," as William Shakespeare's Macbeth decried (5.5.26–28), but rather what Quentin Compson's father refers to as "the mausoleum of all hope and desire" (*Sound* 86).

In practice, reading *The Sound and the Fury* benefits from a prior acquaintance with *Ulysses* through which one can master the necessary techniques of the stream-of-consciousness method. That is to say, Joyce introduces readers to such innovations more slowly and more gently than does Faulkner. Joyce opens with a description of Buck Mulligan about to shave himself on the parapet of the Martello Tower near Dublin while engaged in a mocking dialogue with Stephen Dedalus; it is several pages before readers come upon a passage that might throw them a little and force them to question its placement and meaning. Thus, gradually readers get to explore short runs of Stephen's interior monologues before encountering them full throttle, so to speak. In Faulkner, meanwhile, in his four-day, four-part narrative of the decline of a southern family consisting of an overly philosophical father, a hypochondriac mother, and their four children—obsessed Quentin, promiscuous Caddy, bitter Jason, and mentally handicapped Benjy—readers are first plunged into speechless Benjy's stream of consciousness and must get their bearings within it as best they can. Faulkner was aware of this difficulty and wished to highlight the many transitions of the first section by using different colored print for the several time periods, a desire that was only to be fulfilled in 2012 when such an edition was finally published. In his own time, Faulkner had to content himself with using italics to indicate a transition, much like a modern speed bump in a parking lot, a warning to slow down and pay particular attention to the shift in the narrative.

Joyce, Woolf, and Faulkner are the most famous stream-of-consciousness writers of the twentieth century, and it is the use of this technique that presents the most difficulty for their readers. The term derives from the American psychologist William James and refers to the fact that human consciousness is less an organization of separate compartments—assuming that one is always focused exclusively on the present moment or on one particular thing—than a *stream* in which many disparate and often apparently unconnected items follow one another. Thus, for example, while reading a book, one may also be faintly aware of the temperature in the room, a stray image or memory conjured up by the text itself, a painful encounter from the day before, even a gnawing desire to scratch one's nose—all of these unarticulated and jostling with one another in fragmented ways. This reality of human life is rarely captured in traditional descriptive prose, which tends to select and organize what is most important, converting it into coherent sentences. In this sense, stream-of-consciousness writing is more faithful to day-to-day existence. However, since there is this kind of jumble inside of everyone, when it is translated to the printed page, when it is articulated, it can present numerous problems for the reader. The *art* of stream-of-consciousness writing, then, is to try to impose some order on this stream while still giving a sense of its apparently random workings—to cheat, as it were—so that what seem to be haphazard thoughts nearly always relate to a theme or larger purpose established by the author. The exciting aspect of stream-of-consciousness writing is that narration has moved from being outside the minds of the characters to being inside them, and, at a time when Sigmund Freud's *The Interpretation of Dreams* (1900) was exercising a profound influence in Europe and the United States, the psychoanalyst's presence can be seen broadly in the use of this technique even where the writers themselves denied it.

Given this complexity, it is a commonplace in literary criticism that *Ulysses* or *The Sound and the Fury* cannot be "read" but only "reread." Such works require much more involvement than do so-called realistic novels in order to experience their full effects, to have that modernist sense of dislocation and even bewilderment that is the peculiarity of the disruptive and fragmented twentieth century yet without becoming totally lost. In any case, Joyce and Faulkner presume dedicated readers who are willing to do the work of comprehension. Nevertheless, the difficulties encountered in the works of both novelists are not essentially intellectual ones. When the novels are read with care and attention, many of the problems ostensibly posed by *Ulysses* and *The Sound and the Fury* tend to disappear: one can construct scenes and characters' thoughts that in a hasty reading would seem to be merely an incoherent mishmash. While this is not to say that one needs to read as closely as Faulkner textual scholar Noel Polk and his associates did when they made a "commitment to the principle that readers must understand each word in Faulkner's difficult novels at its most basic, literal level," even to the extent of compiling "their etymologies, their cultural and historical backgrounds, and, not least, their pronunciations," it may help to keep their example in mind (Ross and Polk vii).

Numerous critics have selected passages from Faulkner's novels, and especially from *The Sound and the Fury*, that show Joyce's influence. Again and again, Quentin Compson is compared with his fellow intellectual Stephen Dedalus. In his extensive examination of such parallels, Michael Groden has demonstrated how Molly Bloom's unpunctuated reveries as she slowly fades to sleep beside her already sleeping husband has parallels with Quentin's increasingly jumbled thoughts about his conversations with his father on suicide and incest, which occupy his mind in the closing hours of his last day on earth. Joseph Csicsila has even pointed out several resemblances between Quentin's view of sexuality—the virgin-slut dichotomy—and Bloom's in the "Nausicca" chapter of *Ulysses* (80). Indeed, critic Harold Bloom has summed up a certain disenchantment with mere Joycean imitation in *The Sound and the Fury* in his comment that "Joyce's medley of narrative voices fades in and out of Faulkner's story with no clear relation to Faulkner's purposes" (6). For him, Faulkner's "rather homely story" about the collapse of a single white southern family is "too elaborately wrought" and Faulkner's real achievement lies in his escape from Joyce—or from *excessive* Joycean influence—to write his great novels of the 1930s (Bloom 6). That, however, is for individual readers to judge.

Certainly had Faulkner begun with the Quentin section in the way that *Ulysses* begins with the Stephen Dedalus chapters or ended it with Caddy's stream of consciousness—she remains voiceless, "between the lines"—he could rightly be accused of being too Joycean (Gwin 47). Faulkner not only ignored many things that Joyce had done—after all, his novel is just over a quarter the length of *Ulysses*, and in his talks at the University of Virginia, he cautioned that Joyce "had more talent than he could control" (*Faulkner* 280)—but he also did much that the Irish writer had not attempted. In fact, however much Faulkner may have owed to Joyce's example, he was trying even less to achieve fidelity to a text by another author. The tale took him where it would; as Faulkner himself tells readers, he had to write the story four times in four different ways—the four sections of the novel—in order to clarify its meaning ("An Introduction" 414).

Surprisingly—and unlike *Ulysses*—there is little overt history in *The Sound and the Fury*. The history is there, however, buried in the details of the Compson property's contraction over the decades; in the tension with Mrs. Compson's Bascomb heritage; in Quentin's obsessive code of honor; and, perhaps most of all, in the unspoken relation between Dilsey's family and the Compsons. The New Historicist critics have impressively drawn out such hidden formations in Faulkner so that even a rather extreme example, such as that offered by Cheryl Lester, throws significant light on Quentin's emotional world. Lester shows how the Great Migration of African Americans from the Deep South to the cities of the Northeast and Midwest at the beginning of the twentieth century inflects Quentin's journey from Mississippi to Massachusetts in 1909. In the 1945 "Appendix" that Faulkner wrote for a volume of substantial excerpts edited by Malcolm Cowley, the novelist rather inelegantly introduced the history of the Compsons in a series of semiencyclopedic entries that traced them all the way from the Battle of Culloden in Scotland in 1745, after which the first Compson fled to the American colonies, right up to the present. It is a piece composed with a different mindset from that of the original novel, and though it was routinely attached to *The Sound and the Fury* for decades afterward and hugely influenced the novel's interpretation, it is no longer included. History is, however, brilliantly present in Quentin's mind as he reappears in *Absalom, Absalom!*, and that presence tends to seep into how readers now see the Quentin of the 1929 novel, just as the Stephen Dedalus of *Ulysses* forever mingles with his namesake in *Portrait*.

The most helpful lesson from *Ulysses*, however, is that Joyce is always teaching his audience how to read his story, raising the bar as they advance in their competence. Faulkner does the same. This can be seen, for example, in the Mrs. Patterson incident in the Benjy section. Readers have learned in the previous few pages of the novel how the basic transitions in the narrative function, how a word or incident in the present where Luster is looking after Benjy can prompt a narrative movement, signified by italics, into some past scene (in which the name of the caregiver for Benjy at that time is often given). At this point, Faulkner can ratchet this up and have what initially looks like the same incident follow itself and thus force readers to become aware of large and subtle differences between them. Caddy and Benjy have been sent by their Uncle Maury to deliver a letter to a Mrs. Patterson "without letting anybody see it":

There was a fence. The vine was dry, and the wind rattled in it.
"Only I dont see why Uncle Maury didn't send Versh." Caddy said. "Versh wont tell." Mrs Patterson was looking out the window. "You wait here." Caddy said. "Wait right here, now. I'll be back in a minute. Give me the letter." She took the letter out of my pocket. "Keep your hands in your pockets." She climbed the fence with the letter in her hand and went through the brown, rattling flowers. Mrs Patterson came to the door and opened it and stood there. (*The Sound and the Fury* 15)

Immediately following this scene, in which readers' suspicions about the letter may or may not have been aroused—there are clues in an older Versh not being sent with the letter, its being given to the children, and Caddy's mild puzzlement about it—the narrative transitions to a repetition of the process at another, seemingly later (but likely earlier) time:

Mr Patterson was chopping in the green flowers. He stopped chopping and looked at me. Mrs Patterson came across the garden, running. When I saw her eyes I began to cry. You idiot, Mrs Patterson said, I told him never to send you alone again. Give it to me. Quick. Mr Patterson came fast, with the hoe. Mrs Patterson leaned across the fence, reaching her hand. She was trying to climb the fence. Give it to me, she said, Give it to me. Mr Patterson climbed the fence. He took the letter. Mrs Patterson's dress was caught on the fence. I saw her eyes again and I ran down the hill. (15)

The incident forcefully establishes Benjy's incomprehension about what is going on in his fear that Mr. Patterson is chasing him. No tags help readers along, however, so that without the first scene the second (but chronologically earlier) would be almost incomprehensible (Ross and Polk 16). The implication is that Uncle Maury is sending clandestine love notes to Mrs. Patterson. Readers have to work this out for themselves from the clues given. They get their reward—a good mark from Faulkner—thirty-four pages later when they are proven to have guessed right: Uncle Maury's "eye was sick, and his mouth" because of a visit from the cuckolded and irate Mr. Patterson—though here too readers have to tease out the connection (Faulkner, *Sound* 49).

Things get ratcheted up even further in the way that Faulkner describes Benjy becoming involuntarily drunk (through caregiver T. P.'s negligence) at Caddy's wedding. For Benjy, as he stumbles around the hillside, the cows and the barn appear and disappear because he has no sense of their objective permanence (*The Sound and the Fury* 23–24). Now that readers have mastered this incident, several pages later Faulkner introduces the scene that will eventually cause Benjy to undergo medical castration. In this case, Faulkner introduces first the scene of Benjy running along the fence each day the way he used to when Caddy was coming home from school before she got married and went away; Benjy cannot get out because the fence gate is locked and so the girls passing by do not worry about his moaning and groaning. Readers immediately go from there to a scene in which Mr. Compson and his son Jason are arguing about how Benjy got outside the fence through the unlocked gate. Then the actual occasion when Benjy escaped is introduced through the italicization device: Benjy approached the passing girls, and they began to scream. He was subsequently struck on the head, and imagery reminiscent of the drunken wedding scene follows, except this time it is describing his being in a hospital theater undergoing the castratory operation (58–61). The reader may not be sure of this at the time, but Faulkner confirms the point later in a number of scenes and remarks about a naked Benjy looking at himself in the mirror as he is about to be dressed for bed and hollering and being told by Luster, "*Looking for them aint going to do no good. They're gone,*" and Jason referring to him as a "gelding" and mentioning the use of "ether" in the operation (84, 304–5).

In the Benjy section, Faulkner has been progressively raising the bar but, difficult as it was, these units were discrete and self-contained, objective pictures of the Compson family dynamics in that Benjy is not bringing any judgment to the scenes, though Faulkner himself is obviously manipulating the camera. In the Quentin section, Faulkner mixes things up by not only shifting to a more sophisticated and abstract narrative—Quentin's stream of consciousness—but by having the transitions occur *within* the episodes and only using italics for remembered speech. Just as Bloom can hardly bear to think of Molly's lover Blazes Boylan, who is seducing her as Bloom walks around Dublin, so too Quentin cannot bear to think of Caddy's lover and the probable cause of her pregnancy, Dalton Ames, as he scouts outside Cambridge to find a suitable site for his upcoming suicide: "*I have committed incest I said Father it was I it was not Dalton Ames.* And when he put Dalton Ames. Dalton Ames. Dalton Ames. When he put the pistol in my hand I didn't" (*The Sound and the Fury* 90). It is only later when Quentin lapses into a semicatatonic state and is shortly afterwards knocked out by an athletic Gerald Bland—like Ames another self-confessed philanderer—that he can "remember" the painful scenes from his past: when he failed to commit suicide-incest with Caddy and when he confronted Caddy's lover in a pathetic attempt to run him out of town.

Whether or not Faulkner's depictions derive in part from the "Circe" chapter of *Ulysses* in which Stephen and Bloom are in a brothel and experience a succession of fantasies or hallucinations does not matter much since Faulkner is bringing something new to the table. Quentin, a "half-baked Galahad" motivated by a southern tradition of honor (126), sees suicide as a worthy choice and the fury within him is effectively rendered to suggest that—as, later, his brother Jason will rage against the memory of "the job in the bank of which he had been deprived before he ever got it" by a sister who was "always a bitch" (354, 206). Such furies are quite foreign to Stephen and to Bloom, who has nothing but regret for his father's suicide by poison; as André Bleikasten notes, with Bloom, "we are obviously in less deep and less troubled waters" (105). Maybe Bloom's mundane habit of "watching pennies," as Mr. Compson advised Quentin to do, has preserved him from such an extreme (*Sound* 204). After all, in "The Dead," the most important of the stories in *Dubliners* (1914), Joyce had already dealt with a Michael Furey (a real name, but also one with obvious significance), who shockingly, if indirectly, died because of his youthful love for the heroine of the tale. There, time eventually put his sacrifice into perspective, relieving the main character, Gabriel Conroy, and the reader from its dominance. In *The Sound and the Fury*, on the other hand, Quentin, "under the first fury of despair" (204), cannot escape the "temporary state of mind" that will lead to his suicide over his loss of his sister, not only to marriage but also to a cad (203). That is *his* tragic story, and Faulkner's significant difference from the Joyce that resounds in much of his prose.

Ulysses ends in joy with Molly Bloom repeating the "Yes" of her original consent to Leopold's affections (783/644). *The Sound and the Fury* concludes with "post and tree, window and doorway and signboard each in its ordered place" (371), though the order is merely one that pacifies a mentally handicapped Benjy in a family that seems closer to decline than it was at the beginning of the novel. However, reading Faulkner's narrative, like reading *Ulysses*, is not at all a gloomy experience. Faulkner completed his work in a mood of "ecstasy" ("An Introduction" 415). The attentive twenty-first-century student of *The Sound and the Fury* is likely to share at least some of his exultation.

Works Cited

Bleikasten, André. "Bloom and Quentin." *The Seventh of Joyce*. Ed. Bernard Benstock. Bloomington: Indiana UP, 1982. 100–108. Print.

Bloom, Harold. Introduction. *William Faulkner's* The Sound and the Fury. Ed. Bloom. New York: Chelsea, 1988. 1–7. Print.

Blotner, Joseph. *Faulkner: A Biography*. New York: Random, 1974. Print.

Csicsila, Joseph. "'The Storm-Tossed Heart of Man': Echoes of 'Nausicaa' in Quentin's Section of *The Sound and the Fury*." *Faulkner Journal* 13.1–2 (1997–1998): 77–88. Print.

Eliot, T. S. "*Ulysses*, Order, and Myth." *Selected Prose of T. S. Eliot*. Ed. Frank Kermode. New York: Harcourt, 1975. 175–78. Print.

Ellmann, Richard. *James Joyce*. New York: Oxford UP, 1982. Print.

Faulkner, William. *Absalom, Absalom!: The Corrected Text*. New York: Random, 1986. Print.

___. "Appendix: The Compsons." *The Portable Faulkner*. Ed. Malcolm Cowley. New York: Penguin, 1977. 704–21. Print.

___. *Faulkner in the University*. Ed. Frederick L. Gwynn and Joseph Blotner. New York: Vintage, 1965. Print.

___. "An Introduction to *The Sound and the Fury*." *Mississippi Quarterly* 26.3 (1973): 410–15. Print.

___. *The Sound and the Fury*. 1929. Corrected ed. New York: Random, 1984. Print.

___. *The Sound and the Fury*. London: Folio Soc., 2012. Print.

Groden, Michael. "Criticism in New Composition: *Ulysses* and *The Sound and the Fury*." *Twentieth Century Literature* 21.3 (1975): 265–77. Print.

Gwin, Minrose C. *The Feminine and Faulkner: Reading (Beyond) Sexual Difference*. Knoxville: U of Tennessee P, 1990. Print.

Joyce, James. *Dubliners*. New York: Vintage, 1993. Print.

___. *A Portrait of the Artist as a Young Man*. Ed. Seamus Deane. New York: Penguin, 1993. Print.

___. *Selected Letters of James Joyce*. Ed. Richard Ellmann. New York: Viking, 1975. Print.

___. *Ulysses*. New York: Vintage, 1961. Print.

___. *Ulysses: The Corrected Text*. New York: Vintage, 1986. Print.

Kenner, Hugh. "Faulkner and Joyce." *Faulkner, Modernism, and Film: Faulkner and Yoknapatawpha*. Ed. Evans Harrington and Ann J. Abadie. Jackson: UP of Mississippi, 1979. 20–33. Print.

Lester, Cheryl. "Racial Awareness and Arrested Development: *The Sound and the Fury* and the Great Migration (1915–1928)." *The Cambridge Companion to William Faulkner*. Ed. Philip M. Weinstein. New York: Cambridge UP, 1995. 123–45. Print.

Ross, Stephen M., and Noel Polk. *Reading Faulkner:* The Sound and the Fury, *Glossary and Commentary*. Jackson: UP of Mississippi, 1996. Print.

Sykes, John D., Jr. "What Faulkner (Might Have) Learned from Joyce." *Mississippi Quarterly* 58.3–4 (2005): 513–28. Print.

Walker, Nancy. "Stephen and Quentin." *The Seventh of Joyce*. Ed. Bernard Benstock. Bloomington: Indiana UP, 1982. 109–13. Print.

Weinstein, Philip. "'Make It New': Faulkner and Modernism." *A Companion to William Faulkner*. Ed. Richard C. Moreland. Oxford: Blackwell, 2007. 342–58. Print.

Yeats, W. B. *The Collected Poems of W. B. Yeats*. New York: Macmillan, 1956. Print.

As I Lay Dying, The Time of Man, and the Modern Folk Novel_____

Mark Lucas

When William Faulkner's *As I Lay Dying* appeared to small sales and mixed reviews in 1930, it had been preceded by a widely praised best seller four years before that also featured poor southern farmers enduring barn fires, bad luck, and the wrath of nature. Although out of print and little known now, Elizabeth Madox Roberts's *The Time of Man* was a sensation when it appeared in 1926. Roberts's bildungsroman about the maturation of Ellen Chesser, a downtrodden sharecropper's daughter, "was received with almost universal acclaim," Robert Penn Warren once remarked (Warren 5). Ford Madox Ford and Sherwood Anderson, both literary giants of the day, were among its many admirers. "My love of the book," Anderson wrote Roberts, "is beyond expression" (Slavick viii). Also, given the setting, plot elements, and vernacular of the characters of *As I Lay Dying*, at least one other great writer of the era seems to have read it: Faulkner.

The similarities of the two works in terms of setting are apparent. Both *The Time of Man* and *As I Lay Dying* have journey plots, take place in the early twentieth century, and feature rural southern families who are isolated and poor. Men wear brogans and drink water from cedar buckets. Women milk cows, cook turnip greens, and trade eggs for household needs. Both narratives unfold aboard wagons, along roads, and in dog-run cabins and unpainted barns. Both reveal a Chaucerian spectrum of human nature in the people met as the journey evolves. Both works even have "graphophones," an "Uncle Billy," "barnburners," and someone who has to be hauled by plowline. Such correspondences between the two novels are many. The hill-country part of Faulkner's Yoknapatawpha County may be farther south than Roberts's Kentucky hills, but in folkways, speech, and texture of life the two literary landscapes are remarkably alike.

Overlapping details of setting may or may not indicate influence, of course, and for that matter, Faulkner did not need to read anyone's novel to know about people of the Bundrens' class, namely white "plain folk" or "yeomanry." (Roberts's Chessers and Kents, not owning the land they work, are plain folk of lower status than the Bundrens.) Faulkner grew up a town boy, but he knew the countryside well, especially country talk. He remembered having accompanied his politician uncle on campaigns: "'I would go around with him and listen on the front galleries of country stores and listen to the talk that would go on.'" He also learned country ways and lingo, he said, through "'horses and hunting, things like that, but without carrying a notebook at all, just to remember'" (Gwynn 273). Like Faulkner, Roberts grew up in the small-town South—Springfield, Kentucky, in her case—and came by her knowledge of country life the same way he did, by paying attention. Several years she spent as a young country schoolteacher were of particular importance (Campbell 19–20).

Parallel settings aside, the case to be made for influence begins with certain verbal echoes and a notable plot element. In her introduction to *Annotations to Faulkner's "As I Lay Dying"* (1990), Dianne Luce singles out "the frequency with which Elizabeth Madox Roberts' lyrical novel of country life" is echoed (ii). She specifically cites nineteen such correspondences. There is an analogue in *The Time of Man*, for instance, for Dewey Dell's exposed sense that "they [Darl's eyes] swim to pin points . . . and then my dress is gone" (Faulkner 121, Luce 51). Of Joe Trent's eyes Ellen Chesser observes, "they could draw down into little tubes of looks that went into her dress, under her skin, into her blood" (Roberts 70–71). Another striking echo is the passage in *The Time of Man* when Ellen chants the existence of Jonas Prather out of her mind. "'Jonas, Jonas, Jonas,'" she thinks. "It was nothing but a word, gone out of her body . . . a flat sound without meaning" (Roberts 260). The parallel with Addie's erasure of Anse is remarkable: "I would think: Anse. Why Anse. Why are you Anse. I would think about his name until after a while I could see the word as a shape . . . profoundly without life" (Faulkner 173). Likewise, Addie's yearning response to cries of wild geese "high and wild out of the wild darkness" (Faulkner 170) has its counterpart in Ellen: "Far away some geese, disturbed, were crying, the tones coming as high thin music flaring upward into the dark" (Roberts 72). It is not necessary to attribute conscious borrowing to Faulkner to feel nonetheless that *The Time of Man* was indeed a quarry for him.

Beyond verbal parallels, the plot element of the "barnburner" stands out. In *As I Lay Dying*, Darl's torching of Gillespie's barn is the spectacular climax of the Bundren's travails on the long road to Jefferson. The stigma of being a barn burner is so great—not to mention the Bundren family's potential legal liability for the destroyed barn—that Darl is committed to the state insane asylum. The pariah branding of the barn burner is equally part of the plot of *The Time of Man*, for Jasper Kent, Ellen's man, suffers under the suspicion of having started two barn fires. He is probably innocent, but there is just enough ambiguity that Ellen herself wonders. Barn arson was a feared and hated act of rural violence, and Faulkner made it a key element of *The Hamlet* (1940) later in his career as well as in *As I Lay Dying*. Interestingly, in both *The Time of Man* and *As I Lay Dying*, the patent wrong of destroying stock and property is set against arguments for the barn burnings.

More central than all the above correspondences, however, is the fundamental starting point from which both authors proceed: the artistic decision to believe in, and to find a way to convey, the complexity of provincial characters. Isolated and deprived, thought of by outsiders as "country simple," Ellen Chesser and her literary kinfolk in Faulkner's novel are keenly alive inside their minds. To convey the interplay between inner and outer was crucial to both authors. What Roberts once wrote about her quest as a writer might also have described Faulkner's endeavor in *As I Lay Dying*: "Somewhere there is a connection between the world of the mind and the outer order. It is the secret of the contact that we are after, the point, the moment of the union" (Campbell 33). What particularly electrifies that "moment of the union" in both novels is the extreme contrast between impassive or veiled exteriors and the hyperaware recesses of the mind. Both novels gain a powerful effect from stripping away "hayseed," "bumpkin" exteriors (the epithets are many) to reveal what is sinuous and dynamic below.

High-culture technique combined with folk-culture subject matter is one way to describe the common strategies adopted by Faulkner and Roberts, for both novels' story lines have ballad characteristics. In exploring the unsettling "carnival" mode of *As I Lay Dying*, Richard Gray notes the folk element in the novel, the way the Bundrens "are situated within an accumulating store of legend" in a manner "similar to that of a folksong" (Gray 152–53). The particular type of folk narrative echoed is one of the most venerable, the disaster ballad. "The Ballad of Casey Jones" is a famous example, detailing in verse after verse a spectacular train wreck. The Bundrens' story is likewise a calamitous tale delivered in unfolding detail, fifty-nine "verses" in fact, with flood, fire, mules, buzzards, and concrete cast all given their due in the communal telling.

Ellen Chesser's story is balladlike too, though reminiscent of another type. It is a rewriting of the false-hearted lover narrative. "Come All You Fair and Tender Ladies" is a classic of this mode. "Take warning how you court your men," sings the betrayed young woman of the song, for "away they'll go and court some other." Ellen knows and loves such ballads; they are what she has instead of books. Art becomes fact when Jonas Prather's desertion makes Ellen the girl of the ballad. Unlike Cassie MacMurtrie, also the victim of a false-hearted man, Ellen refuses to die for love, as happens in so many of the ballads. The larger artistic pattern is twofold: both Faulkner and Roberts embrace traditional folk elements in these novels, but their shared next impulse is not "folk" at all, for both also embrace modern notions of the mind and its presentation.

Nonetheless, for all they share, the two works diverge in style and tone. Roberts's way of penetrating the flint surfaces of rustic characters is quiet, rhythmic, and tender. Faulkner's way, despite essential parallels, is so heightened and multifarious as to be a phenomenon of a completely different order. Since *The Time of Man* is relatively unknown today, examining it first and at a little length will be a useful prologue to exploring the parallels and departures in the narrative strategies of *As I Lay Dying*. To think about Faulkner's novel in the context of Roberts's is a way to look afresh at a key part of the reading experience of *As I Lay Dying*, the delightfully complex intersection of characterization, point of view, and tone.

Roberts's Southern Folk

Even before the country schoolteacher Roberts went to the University of Chicago and became a modern artist, she already admired the Irish playwright John Millington Synge and the way he found music in the peasant speech of rural Ireland. She saw as well that the strategy could be transferred to the Knob Country of Kentucky (Slavick xi). The stoic, uneducated folk who populate *The Time of Man* voice themselves in a resonant language, however haltingly delivered. "'A big ripe peach is like a promise in the wilderness,'" says the wandering tree salesman (Roberts 377). Most of Ellen's life passes inarticulately, inside "feeling [that] could not take words" (Roberts 73), but in such moments as her father's chance remark that "'no plow iron ever cut this-here hill afore, not in the whole time of man'" (Roberts 87), the relentless now of one hardscrabble situation after another opens out into mythic dimensions, into deep wells of feeling and context.

A remarkable example of the sleight of hand by which Roberts turns low diction to epic purposes may be found in the porch talk of Ellen and Jasper in the autumn before they marry. One notes its curious ebbs and flows, repetitions and disconnections:

"Hear the dogs howl," she said, "off toward Stigall's it is. It's a lonesome sound, like the end of the world. Are you afeared of the end of the world?"

"I feel like I could pick up a hill or I could break open a mountain with my fist, and what call have I got to be afeared of a lonesome sound to-night? But it's a lonesome one."

"Lonesome like doves a-callen in trees to each other. Did you ever in your time hear a dove call and then another one answers?"

"I could pick up a hill with my strength."

"One asks the question, the doves, and then the other comes right along with the next call."

"I could pick up a hill or I could break open a rock with my fist."

"It's the sorrowfulest sound there is, as if it knowed what would come. Fair and sorrowful all together. It calls to mind good times that are lost and bad sorrowful ones, both gone together somehow."

"I take notice of doves a heap in spring. A dove call denotes spring is come for sure, and it's safe then to plant corn."

"And a dove has got one drop of human blood in its body somewheres, they say." (Roberts 284)

The vernacular diction of the dialogue is as real as dirt. However, the disconnected planes of musing utterance, what might be called the dialogue's poetic quality of strophe and antistrophe, are strangely stylized and repetitive, a strategy from the modernist toolbox that Roberts blended with her realism. Ellen's is the voice of longing and wonderment, Jasper's of muscle and fact. The two voices run parallel, do not intersect or engage. What they do share, however, is dreaminess. Interestingly, Jasper's Samson-like dream of indomitability will be shattered by novel's end, and Ellen's premonition of sorrow will prove true.

The passage accomplishes more than foreshadowing, however. Its principal contribution is tonal. It constitutes a kind of verbal music that is poignant and enlarging in tone. Doves are augurs and part human. There are mountains to "break open" with a hero's fist. Distant hounds sound like "the end." Great doings and magic seem to live. There is nothing comic or deflating or even realistic, for that matter, in the gaps of the exchange. Rather, the effect of its counterpoint is to lift the narrative into the epic register that Roberts sought.

In journal notes, Roberts wrote that her aim was to make "the wandering tenant farmer of our region . . . a symbol for an Odyss[e]y of Man" (Rovit 9). Elucidating Roberts's idea of a modern odyssey, Earl Rovit highlights Ellen Chesser's "epic struggle for life against the fatal forces of nature" (Rovit 10). She is an Odysseus of the lowly, and endurance is her heroic virtue. Hers is a twenty-year wander, beset not by gods and monsters but by "the spectacular panorama of nature" and its inexorable cycles (Rovit 11). The wind and the rain, the field and the well, the seed and the hoe—these are the constants of her journey.

Ellen is indeed an emblematic hero, yet, as Rovit says, it is by a strange inversion that this is accomplished. She is "the lowest common denominator of mankind," stripped of "every refinement of culture not absolutely essential to that which makes her a human being" (Rovit 15)—prefiguring in this the burned and broken Bundrens grinding on toward Jefferson "as though the very earth would hush our entry" (Faulkner 229). Hunger, isolation, betrayal, and humiliation are Ellen's lot in life. The story's outer trajectory is but rags to rags. It ends as it began: a poverty-stricken family on a wagon. Yet Ellen trudges on with her tenacious life force. Over and again she flowers out of stone.

Despite the sorrow of Ellen's young family's expulsion from Rock Creek in the narrative's closing sequence, the children's wagon chatter is a reprise of the strains of lyricism that thread the whole work. "'Where are we a-goen, Mammy?'" asks Nan. The question of destinations unleashes flights of longing and wonder from one voice after another: "'I heared it said one time that all the stars have names.'" "'You could learn that in books.'" "'And all the sky and how deep it goes, and whe'r it's got an end or not?'" (Roberts 393–94). The undaunted notes of the close of the novel connect with and redefine one of the book's darkest passages. In a wretched interval of her past, Ellen had found herself living in poverty in yet another exploitative tenant situation, this time at the Goddard place. Rain dripped through the roof and her children grew hollow-eyed in want while they all waited "upon the hazards of the seasons" (331). In the misery of this bad time, she had had a troubling vision of her children grown to adulthood, "all standing about the cabin door until they darkened the path with their shadows, all asking beyond what she had to give, always demanding, always wanting more of her and more of them always wanting to be." "'Out of me,'" thinks Ellen, "'come people forever, forever'" (Roberts 333). It is a symbolic moment. Out of her indeed come people forever: the salt of the earth from the dirt-born enduring Everywoman. Call her poor white, but she is not, in her own mind or Roberts's, trash. "Out of me come people forever." Who are those "people"? They are the children in the wagon dreaming about stars and books and a crop of their own. Ellen may not always be able to feed them meat, but she has fed them her dreams. The close of the story recasts and resolves the season of despair. The verbal music typified by the ending is Roberts's signature. She risks the shoals of sentimentalism perhaps, but the passage succeeds because the vernacular remains true, and most of all, because the golden moment is so hard-won. Long seasons of woe lie both behind and ahead.

There are triumphs of character in Roberts's created world but no triumphs over circumstance. Jasper's strength goes for naught. Ellen's goodness secures nothing. Yet Roberts lifts her humble nobody up to heroic stature by powerfully rendering her interior life. Ellen's thoughts may typically lie too deep for utterance, but Roberts opens Ellen's mind to the reader in ways that suggest the girl's moil of feelings, impressions, and sensations, something near subjective consciousness itself. Trying to fall asleep one night on a cabin floor, for instance, young Ellen replays the long day's fields and toil and farmer's orders, seeing again "little grains of soil swimming past her tired eyes" until "the farmer was there with his stiff legs and square butt, bending over the plant bed, urging everyone forward, trying to be both familiar and commanding. Across the mud and the swimming grains of soil ran his yellow house, off past trees, ran mist, roof-shapes, bobolinks over a meadow, blackbirds in locust trees, bumblebees dragging their bodies over red clover" (Roberts 15). Images reel by in dreamlike liquidity. Actual words spoken may be as simple as "'I look for spring'" (186) or "'I couldn't say e'er word for sure'" (Roberts 193), but the accompanying thoughts spin through chains of complex cerebration: "She could not think why one would quit life," she reflects when Cassie MacMurtrie commits suicide. "A great will to live surged up in her, including the entire assembly—the coroner, Squire Dorsey, Henry, Miss Tod, Mr. Al, all of them. They would all live. She was living. Only life was comprehensible and actual, present. She was herself life. It went with her wherever she went, holding its abode in her being" (Roberts 193). Ellen would not use the word "comprehensible" in speech—in fact she probably does not even know the word—but her internal life is so vivid and sensitive that almost no vocabulary is off-limits for conveying it. Ellen can feel what "holding its abode in her being" expresses even though she would never use the phrase. This is simply a convention of Roberts's narration, one that Faulkner will use as well.

One other strategy for rendering Ellen's interior life is via the lonely girl's habit of silently talking to herself. There is a whisper inside her brain on occasion, a "mind-voice" that rattles through transitionless impressions, memories, and fantasies. "'People a-dyen in ships at midnight,'" she "talk-thinks" from a creek rock one August afternoon, "'and people a-goen to a foreign country with pots made outen gold and skillets made outen silver on the pack-horse, and gold cups. People a-goen to London-town—Is this the way to London-town?—and an old, old queen. And a story about a horse could talk'" (Roberts 45). Adolescent confusion erupts in similar passages. "Unable to gather her sense into a thought" one melancholy evening as she nears sixteen, Ellen begins silently to "talk" her consciousness instead: "'What is it is a-beaten down on my breath? I'm a-fallen through the world and there's no end to the top and no end to the bottom. Mammy a-getten up and a-cooken and a-goen to bed and Pappy works all day, and we have to eat and we have to wear and we have to have a fire, and there's no end to anything'" (Roberts 96). At such junctures the narrative becomes more first-person monologue than third-person limited. The parallel in *As I Lay Dying*, cast completely in first-person interior monologue, is striking.

The Inner Voice in *As I Lay Dying*

Elemental struggle yoked with deep-mind poetry, homegrown folk material blended with intense subjectivity—it is hard to imagine Faulkner reading *The Time of Man* without seeing exciting possibilities for his own imagination. Here was inspiration close to home. *As I Lay Dying* would certainly embrace Roberts's governing notions: the idea of an endurance trial so primordial that it creates its own epic atmosphere and the idea of the untutored mind possessed of deep capacities. How it would embody those notions was pure Faulkner. To consider the two works side by side now, especially in terms of technique and, finally, tone, is revealing.

As I Lay Dying spins a shrewdly plotted, generally chronological story. As psychological as it is in focus, it is not at all short on action. Addie Bundren, the mother of the backcountry Bundren clan, oversees the building of her own coffin as she lies dying. The doctor arrives, hauled up the bluff by plowline, but it is too late. Addie dies, is put in her wedding dress and then the pine box. Her youngest child, after beating the doctor's horses, drills holes in the coffin lid and on into his mother's face. Then the body is loaded into the family wagon to honor Addie's wish: to be buried in town. However, torrential rains have taken out the bridges. The trip swiftly becomes an Underworld journey complete with a harum-scarum river crossing, dead mules, a hay-barn inferno, a shocking flashback revelation, an audibly decomposing corpse, and a son declared insane. Then in the final paragraph a twist ending: the husband remarries the day after putting his wife in the ground.

One can imagine a highly readable conventional novel made from these materials. But *As I Lay Dying* is not conventional. Where *The*

Time of Man has the traditional continuity of the consistent third-person-limited narrative, *As I Lay Dying* is fractured into fifty-nine short chapters delivered from fifteen first-person points of view. Faulkner ran a risk. The technical intricacy might have spoiled a good story. But instead it intensifies it. What makes the novel such a dazzling reading experience, far more in truth than the audacious plot, is the multiplicity of complex voices. Faulkner brings the bright, jagged pieces together in a brilliant, if disorienting, mosaic. It is as if the subjectivity subtly employed by Roberts has entered a house of mirrors.

Each chapter is a character's name and then anywhere from a sentence to nine pages of interior monologue. The monologues address no one, yet work steadily in service of the reader as they advance the what and the why of the story. The technique here has reasonably been called stream-of-consciousness narration, plugged in as the reader is to each narrator's silent thoughts and feelings, but one notices that the consciousnesses represented only intermittently "stream" in the unordered, spontaneous way such a word suggests. The monologues accelerate into "streaming mode" only in heightened moments that are all the more arresting for being wavelike and passing.

Like Roberts, Faulkner employs a polyphony of inner and outer—multiple melodies at once, one could say, borrowing from music terminology. In *The Time of Man* Roberts achieves a striking effect from the contrast between Ellen's simple country speech and her complex language of thought. The scene cited earlier in which she is questioned by the coroner is a good example: "Did she know of any reason Cassie MacMurtrie might have for hanging herself?" In the matter of seconds before she replies, her mind swirls through layers of reflection. She visualizes Cassie's discovery of her husband's adultery; she detours into thoughts of Jonas; she opens out into a great, encompassing will to live. All of this cerebration the coroner will never know. Ellen's reply is simply, "'Miss Cassie didn't say e'er word to me about her trouble'" (Roberts 193).

Faulkner, too, employs this kind of polyphony, but with a multi-voiced exuberance that is a symphony next to Roberts's piano. The strategy is multiplied and intensified with astonishing results. The external action of Darl's second chapter, for instance, consists merely of his getting a drink of water and being asked, "Where's Jewel?" In the brief interval before Darl gives his demotic reply—"Down to the barn . . . Harnessing the team"—his mind darts through at least seven layers of reflection: the taste of water from a cedar bucket, the look of stars reflected in a gourd dipper, a pubescent memory of nighttime silence "blowing upon [his] parts," an intuition of coming rain, a quick history of his father's wrecked toes, a visual deduction of Tull's henpecked home life, and a wildly inventive mental snapshot of his father's brogans looking "as though they had been hacked with a blunt axe out of pig-iron" (Faulkner 11). Nor is that the end of the psychological pyrotechnics, for the flat seven-word reply, which is actually a cover-up lie, is followed by nothing less than a vision. Darl sees in his mind's eye "a tableau savage in the sun": Jewel's violent ballet with his horse, which is what in all likelihood is really happening "down to the barn." It is an intensely detailed, two-page description, complete with dialogue, looped chains of participial phrases, and words like "curvetting," "myriad," and "hiatus" (Faulkner 12–13). Moreover, the tableau unfolds as if Darl were an intimate observer, but he is not there.

Narrowly speaking, the episode might be said to disrupt credibility. However, the reader recognizes and swiftly follows the shift from one level of thought to a deeper one and enjoys both the fuller revelation of character and the freshness of a new way of "telling." One need not exactly share Stephen Ross's view that the novel is "fundamentally spoken" (Ross 111) to agree with his sense that the deviations from a character's normal diction and syntax are deeply revealing. As I Lay Dying is indeed, as Ross argues, a tour de force of "differing registers of fictional discourse" (Ross 111). Rather than experiencing such deviations as breaches of verisimilitude, most readers take them simply as expansions of perceptual reality, not violations. With subtle tense and tone shifts, Faulkner handles the transitions so shrewdly that the reader follows the modulations without pause. There is a jolt of excitement but not of resistance. As in Roberts, the reader understands the character's mind to know and feel with a hypersensitivity indicated by language beyond its actual vocabulary.

The polyphony between inner and outer is even more fundamental to the reading experience of *As I Lay Dying* than to that of *The Time of Man*. As spectacularly dysfunctional as the Bundrens are as a family unit, they are none of them "simple," not even Anse. He may have the one-note quality of the "flat" comic character, the single note in his case being self-interest, but consider his communism-of-the-afterlife theology (Faulkner 110–11), the nimbleness and success with which he plays his Job card beginning to end ("for who He loveth, so doeth He chastiseth" [Faulkner 110–11]), and his amazing replacement-drudge detector. "He'll get it, too," Darl says in homage when they stop at the duck-shaped woman's house for a shovel. "Ay," says Cash, foreseeing all: "It was just like he [Anse] knew, like he could see through the walls and into the next ten minutes" (Faulkner 236).

Such passages as the love-duet porch talk in *The Time of Man* have no counterpart in *As I Lay Dying*, albeit Anse comically mouths one side of such a conversation ("The somebody you was young with and you growed old in her and she growed old in you" [Faulkner 234]). Faulkner seldom goes for Roberts's shimmer effect in his dialogue. The talk is plain. Only the phonies—Anse, Whitfield, and Cora—indulge in spoken eloquence, their florid locutions the index of their hollowness. The laconic quality of most of the dialogue does not mean, however, that Faulkner hears no poetry in his characters.

There are many passages of dreamy wonderment in *As I Lay Dying*, all the strife of the action notwithstanding. Darl's mind is filled with such, from remembered stars in the water bucket to a sun "poised like a bloody egg upon a crest of thunderheads" (Faulkner 11, 40); from reflecting that a woman's legs are "that caliper which measures the length and breadth of life" to his thought before the last rise into town:

"Life was created in the valleys. It blew up onto the hills on the old terrors" (Faulkner 104, 227). Even literal-minded Cash can be figurative, such as in the carpentry metaphors of his internal homily on "the olden right teaching" to "drive the nails down and trim the edges well always like it was for your own use" because "it's better to build a tight chicken coop than a shoddy courthouse" (Faulkner 234). The fascinating oddities of Vardaman's juvenile perceptions are another slice of the journey's incongruous poetry: "Darl and I go across the moon"; streetlights "roost in the trees"; the burning barn collapses "swirling, making the stars run backward" (Faulkner 214, 249, 225). None of the Bundren siblings are dull to experience. Darl is a bard in overalls, Cash a stoic philosopher, Dewey Dell a quivering web of feeling. And their mother, her one monologue reveals, is a ferocious priestess of freethinking. The underlying point is that these characters are all full of potential, however frustrated. They can certainly look like simpletons to the casual observer or seem "stone-hearted," as Cora judges them (Faulkner 23), but they are not.

Faulkner and Roberts share a key premise: one's deepest life is lived "in the head." The engine of thought churns inside a self that is all the more alive for being secret. The landowner may bark at Roberts's heroine about an escaped pig, for instance, but "the deep-running currents of her life [hold] him in but very little place" (Roberts 315). Samson in *As I Lay Dying* tries to tell himself that men, unlike women, take life "as it comes," without brooding. Then he promptly spirals into a knot of hallucinatory overthinking (Faulkner 118). Similarly, Vernon Tull has a virtual credo of thought suppression—"For the Lord aimed for [men] to do and not spend too much time thinking" (Faulkner 71)—but he tramples it to shreds in one of the most intricately thoughtful chapters of the novel (Faulkner 68–74). The crowning moment of this clinic in the primacy of the silent but whirling mind is when, in a bout of insomnia, Darl reasons out his homespun version of Descartes's famous "cogito ergo sum": "And then I must be, or I could not empty myself for sleep in a strange room. And so if I am not emptied yet, I am is" (Faulkner 81).

Darl is the most extreme example of narrative polyphony, but one might just as readily turn to a character whose reflectiveness is sometimes sold short, Dewey Dell. To begin by considering her in parallel with Ellen Chesser, her counterpart (sans pregnancy) in *The Time of Man*, one notes that they are both denigrated as "people like that" by the larger world (Roberts 19). "We are country people, not as good as town people" (Faulkner 60), thinks Dewey Dell herself, resigned to the prejudice that Ellen also knows. Roberts and Faulkner explode the stereotype to reveal characters of stunning depth. Both girls are ungrammatical and inarticulate by parlor-talk standards, but they possess anything but flat psyches. For instance, Ellen can only stutter, "'Mr. Bodine told Pappy'" (Roberts 37), when shooed away from the blackberries by the farmer's wife, yet immediately afterward her mind fills with minute perception of nature, ballad lyrics, a fortune-teller's patter, and, finally, a summing-up of Mrs. Bodine: "'I know about everything she does, in and out of her big ugly house, a-planten her late cabbage one day and a-putten up jam the next, with Pappy to cut her stovewood'" (Roberts 38–39). Even when Ellen's tongue is not articulate, her perceptions are.

Dewey Dell's interior life is equally alive, often neurotically so. Because her naïveté and desperation make her gullible, critics sometimes forget how rich her mind can be. The Dewey Dell monologue during the family's silent refusal of the turnoff for the New Hope churchyard, for instance, is virtually psychedelic. Her panic about being pregnant colors everything, including her desperate desire to keep the journey moving toward town and the abortion medicine Lafe says is there. Narrative description ("The signboard comes in sight") escalates into hallucinatory thought language as inanimate objects come to life: signboard and road "look" and "wait." Everything has the "time" that Dewey Dell does not. She wants to grieve for her mother ("I wish I had time to let her die"), but "the womb of time" has become her own expanding pelvic girdle: "the agony and the despair of spreading bones." Even in her agitation she is capable of sympathetic imagination, for she notices a quality "pale empty sad composed and questioning" in Cash. Then in one instant she sees Darl's vision as a strange projector ("The land runs out of Darl's eyes") and in the next as an x-ray ("[his eyes] swim to pin points . . . and then my dress is gone"). Her mind divides into three essentially simultaneous layers of consciousness, Faulkner using italics to indicate the layers: (1) telepathic "eye-talk" from Darl in the present, (2) freeze-frames from a memory of a bloody midnight hallucination, and (3) recollection of a nightmare she once had, a nothingness scenario that repeatedly haunts her in one form or another. Punctuation disappears at the frenzied height of the sequence, the nightmare (Faulkner 120–21), which coincides exactly with the crisis of choice adjacent to the dreaded turn.

The chapter has a musical dynamic—crescendo and diminuendo—that follows the curve of Dewey Dell's rising and falling hysteria. Once the New Hope crisis has passed, her mind quiets, but not without one last tremor. "I believe in God, God," she thinks. "God, I believe in God" (Faulkner 122). The repetitions of the profession of faith suggest anxiety more than conviction. What Dewey Dell feels throughout the chapter is not garden-variety "worry." As her barn monologue earlier underscores, she has become worry itself, the raw experience, what Addie terms "the dark voicelessness in which the words are the deeds" (Faulkner 174): "I said You dont know what worry is," Dewey Dell thinks. "I dont know what it is. I dont know whether I am worrying or not. . . . I feel like a wet seed wild in the hot blind earth" (Faulkner 64). The addressed "You" is Lafe, her fleeing lover and a mere mouther of the word "worry." Dewey Dell is the thing itself.

One of the saddest and most subtly rendered passages in the novel is Dewey Dell's final monologue, during which Anse takes the money package she has been bearing like an amulet. Not a single thought emerges, only a verbatim transcript of the brief dialogue and then the blank report, "He took the money and went out" (Faulkner 257). Her defeat is complete. Her driving mind has been blotted out.

The Elevation of Southern Fiction

The Time of Man is a love story. It tells the story of the three loves of Ellen Chesser: Jonas Prather, Jasper Kent, and life itself. The third is the central thread of everything in the narrative. Ellen lives in poverty and endless toil, yet her highs are as high as anyone's. She is mere "road trash" in the eyes of the propertied farmer or the educated town dweller, yet her interior life is subtle, intense, and open to wonder. Thus it is that even though the plot of *The Time of Man* is a litany of setbacks, its tone is not dark. Ellen loses her childhood friend. Her father is a serial failure. Ellen suffers betrayal in love. New love is thwarted by catastrophe. That much is the first three quarters of the book. Then after the brief and dreamlike elopement sequence, the outer story turns to adultery, a lost child, mob violence, and exile. Nonetheless, the narrative embodies what Rovit terms a "fundamental faith in the essential nobility of man" (Rovit 22). The epic elevations of style offer a dignity to humble material. The resilience and aspiration of Ellen, and then in turn her children, are a testimonial to character. What might have shrunken into bitterness and frustration has not. The lyrical tone of Roberts's love narrative is its harmonic center beginning to end.

Unlike *The Time of Man*, however, *As I Lay Dying* is extremely resistant to classification of mode or tone. Where one commentator speaks of Faulkner's "most affectionate" novel (Howe 189), another sees an "ending [that] makes us feel as though we had been tricked into caring at all" (Thompson 9). "Are we to laugh or cry over the Bundrens' exploit?" asks Cleanth Brooks (93). The novel's "turgid thickness of meaning" is breathtakingly "patternless," says Calvin Bedient (62–63). Warwick Wadlington finds in the work's wild mix of "epic storytelling, tragedy, and grotesque humor" a deliberate "outrageousness" (36). There is a long tradition of finding it difficult to designate the book's tone, much less say what kind of story it is.

However, there are affirmations of character in *As I Lay Dying*, with an accompanying sympathy and seriousness, even the stately dignity of tragedy. One thinks of the heroism of Jewel, the stoic suffering of

Cash; the Good Samaritanism of all the Tulls, Armstids, and Peabodys; and the remarkable depth beneath one humble exterior after another. The book's very title is epic, a quotation from Homer's *Odyssey* (ca. 725 BCE; English translation, 1614).

Nonetheless, the novel has a withering side, half comic and half darkly absurd. What Anse calls a sacred promise was actually Addie's practical joke. The one Bundren who tries to halt the family's suffering and humiliation is straitjacketed and institutionalized. Dewey Dell's laughable "cottonsack reasoning" for coupling with Lafe culminates in her de facto rape in a Jefferson drugstore, the butt of a farmer's daughter joke. And who wins in the world bodied forth in this novel? Anse Bundren, the human cockroach. The Homeric title is suddenly parody.

Perhaps the tonal quandary is a way of saying Faulkner's cup of invention runs over. *As I Lay Dying* is a Roman candle of sixty flares: fifty-nine surprise-laden monologues and then whatever happens in the reader's mind at the end of the show. *The Time of Man*, by contrast, has a single, central consciousness that keeps the book all in the key of nature. Roberts's romanticism is tough, but it is still romanticism. Enduring all weathers, Ellen becomes all weathers and catches up the glow of the nature goddess Luke Wimble sees in her. She's a flower, an apple, wild honey. *As I Lay Dying* has no such presiding presence. What it does share with Roberts's novel, though, is a profound sense of the interior lives of humble characters. Roberts was a door opener in the house of southern fiction. The ruckus Faulkner raised beyond that door is astonishing.

Works Cited

Bedient, Calvin. "Pride and Nakedness: *As I Lay Dying.*" *Modern Language Quarterly* 29 (1968): 61–76. Print.

Brooks, Cleanth. *William Faulkner: First Encounters.* New Haven, CT: Yale UP, 1983. Print.

Campbell, Harry Modean, and Ruel E. Foster. *Elizabeth Madox Roberts: American Novelist.* Norman: Oklahoma UP, 1956. Print.

Faulkner, William. *As I Lay Dying*. 1930. New York: Vintage International, 1990. Print.

Gray, Richard. *The Life of William Faulkner: A Critical Biography*. Oxford: Blackwell, 1994. Print.

Gwynn, Frederick, and Joseph Blotner, eds. *Faulkner in the University: Class Conferences at the University of Virginia 1957-1959*. Charlottesville: UP of Virginia, 1959. Print.

Howe, Irving. *William Faulkner: A Critical Study*. 4th ed. Chicago: Elephant, 1991. Print.

Luce, Dianne. *Annotations to Faulkner's* As I Lay Dying. New York: Garland, 1990. Print.

Roberts, Elizabeth Madox. *The Time of Man*. Lexington: UP of Kentucky, 1982. Print.

Ross, Stephen M. *Fiction's Inexhaustible Voice: Speech and Writing in Faulkner*. Athens: U of Georgia P, 1989. Print.

Rovit, Earl H. *Herald to Chaos: The Novels of Elizabeth Madox Roberts*. Lexington: U of Kentucky P, 1960. Print.

Slavick, William H. Introduction. *The Time of Man*. By Elizabeth Madox Roberts. Lexington: UP of Kentucky, 1982. Print.

Thompson, Lawrance. *William Faulkner: An Introduction and Interpretation*. New York: Barnes and Noble, 1963. Print.

Wadlington, Warwick. As I Lay Dying: *Stories out of Stories*. New York: Twayne, 1992. Print.

Warren, Robert Penn. "Elizabeth Madox Roberts: Life Is from Within." *Elizabeth Madox Roberts: Essays of Reassessment and Reclamation*. Ed. H. R. Stoneback and Steven Florczyk. Nicholasville, KY: Wind, 2008. Print.

"Shall Not the Judge of All the Earth Do Right?" William Faulkner, Cormac McCarthy, and Jurisprudence____

Bryan Giemza

Literary criticism bearing on Cormac McCarthy has tended to break his writing career into two distinct phases: a William Faulkner phase and an Ernest Hemingway phase. At various times, the signature style of one of these two writers seems to predominate in his work. McCarthy had certainly read both writers even as he commenced his own writing career, and there are good examples of both influences in his early work. The formally playful first phase, which is characterized by richly descriptive, extended passages, run-together coinages, and, to some degree, stream of consciousness, operates in a familiar southern gothic mode. Critical consensus deems this McCarthy's "Faulkner" phase, exemplified in his earlier Appalachian works, culminating perhaps in *Suttree* (1979), and tapering off in the spare, slimmed-down prose of the works that followed *Blood Meridian* (1985). Critical consensus also holds that this marked the beginning of McCarthy's "Hemingway" phase.

In fact, McCarthy was so much under the spell of Faulkner's influence that Harold Bloom observed of this earlier phase, "It seemed to me to be Faulknerian in a way that was not really integrated in a way that made it McCarthy's own. It may have been *Suttree,* in fact, a book that I haven't read since. It was a strong book, but you had the feeling at times that it was written by William Faulkner and not by Cormac McCarthy" (Bloom). If it sounds like Bloom is suggesting that McCarthy's work is "merely" derivative, bear in mind that Bloom also proclaimed *Blood Meridian* to be "the greatest single book since Faulkner's *As I Lay Dying*" (ibid.) and that *Suttree* pays obvious tribute to Joyce's *Ulysses* (1922). In fact, that influence prevails so thoroughly that McCarthy could be accused of "borrowing" from Joyce in *Suttree* as well.

The anxieties of influence indeed proliferate, but they are somewhat beside the point, as they are incontrovertible. Anyone who reads McCarthy's earlier novels will detect Faulkner's presence on virtually every page. There is kinship in McCarthy's winding syntax, his lengthy sentences and Latinate vocabulary, and even in his unorthodox punctuation. While everyone seems to agree that Faulkner's work is the major literary progenitor of McCarthy's earlier work, the critical commentary has been somewhat impressionistic in describing the exact nature of their kinship. The objective of this essay is to make these relationships more tangible by narrowing the field of focus and mapping their shared interest in the parlance and ethical questions of law.

Certainly the common link in the subject of law is arbitrary; there are myriad ways to connect the two writers in their concerns. Little has been written, however, about the way that their legal themes unite them. In this legal resonance one sees how the two writers share a common interest in bounded language and the testamentary power of writing. Also, in the legalistic nature of their texts, they explore the power of the word, investigate the relationship between human law and natural law, and interrogate the limits of reality itself.

Influence of Lawyers on Faulkner and McCarthy

Both Faulkner and McCarthy had close mentors who were lawyers. In Faulkner's case, he "read" in law and absorbed some of its lingo through his friend Phil Stone. McCarthy's father, Charles Sr., was a *Yale Law Journal* editor and chief counsel for the Tennessee Valley Authority (TVA). Michael Lahey writes that "Faulkner arrived at his insistent legal concerns both by way of family history. Through the cultural milieu of Mississippi, which was complexly characterized by traditional respect for lawyers . . . and by infamous contempt for and mass resistance to the rule of law itself" ("Law" 224). Interestingly, this characteristic is precisely true of McCarthy as well. A respected and respectable man, McCarthy's father arrived in Knoxville as a Tennessee Valley Authority lawyer, placing him at the nexus of what was then perhaps the most important legal and economic concern in the region. He also understood southern ambivalence toward lawyers and the law: "The average American is not noted for his respect for authority," he wrote in a 1950 law-review article on the TVA, "and regulatory laws which restrict the freedom of the citizen cannot be enforced unless supported by public opinion, as the United States learned to its sorrow during the days of national prohibition" ("Law" 129).

No surprise, then, that split attitudes toward the law—as between the lawlessness of rebellion and the legalism of the "one drop" rule, as the glue that bound southern society, on one hand, and that which ensnared the ordinary person, on the other—can be traced in the work of both of these southern writers. Before delving more deeply into the divided attitude toward the law in the work of Faulkner and McCarthy, however, it is necessary to understand a little more about how profoundly their lawyer mentors shaped the two writers.

Stone was hardly the only lawyer of Faulkner's acquaintance; he could claim many family members in the legal profession, including his great-grandfather, grandfather, and uncle, not to mention a number of close family friends who were lawyers (Watson 7). However, Stone was almost certainly the most influential of the lot. His life is documented most extensively in Susan Snell's *Phil Stone of Oxford: A Vicarious Life* (1991), and is widely commented upon by Faulkner biographers. Stone's enthusiasm for literature, dating to his days as a teenager, was intense, yet he was aware that he did not possess writerly gifts (or at least not the necessary dedication). Seeing these qualities in Faulkner as early as 1914, when Faulkner was seventeen, Stone began a campaign to encourage his soft-spoken friend, taking the first steps of what Snell calls "a vicarious life." Stone came from an established family and was educated at the University of Mississippi and at Yale. He gave Faulkner access to his family's extensive library, recited poetry for him, and introduced him to his circles of friends, in later years granting Faulkner critical access to emerging literati in places beyond Oxford, Mississippi. In the first decade of their friendship, the two would sometimes be roommates, explore the possibilities of military service, and travel widely together, including excursions to the criminal Memphis underworld. All of this experience proved invaluable to Faulkner's literary imagination, and "more valuable an intellectual education than any institution would provide," observes biographer Judith L. Sensibar (242). Stone was a constant sustaining presence in Faulkner's life; through his connections he would secure for his friend a writer's "day job" as a postmaster, defend him in legal affairs, orchestrate the publication of his early poetry, and serve as nothing less than a literary agent and critic. In short, he fulfilled all the sustaining roles necessary to the cultivation of a writer at the beginning of his career. Decades later, when the Stone family legal practice was mired in debt, Faulkner returned the favor by loaning money to Stone without expectation of repayment. The Snopes trilogy is dedicated to Stone.

However, Stone's support could become "insufferable," in the term of Philip Weinstein, and was often clouded by jealousy (230). Biographers usually acknowledge Stone's role in Faulkner's self-discovery of his inner writer; Snell points out, quite rightly, that Faulkner was instrumental in helping Stone to discover his own inner character, and Stone's family provided, in some respects, a stock of characters that surpassed Faulkner's own family in eccentricity. Of course, more than one biographer has likened the relationship of Faulkner and Stone during those early years to a type of "marriage" (Sensibar 391). The first decade of their friendship was intense, in the way of young men; they were busy courting, partying, and exploring the world—and, in Stone's case, reputedly drinking a quart of bourbon a day (Sensibar 304).

After the first decade, the relationship was more complicated. Founded in the southern male world of drink and intellectual companionship, their friendship changed in tenor with their respective marriages. Their correspondence fell off by the end of the 1920s. Stone became preoccupied with his family's law practice and the unfolding of a productive legal career that included the presidency of the Mississippi bar; Faulkner, with the business of being a family man who was an unprofitable professional writer and sometimes writer-for-hire. If alcohol had drawn them closer as young men, it was increasingly problematic in their separate lives. Stone developed a habit of making slighting statements to the press, saying, for example, that Faulkner had developed "Nobelitus in the Head" after he received the Nobel Prize in Literature (Blotner 562). Moreover, according to Stone, Faulkner was given to grandiose language and "using big words he doesn't know the meaning of" (ibid.). The irony was that Stone had done so much to instill that vocabulary in Faulkner, enlarging it by exposing his friend to the specialized parlance of the law office, and giving him, as Snell puts it, his "whole life and word hoard" (10). Lawyer Tom Freeland, the son of Hal Freeland, who was one of Stone's law partners, observes:

> The accuracy of his observations about what lawyers do, the details about the way which lawyers talk among each other, are just remarkable. It's a really pitch-perfect observation about stuff that lawyers do and stuff that judges do and the way lawyers talk about good and bad judges, the way lawyers talk about cases. He just gets it dead-on. And a major source of that material would have been from hanging out with Stone. (Simonson)

One of Faulkner's most memorable characters, Gavin Stevens, a classics-reading, gadfly "country lawyer," "loose-jointed" with untidy hair, owes much to the double-jointed, real-life Stone (Snell 213). Elements of the lawyer persisted in the ineffectual intellectuals of Faulkner's fiction, including Quentin Compson, Darl Bundren, and Horace Benbow (Watson 8). While Horace Benbow and Gavin Stevens are Faulkner's best-known lawyer protagonists, Jay Watson offers more than twenty examples of other legal professionals in the Faulkner canon, ranging across genres as varied as his screenplays, short stories, and novels (3–4).

In this sense, Stone is not merely present in Faulkner's fiction; he is very nearly *omnipresent*. In the opening pages of Snell's biography of Stone, she describes how Faulkner "ransacked" details from Stone's life for his books: "Phil's great-uncles Amodeus and Theophilus, his roadster Drusilla, his sojourns in the Ivy League, his father's Delta hunts, his friends among the gamblers and prostitutes in Clarksdale and Memphis—only begin the reckoning" (3). The remoteness of Caroline Compson and Addie Bundren is perhaps more accurately modeled on Stone's mother, Rosamond Alston Stone, than his own, Maud Butler Falkner, argues Snell. Even the fiery destruction of the Stone antebellum home, she points out, seems to be detailed in *Absalom, Absalom!* (1936). Faulkner would even represent some of the remarkable events of Stone's life as his own, including, for example, Stone's childhood encounter with General James Longstreet at the Hyde Park Hotel (34). In *The Town* (1957), all pretense of veiled allusion is dropped when a lawyer, Mr. Stone, is referred to by name.

Viewed over the long arc, the lifelong friendship between Stone and Faulkner was complex, shifting, and possessive. As is typical of such long-term friendships, there was inevitably some blurring of their identities. Also typical of them, the soundness of the friendship permitted it to endure even as the two pursued divergent paths. Faulkner's "walk with the law," so to speak, can be charted in his biography.

Less is known about McCarthy's life in general, and little can be documented about the relationship between him and his lawyer father. Anecdotally, there is considerable evidence that their relationship was a difficult one. Though he was his father's namesake, Charles Jr. changed his name to Cormac and charted a course that expressly rejected his father's path. The tensions of their relationship appear to be reflected in some of the biographical details of McCarthy's novel *Suttree,* as evidenced in a scene describing an essentially disinherited son's last communication with his father:

> In my father's last letter he said that the world is run by those willing to take the responsibility for the running of it. If it is life that you feel you are missing I can tell you where to find it. In the law courts, in business, in government. There is nothing occurring in the streets. Nothing but a dumbshow composed of the helpless and the impotent. (13–14)

However, it was to that "dumbshow" that the younger McCarthy was attracted and would spend his twenties examining, much as Faulkner spent his youth rambling around with Stone.

Even as McCarthy was exploring the underside of Knoxville, with no visible means of support, his father was accepting his part in civic stewardship and the "running of the world." McCarthy's father was nearly contemporaneous with Stone and Faulkner. Born June 19, 1907, in Providence, Rhode Island, he received his LLB from Yale in 1930, some twelve years after Stone graduated with his (Blotner 60). In the fall of 1934, after working in private practice for four years, he was hired as a senior attorney for the TVA and was appointed assistant general counsel in October of 1939. In 1953, he was named the TVA's solicitor and served as general counsel from 1958 until 1967, when he retired to establish his own private practice in Washington, DC (McCarthy, "Tennessee").

When he was interviewed for the TVA's oral history collection on May 4, 1983, the senior McCarthy acknowledged that he "knew very little about TVA" before he took the position, and that he was primarily attracted to the salary. That was understandable in light of the six children of the McCarthy family. There are some indications of McCarthy's personality in that record, and the portrait that emerges is of a moderate and perhaps even cautious man, as befits someone in a quasi-political position. McCarthy served the public, the courts, and the politicians. He acknowledged that environmentalism "was not a big deal" at the time—though it would become a more acute issue for the TVA in the wake of the 1960s—and he expressed his admiration for Franklin D. Roosevelt's leadership and especially for the women with whom he worked (who at that time were few in number). In 1982, McCarthy Sr. published an article in *Tennessee Law Review* in which he looked at the long history of efforts to curtail the powers of the TVA, arguing that it should continue to be "unshackled" in order to work effectively (McCarthy, "Tennessee").

So how is McCarthy Sr.'s experience relevant to his son's writing? For one thing, a significant portion of McCarthy's work is set against the positions his father took. McCarthy's work suggests a far more skeptical view of the "good" accomplished by the TVA. If *Suttree* is largely an autobiographical reflection of years spent "slumming" in Knoxville's underworld, it is also a book set on the Tennessee River as it winds through Knoxville—the primary exhibit in the TVA's publicly proclaimed successes. The portrait offered by McCarthy was far from flattering, however; Buddy Suttree's river flows with any imaginable sort of offal, and the novel begins with the dredging of a body from its waters. Later, a dead baby will drift by, and another corpse will be committed to it. Meanwhile, the poor and dispossessed, like the character Eugene Harrogate, are imprisoned or marginalized as squatters along its banks, even as social reformers come across as ineffectual, bigoted zealots. Their campaigns of false baptism, false imprisonment, and false social reform course through the novel like the river. Also, a significant undercurrent is the city's restlessness to discard its past along with the dead. The novel closes with the sort of large-scale engineering schemes that the TVA brought to Knoxville: "the destruction of McAnally Flats," a poverty-ridden section of town, as "yellow machines groaned over the landscape" (470).

In Suttree's final farewell to Knoxville, he walks away from a road-building project where "the white concrete of the expressway gleamed in the sun where the ramp curved out into empty air and hung truncate with iron rods bristling among the vectors of nowhere" (471). Throughout the novel the older orders and rhythms of southern culture are under threat from mechanized forces beyond, and so there is a trenchant critique of the world that the TVA brought to Knoxville. The spoilage is not merely of the material ruin but points to an underlying nothingness, as Robert Rudnicki explains in "Turtles All the Way Down: Foundation, Edifice, and Ruin in McCarthy and Faulkner." Both Faulkner and McCarthy inhabit a world where edifices are relentlessly torn down, so that the bulldozer is as much a menacing presence in McCarthy's work as it is in Faulkner's. What might persist, both writers suggest, is the story of the destruction, the narrative itself.

Such a view is characteristically different from the one espoused by McCarthy's father, who admitted in a law review article that, "Like the elephant in the fable of the blind men, TVA is all things to all people" ("Tennessee" 116). Though the article offers something of a march of statistics, the elder McCarthy would also write, "The effects of the program have been dramatic. Figures do not tell the story adequately. To understand what has happened, one has to drive through the Tennessee Valley and contrast its appearance today with its appearance 15 years ago" (125). Pointing to a common theme of mid-twentieth century development in the American South, he notes that the "the hungry-looking mule is being replaced by modern machinery. The look of poverty has left the land" (128–29). Ironically, the whole of *Suttree* is devoted to showing how the *look* of poverty might have left, but the fact of poverty remained—and one did not need to look far to find it.

Along these lines, the senior McCarthy goes on to tout successes in disease control: "The old muddy river has gone and with it have gone the annual threat of floods and the scourge of malaria. In its place are beautiful lakes which carry an increasing amount of commercial navigation and support a rapidly growing recreation and fishing industry" (128). In *Suttree*, though, waterborne diseases are alive and well, including typhoid fever, not to mention nonwaterborne ailments such as rabies and venereal disease. In *Suttree* there is an atmosphere of wistfulness for the lost civilization of trains, American Indians, and the simple agrarians and pioneers who built Knoxville. However, the book is skeptical of any claim to human "civilization" in its obsessive return to the poor, the malnourished, the mentally ill, the addicted, the sick, the discarded, and the imprisoned—all of the elements of society that run just under the surface. In other words, *Suttree* is devoted to exposing those very things that the law hopes to remedy, and that McCarthy's father had hoped to alleviate over the course of a career in public service.

At the same time, the young McCarthy's intellectual horizons and exposure to culture were almost certainly enhanced by his father's work. One finds a glimpse of this in the "old tattered barrister" whom Suttree meets, a man "who'd been chief counsel for Scopes, a friend of Darrow and Mencken and a lifelong friend of doomed defendants, causes lost, alone and friendless in a hundred courts" (366). The character in real life was John Randolph Neal, once a University of Tennessee law professor, supporter of the TVA, and, remarkably, a Scopes trial defender. The eccentric lawyer exhorts Suttree, "Follow the trade that you favor and you'll have no regrets in your old age" (367).

Simultaneously, some of McCarthy's skepticism regarding the law might come from the lawlessness of Knoxville itself. Consider an eyewitness account he sent to Howard Woolmer in 1981:

> Went downtown yesterday & suddenly found myself surrounded by fleeing felons firing off revolvers, police running up the street returning the fire, several detectives dragging another man from an alley & fastening handcuffs & leg irons to him, etc. A newsboy rushed up to me with a microphone & a tape recorder & asked me what was going on. I told him I had no idea, but it certainly seemed like the good old days for a few minutes.[1]

For his part, McCarthy was fascinated by the aspirations of the law, in contrast to its application, in the often sordid world of human reality. He decided to live so simply that he remained in or close to poverty throughout most of his early life. The rejection of his father's career path, and perhaps even some of the elusive pomps that accompany legal careers, was not the same thing as the wholesale rejection of his father, however. On the contrary, as with the relationship between Faulkner and Stone, his father (and his father's career) became a shaping force in his fiction.

Forensic Language in Faulkner and McCarthy's Fiction

If one wishes to argue that Faulkner is especially preoccupied with the law in his writing, there needs be some proof to bear out such a generalization. After all, one might say that John Grisham typifies the legalistic writer and this would hardly come as a revelation or even a useful observation. We could derive a formula to quantify the "legalness" of a writer's work based on its subject matter. Furthermore, it could be argued that some subjects are more legal in nature than others—and it is true that *The Town* features a protagonist who is a lawyer. One might expect the count of forensic terms to run high.

On the other hand, Faulkner used some legal terms on a recurrent basis. "Abrogate," for example—a term that does not have much application beyond the parlance of law—appears in no fewer than eleven Faulkner novels (by my count) as well as some in his short stories. "Relinquish," in a legal register, occurs in six novels and stories. What is worth examining is whether Faulkner's writing is profoundly and innately forensic in a way that penetrates beyond the surface of his subject matter, and if so, why he writes that way. Similarly, McCarthy uses legal terms throughout his oeuvre, particularly in *Blood Meridian*.

Both McCarthy and Faulkner draw on the word stock of *Black's Law Dictionary* (if not the actual reference volume—it is not listed among the reference books in Faulkner's library). *Blood Meridian*, for example, has a major character, the judge (McCarthy does not capitalize his name), who speaks from the bench, as it were, and instructs others in the law: "He and the judge sat together and the judge went over points of law with him. . . . The judge translated for him latin terms of jurisprudence. He cited cases civil and martial. He quoted Coke and Blackstone, Anaximander, Thales"—the former two being classical authorities familiar to any student of law (239). One might, therefore, expect to encounter a lot of legal language and for the judge to have the diction of a judge, as indeed he does, for example, when he tries to cajole the kid into giving up his steed: "He called out points of jurisprudence, he cited cases. He expounded upon those laws pertaining to property rights in beasts mansuete and he quoted from cases of attainder insofar as he reckoned them germane to the corruption of blood in the prior and felonious owners of the horses now dead among the bones. Then he spoke of other things" (305). Here again, the more interesting question is, why the fascination with legal matters?

In fact, both McCarthy and Faulkner have attracted their share of critics who fault them for never using a simple word when a Latinate one will do (B. R. Myers initiated this school of thought in "A Reader's Manifesto," a withering critique of McCarthy's prose that appeared in the *Atlantic Monthly*). Take, for example, McCarthy's use of the word "instanter" in this passage from *Suttree*:

> They lifted him onto the deck where he lay in his wet seersucker suit and his lemoncolored socks, leering walleyed up at the workers with the hook in his face like some gross water homunculus taken in trolling that the light of God's day had stricken dead instanter. (9)

Why "instanter," and not "instantly"? "Instanter" is a word of exclusively legal connotation. When a court's order is for something to be carried out "instanter," it generally means before the court convenes the next day. In this passage, a corpse is discovered of a man whose wristwatch is still running. Concerned as the novel is with the passage of time, both in the human and larger orders of the world, the word choice is an arresting one. "The light of God's day" suggests that the Almighty is in the seat of judgment, and that the reckoning of the drowned man would be carried out before another day passed.

This hints at McCarthy's understanding of the legal import of the word, which is not incidental in a text that raises all manner of questions about the judgments passed by God, by courts, and by society. More to the point, McCarthy invokes (but does not necessarily endorse) the possibility of natural law as a governing force in human affairs in a dialogue that ranges across his novels. The maestro of *Cities of the Plain* (1998), for example, declares, "We have only God's law, and the wisdom to follow it if we will" (195). The child of *The Road* (2006) is attuned to natural law, and Sherriff Bell of *No Country for Old Men* (2005) affirms that "the truth is always simple. It has pretty much got to be. It needs to be simple enough for a child to understand" (249). Such a view is in stark contrast to *Blood Meridian*'s judge, who altogether rejects natural law as an arbiter of human affairs: "Moral law is an invention of mankind for the disenfranchisement of the powerful in favor of the weak" (250). *Blood Meridian* suggests that the rule of law is itself a fiction. To the rhetorical question famously posed in Genesis 18:25 of the King James Version of the Bible—"Shall not the judge of all the earth do right?"—the text suggests that there is no judge, but rather, a destructive force that is far beyond the reach of human law.

How far does natural law prevail in Faulkner's work? Where does the voice of judgment come from in his texts? As with McCarthy, the issue is complex. Unusually, much of *The Town* is narrated in first-person plural. Faulkner's "we" is not the royal we; it is the voice of the town itself, passing judgment, deciding what should be done, and meting out justice. Faulkner rarely makes the "we" explicit; he leaves the reader to infer that it is the voice of the speaker plus the opinion of the town. There appears to be only one place in the novel where the "we" is elaborated, and from that place the work might take its title: "and we—the town—gathered at their little house" (344). This passage describes the fallout when Mrs. Snopes kills herself. The townspeople wait to see if her lover will resign his post at the bank and make a graceful exit from the town, once and for all:

> After his guilty partner had paid with her life for her share of the crime, he didn't even lose that key to the back door of the bank to pay for his.
> We all knew that. So did he. And he knew we knew. And we in our turn knew he knew we did. So that was all right. He was finished, I mean, he was fixed. His part was set. (339)

There are many layers of mutually reinforced awareness, as between the collective (the town) and its constituents. One of the results of this system is that public consensus upholds a face-saving honor code that in turn permits vigilantism and the settling of scores with violence. When a hotheaded boxer woos Linda Snopes, he winds up in a drunken brawl with Anse McCallum that lands both in jail. The next day Anse's father posts bail for both for the sole purpose of settling the dispute in a "fair fight." This is consistent with Eula Varner's values:

> If you are a man, you can lie unconscious in the gutter bleeding and with most of your teeth knocked out and somebody can take your pocketbook and you can wake up and wash the blood off and it's all right; you can always get some more teeth and even another pocketbook sooner or later. But you cant just stand meekly with your head bowed and no blood and all your teeth too while somebody takes your pocketbook because even though you might face the friends who love you afterward you can never face the strangers that never heard of you before. (331)

Such a society, by definition, approves the notion of extralegal justice—if such a thing exists. In another incident from *The Town,* when a local moonshiner named Wilbur Provine is arrested, he claims complete ignorance, and that "he didn't even know what the word 'still' meant" (168). Confronted with evidence of a well-beaten path from his doorstep to the still beside a spring a mile and a half distant, he changes tactics, suggesting that perhaps his wife had worn the trail in fetching water from the spring. Judge Long finds an expedient solution: "I'm going to send you to the penitentiary, not for making whiskey but for letting your wife carry water a mile and a half from that spring" (169). As Gavin Stevens says to Ratliff, "You're like me. . . . You don't give a damn about truth either. What you are interested in is justice" (176). In the words of Lahey, Faulkner implicitly "define[s] law as that which legal officials decide to do about legal disputes" ("Law" 224).

Something of the same may be said of the judge in *Blood Meridian,* who operates as a plenipotentiary: lawgiver, law enforcer, and scofflaw. In the world of *Blood Meridian,* however, there is no pretense of justice; might makes right, and McCarthy seems to suggest that the chaotic forces unleashed by war merely point to the law as a trifling defense to barbarians at the gate. After all, if it was lawful to place a bounty on Indian scalps, the scalp hunters merely enlarged the doctrine to include any civilian head, Indian or otherwise. The pronouncements of the judge and of the legal officials of McCarthy's novel in some respects resemble what Lahey calls Faulkner's parody of "the often arid (often absurd) rationality of legal judgments" ("Law" 223). In McCarthy's work the parody of jurisprudence is just as savage: In *Suttree,* a teenager, first shot and then convicted for "molesting" melons, is effectively sentenced by the state to a cycle of hard labor and incarceration. When the boy is faced with a charge of bestiality, his "smart" lawyer "told em a watermelon wasnt no beast" (49). A later portion of McCarthy's *Suttree,* based on the Circe chapter of Joyce's *Ulysses,* puts the protagonist on trial for nonconformity in a hallucinatory sequence.

Conclusion

Stylistically, both Faulkner and McCarthy use the language of law to confer a sense of testamentary timelessness to their prose, and both have occasionally been faulted by critics for this tendency. Both writers are highly influenced by mentors who were lawyers, and both are driven to investigate the paradoxes inherent in the law in southern society and to understand the sort of farcical jurisprudence that underwrites the region's history (a jurisprudence that decreed that slaves were not persons in a legal sense). Both writers have a habit of truing the human application of law against notions of natural law or some higher order, even when their work indicates a skepticism about appealing to some higher authority. Both, in turn, are famously suspicious of "facts." Whereas language tends to divert "the truth" into competing narratives, McCarthy's plainspoken cowboy John Grady insists in *All the Pretty*

Horses (1992), "There aint but one truth," and "The truth is what happened. It aint what come out of somebody's mouth" (168). In *The Town*, Gavin Stevens points out that "poets are almost always wrong about facts. That's because they are not really interested in facts: only in truth: which is why the truth they speak is so true that even those who hate poets by simple natural instinct are exalted and terrified by it" (93).

Finally, and perhaps most subtly, both writers appreciate that the law is a meaningful force to be exerted upon human lives—even if it is reducible to language (and the fallibilities of language). In this understanding there is an implicit connection to the part of the writer as a determiner of "the" story, and it is no accident that Faulkner's stories often unravel according to such facts as are available, and their interpreters—consider, notably, the way that the narrative of Faulkner's *Absalom, Absalom!* (1936) is synthesized in this way. In *The Town* Faulkner writes of the capacity of women to avoid the snares of "cold moralities and colder facts" (203), a response to the idea that a juror is fact finder. Likewise, it is no accident that many of McCarthy's most villainous characters pervert the language of the law in order to pass down "sentences" (think not just of the judge in *Blood Meridian* but of the "trials" of *All the Pretty Horses* and the character of Anton Chigurh in *No Country for Old Men*). In *Cities of the Plain*, the villainous padrone of the White Lake brothel, Eduardo, demonstrates the power of forensic language as he conjures a prison for the prostitute, Magdalena, out of thin air:

> He spoke in reasoned tones the words of a reasonable man. The more reasonably he spoke the colder the wind in the hollow of her heart. At each juncture in her case he paused to give her space in which to speak but she did not speak and her silence only led inexorably to the next succeeding charge until that structure which was composed of nothing but the spoken word and which should have passed on its very utterance and left no trace or residue or shadow in the living world, that bodiless structure stood in the room a ponderable being and within its phantom corpus was contained her life. (212)

Such is the trial of Magdalena, made of words and their nothingness, reducing her to nothing, and yet real all the same. In the only full-length study of the law in Faulkner's fiction, Jay Watson writes,

> Language is itself a form of action, perhaps the most pervasive and powerful means by which we involve ourselves in our own and each other's lives. Lawyers, and especially, litigators, do not choose between language and action. . . . They choose language *and* action, language as action. They know how to do things with words (though there is of course no guarantee that what they do will not be harmful or wrong), and I am convinced that the deeply performative nature of their craft contributed to, or at least confirmed, Faulkner's sense of his own. (5)

McCarthy views the generative power of language in much the same way. Both Faulkner and McCarthy are distinguished in creating novels that are testimonies to the ability of language to *create* reality, and in the final attempt, to impose order on chaos by the construction of narrative. The law is narrative, and narrative is the law: this is the simple version of the statute that defines the order of Faulkner and McCarthy's respective fictional universes.[2]

Notes

1. June 22, 1981. Woolmer Collection, Box 1, Folder 4. Southwestern Writers Collection, The Wittliff Collections, Alkek Library, Texas State University–San Marcos.
2. The author wishes to express his gratitude to Nancy Proctor of the TVA archives in Knoxville, Tennessee, for her generous assistance in furnishing archival materials.

Works Cited

Bloom, Harold. "Harold Bloom on *Blood Meridian*." Interview by Leonard Pierce. *A.V. Club*. 17 Jun. 2009. Web. 23 Jul. 2012.

Blotner, Joseph. *Faulkner: A Biography*. New York: Vintage Books, 1991. Print.

___. *William Faulkner's Library: A Catalogue*. Charlottesville: U of Virginia P, 1964. Print.

Duvall, John N. *Faulkner's Marginal Couple: Invisible, Outlaw, and Unspeakable Communities*. Austin: U of Texas P, 1990. Print.

Faulkner, William. *The Town*. 1957. New York: Vintage Books, 2011. Print.

Lahey, Michael. "The Complex Art of Justice: Lawyers and Lawmakers as Faulkner's Dubious Artist-Figures." Eds. Donald M. Kartiganer and Ann J. Abadie. *Faulkner and the Artist*. Jackson: UP of Mississippi, 1996. 250–68. Print.

___. "Law." *A William Faulkner Encyclopedia*. Eds. Robert W. Hamblin and Charles A. Peek. Westport, CT: Greenwood, 1999. 222–23. Print.

McCarthy, Charles J. Interview by Mark Winter. TVA Employee Series, Tennessee Valley Oral History Collection. May 1983. Transcript.

___. "The Tennessee Valley." *Town Planning Review* 21.2 (1950): 116–130. Print.

McCarthy, Cormac. *Blood Meridian: Or the Evening Redness in the West*. New York: Vintage, 1985. Print.

___. *The Border Trilogy*. New York: Knopf, 1999. Print.

___. *No Country for Old Men*. New York: Knopf, 2005. Print.

___. *The Road*. New York: Knopf, 2006. Print.

___. *Suttree*. New York: Vintage, 1992. Print.

Moreland, Richard C. *Faulkner and Modernism: Rereading and Rewriting*. Madison: U of Wisconsin P, 1990. Print.

Morris, Wesley, and Barbara A. Morris. *Reading Faulkner*. Madison: U of Wisconsin P, 1989. Print.

Myers, B. R. "A Reader's Manifesto." *Atlantic Monthly* July-Aug. 2001: 104–122. Print.

Rudnicki, Robert. "Turtles All the Way Down: Foundation, Edifice, and Ruin in Faulkner and McCarthy." *The Faulkner Journal* 25.2 (2010): 23–52. Print.

Sensibar, Judith L. *Faulkner and Love: The Women Who Shaped His Art*. New Haven: Yale UP, 2009. Print.

Simonson, Sarah. "Phil Stone and Faulkner." *NMissCommentor*. 17 May 2012. Web. 23 July 2012. Film.

Snell, Susan. *Phil Stone of Oxford: A Vicarious Life*. Athens: U of Georgia P, 1991. Print.

Watson, Jay. *Forensic Fictions: The Lawyer Figure in Faulkner*. Athens: U of Georgia P, 1993. Print.

Weinstein, Philip. *Becoming Faulkner: The Art and Life of William Faulkner*. New York: Oxford UP, 2010. Print.

"Far from Home across the Sea": William Faulkner, Randall Kenan, and Taboo Sexualities_____

Mary Alice Kirkpatrick

With Randall Kenan's creation of rural Tims Creek, modeled after his hometown of Chinquapin, North Carolina, scholars have noted the African American writer's connections to William Faulkner and his fictional world of Yoknapatawpha. Kenan almost insistently places his characters within a distinctly southern landscape; both his first novel, *A Visitation of Spirits* (1989), and his later collection of short stories, *Let the Dead Bury Their Dead* (1992), feature Tims Creek and its inhabitants. Consider his title story, elaborately—and certainly tongue-in-cheek—subtitled, *"Being the Annotated Oral History of the Former Maroon Society called Snatchit and then Tearshirt and later the Town of Tims Creek, North Carolina [circa 1854–1985]"* (Kenan 271), compiled by lifelong local resident, the Reverend James Malachai Greene. According to Reginald Gregory Kain, the oral history's ostensible editor, Baptist preacher Jimmy Greene remained fascinated by "the origins of Tims Creek; his family's slave past; the intermingling of the two [founding] families, black and white; folklore and the supernatural; thanatology; issues of community leadership and decay" (279). Is it any wonder, then, that readers and critics alike invoke Faulkner when reading Kenan?

In a 1997 interview given while writer-in-residence in Oxford, Mississippi, and published in *Callaloo* (1998), Kenan himself speaks to such intersections. Nearly halfway through the conversation, interviewer Charles Rowell remarks, "I am so happy to hear one Southern writer speak without invoking the name of William Faulkner. Even though you are presently in his country, I am so happy that you learned to write without having to know William Faulkner" (Rowell 139). Contextualizing the influence that the writer had on him, Kenan replies, "I came to him as one country boy to another, and the work just sang out; it seemed inevitable and right and huge" (140). Arguably, he profiles Dean Williams, the central protagonist in his story "Run, Mourner, Run," in much the same way—"as one country boy to another." Yet the author also distinguishes his voice from Faulkner's: "Faulkner came from Oxford, Mississippi. He was a Southern White Aristocrat. He came from a very specific time. I came from a very different time and place. My influences were quite different. It would be utter hubris for me to attempt to copy him. He's a mountain. But the influences are there. Unspoken. I believe we're all standing on that mountain in a way" (140).

Even as he acknowledges this unspoken presence, Kenan intentionally underscores the issue of subject position—the complex intertwining of regional location (Oxford vs. Chinquapin), racial identity (white vs. black), socioeconomic class (namely Faulkner's "aristocratic" status), and historical placement. To this specific catalogue, he might have added sexual orientation as well. Such deliberate attention to individual location, of having come "from a very different time and place," evokes Paul Gilroy's articulation of identity as "an ongoing process of self-making and social interaction"—not "a thing to be possessed and displayed" (103).

In a similar fashion, the concept of place might be recast not as rigidly unchanging but as actively becoming vis-à-vis embedded social, political, historical, and cultural interactions across permeable borders. Toward the conclusion of "Dismantling the Monolith: Southern Places—Past, Present, and Future," Barbara Ladd ponders whether place is "something phantasmagoric," "something lost and longed for," or merely "the locus of desire" (56). Yet she quickly moves to matters of agency, reflecting upon the ways radically rethinking place—as "a dynamic and vital force"—would alter the landscape of literary studies (56). Her appeal for place as "something more provisional, more fleeting, more subversive," and thus as "*a site of memory and meaning for both the past and the future*" (56), posits an interpretive mode that extends this discussion not only back to redress history but also forward through time. Further, proposing a notion of place that operates against inert, static fixity reanimates geographic boundaries. For "the character of the place itself," cultural geographer Doreen Massey maintains, "the very formation of the identity of a place—its social structure, its political character, its 'local' culture—is also a product of interactions," not only within but also outside its borders (120).

This essay, rather than focusing on the intersections between Faulkner's and Kenan's preoccupations with the history of the South, agrarian tradition, or rural community, instead examines their treatment of taboo sexualities through a dynamic, interactive prism of place. Both Faulkner's "Divorce in Naples" and Kenan's "Run, Mourner, Run" teem with forbidden desire, secret seductions, and ruinous betrayal. Faulkner's tale, which foregrounds the romance between two Victrola-dancing seamen early on, contains "the most overtly homosexual relationship in his fiction" (Ferguson 66). Both short stories similarly oscillate between movement and stasis, innocence and corruption, home and away. Even as blond virginal Carl openly embraces dark Greek George, their union first unfolds aboard a nomadic vessel and later unravels upon a foreign shore. Their relationship seemingly takes center stage when geographically placed at the periphery.

By way of contrast, Dean Williams may hum lines from a childhood nursery rhyme, *"Far from home across the sea / To foreign parts I go"* (Kenan 177), but he never crosses state lines, much less journeys across the sea. His sexual liaisons with Raymond Brown and the subsequent shattering of their secret affair transpire at home. In addressing questions of sexual difference, Faulkner's "Divorce in Naples" and Kenan's "Run, Mourner, Run" depict characters that remain vexingly adrift, unveil triangulated desires that interrupt stasis, and craft porous margins that intensify the dynamic interplay of place. Yet while Carl and George flirt at sea, Dean and Ray frolic at home. Kenan relocates the site of transgressive love—transported from a distant foreign shore and firmly planted in the soil of the American South.

Faulkner's Traveling Tale

Framing "Divorce in Naples" as a tale in motion emphasizes departures and returns, literal and figurative passages, as well as the unresolved textual tensions that create disruptive possibilities. This approach also explores how fiction set abroad unsettles discourses at home. Cultural critic Trinh T. Minh-ha similarly ponders crossings, both physical and psychological, that yield multiple traveling selves. She suggests: "Every voyage can be said to involve a re-siting of boundaries. The traveling self is here both the self that moves physically from one place to another, following "public routes and beaten tracks" within a mapped movement, and the self that embarks on an undetermined journeying practice, having constantly to negotiate between home and abroad . . . between a here, a there, *and* an elsewhere" (9).Trinh largely speaks to the vexing strains that characterize diasporic migration, the experience of being "a stranger in a strange country" (11), a wanderer in an unfamiliar place, or a foreigner displaced from home. Faulkner's five seamen—an unidentified narrator, Monckton, "the bosun" (i.e., the pronunciation of boatswain), Carl, and George—only travel provisionally: "thirty-four days of sea time which we had but completed" (*Collected Stories* 877). Yet even when not charted across navigational maps, the story's negotiated movements—whether comings and goings on the ship, adventures in the city of Naples, or references to far-off ports in Galveston, Philadelphia, and the Tortugas—proliferate. Even transient voyages, readers soon learn, can reposition borders.

To a certain degree, "Divorce in Naples" as a text inhabits outlying spaces, within both Faulkner's oeuvre and the critical discourse. Written sometime after the author's European travels, the tale, Theresa M. Towner and James B. Carothers note, "makes its first certain appearance in Faulkner's short story sending schedule on 21 May 1930, but there were two manuscript versions, one of them entitled 'Equinox,' which may date from much earlier" (448). Although *Forum* rejected "Equinox," Faulkner would send "Divorce in Naples" (with two additional stories) to his agent Ben Wasson in April 1931 (Blotner,

1974 655, 689). Even so, the story was not published until September 21, 1931, as part of his first collection, *These Thirteen*. Perhaps Joseph Blotner's droll observation, "by now he was craftsman enough to know that most of the early work was apprentice work," and wry comments concerning his "frugality" and "dogged confidence" reflect the author's own ambivalence toward writing short stories (1974 687, 693). Numerous letters reference the pecuniary strains that necessitated steady submissions to literary magazines. Whether due to gambling debts or increased financial responsibilities, Faulkner, more often than not, simply needed the money. In both private musings and official correspondence, he routinely complains about gnawingly persistent "money pressure" (*Selected Letters* 123).

A December 1928 note to Alfred Dashiel betrays the writer's mixed feelings about the short story genre itself. As he confides, "I am quite sure that I have no feeling for short stories; that I shall never be able to write them, yet for some strange reason I continue to do so, and to try them on Scribners' [sic] with unflagging optimism" (*Selected* 42). Here Faulkner questions not only his inclination but also his facility for crafting short fiction. Whether his "unflagging optimism" reflects financial need or the "dogged confidence" Blotner mentions, Faulkner's feelings fluctuate. Years later, when asked about the relative difficulty of this genre, he almost idealizes the form: "In a short story that's next to the poem, almost every word has got to be almost exactly right. In the novel you can be careless but in the short story you can't. . . . That's why I rate [the short story] second—it's because it demands nearer absolute exactitude" (Gwynn and Blotner 207).

Certainly where "Divorce in Naples" is concerned, the author gave its *placement* a great deal of thought, for the story reappears in the final "Beyond" section (Part VI) of *Collected Stories*. Letters dating well before the collection's publication in 1950 demonstrate its purposeful organization, the care with which Faulkner made his selections. Correspondence with Malcolm Cowley (dating November 1, 1948) reveals his meticulousness. He formulates six divisions loosely arranged thematically and geographically: "The Country," "The Village," "The Wilderness," "The Wasteland," "The Middle Ground," and "Beyond," with the final section emphasizing the "wide variety of geographic and imaginative landscapes, concentrating on problems of psychological aberration" (Carothers 59). After professing an increased fondness for the collection, "which the more I think about, the better I like," Faulkner underscores its deliberate arrangement: "even to a collection of short stories, form, integration, is as important as to the novel – an entity of its own, single, set for one pitch, contrapuntal in integration, toward one end, one finale" (*Selected* 277–278). Intriguingly, *Collected Stories*, which "practically marks the end of his work in the short story form" (Carothers 58), concludes with precisely the same three tales in *These Thirteen*'s final section: "Mistral," "Divorce in Naples," and "Carcassonne." To incorporate "Divorce in Naples" as the 1950 collection's penultimate tale, given Faulkner's insistence upon unity and harmony directed toward "one end, one finale," seems significant.

Within the critical discourse, however, this short story habitually hovers in parenthetical spaces. Among contemporary reviews of *These Thirteen*, it garnered minimal attention. Robert Cantwell calls the final three narratives "largely literary experiments," while the Durham *Herald* merely makes a passing reference to "three Italian sketches" (Inge 68, 72). George Smart, writing for the *Boston Post*, notes that *Collected Stories*'s final "Beyond" section contains "stories built around a kind of psychological mysticism almost impossible to define" (Inge 316). Echoing the sentiments of early reviewers, Hans Skei labels "the final group of stories [in *These Thirteen*] . . . enigmatic" and "experimental departures from the rest of the volume" (*Reading* 14). In perhaps the only article devoted exclusively to "Divorce in Naples," Edward Volpe offhandedly comments, "though I hesitate to give too much weight to a minor short piece of comic fiction, I would suggest that the story does seem to point to the homosexual overtones that are implicit in the Faulkner drama of lost innocence" (45). These same overtones, Robert Dale Parker suggests, contribute to the relative dearth of scholarship, a claim he curiously brackets in parentheses: "(their [referring to Carl's and George's] sexuality has probably frightened off critical discussion)" (79). Thus, if "we begin to ask why [Faulkner] would grant this story . . . such an important place in his most important collection" (Towner and Carothers 448–49), a related line of inquiry surfaces: to contemplate why the story has received but nominal scrutiny by scholars.

Set well outside the established ground of Yoknapatawpha, "Divorce in Naples," despite announcing its major preoccupations—a romantic relationship, a probable breakup, and an overseas backdrop—in the title, remains a slippery tale. A story of devastating heartbreak and tentative reunion should strike a universal chord. William Peden's 1950 review even lists Faulkner's "greatest achievements" as "his sure, penetrating, and frequently devastating comprehension of the universal, translated into fictional terms by means of the local and the specific" (Inge 306). Peden primarily refers to the local specificity of Faulkner's Mississippi county, yet the noisy European café presents a recognizable stage for the opening action: raucous flirtation between the ship's crewmen and "three women of that abject glittering kind that seamen know or that know seamen" (*Collected* 877). Even in an atmosphere well outside the American South, Faulkner's unnamed narrator peppers the Naples port with regionally inflected flavors. Consider his precise description, surely drawn from the author's own 1925 sojourn through Italy, of the *carabinieri* (Italian military police) who arrest George: "two Napoleons in their swords and pallbearer gloves and Knights of Pythias bonnets" (885).

Yet recognizable tropes and descriptions cannot offset the story's tendency to render the familiar uncanny. Chatting in the café, the narrator casually explains, "We were talking about Carl, to George" (*Collected* 877). To the bosun's query as to *why* George brought Carl with him, Monckton snidely remarks, "Yes . . . I sure wouldn't bring my wife to a place like this" (877). A seemingly innocuous conversation abruptly shifts direction when Carl is identified as George's wife. The seductive exchanges between American sailors and Italian prostitutes, a relatively known quantity, unexpectedly alters. The men's ribald teasing presumably establishes a lighthearted atmosphere, in which case George's fury—he "cursed Monckton: not with a word or even a sentence; a paragraph" (877)—denotes an exaggerated response to good-natured ribbing. Yet George's profound anguish later, "the outrage, the despair, the sense of elapsed time, an unfamiliar city at night" (884), when he returns from the lavatory only to find Carl (and the gold-toothed woman) missing, suggests that the surface jocularity belies genuine attachment. As George forlornly recounts, "They ducked out on me. I never thought he'd a done me this way. It was her. She was the one made him done it. She knew what he was, and how I . . ." (883). Trailing off, the sea-roughened sailor then weeps, "quietly, in that dull, detached way" (883). Thus, the story oscillates between discomfiting emotional registers, ranging from lowbrow comedy to deep despondency.

This pattern of narrative upheaval recurs in part four, when the promise of marital rupture—divorce—finally materializes. Almost as an aside, the narrator remarks, "This is the most difficult moment in marriage: the day after your wife has stayed out all night." The bosun immediately counters, "You mean the easiest, [for] . . . George can quit him now" (*Collected* 889). Once again, Carl and George's relationship is framed as a marriage; once again, Carl is cast as the wife. Feminizing Carl might, Parker argues, illustrate Eve Kosofsky Sedgwick's "inversion model of homosexual or queer desire, in which gay men are gendered as women" (80). Reiterating Monckton, the bosun insists, "I sure wouldn't bring my girl to a dive like this, even if he did wear pants" (*Collected* 878). Later, he imitates Carl's supposedly effeminate behavior: "steadily and deliberately, his body thrown a little back and his head tilted . . . with that air of Carl's, that grave and cosmopolitan swagger" (879). Even as the men cast Carl in a feminine role, stating that he organizes his cabin "with the meticulousness of an old maid," his childhood aspirations are decidedly masculine: to "be a ballplayer or maybe a prize fighter" (879, 880). To characterize him as "a sophisticated baby,"

"*È innocente*," an altar boy, or even a saint speaks to his virginal status, thereby invoking the trope of sexual initiation and another transitional passage in the narrative (878, 880–881). Carl's depiction and the language here evoke Quentin and his Harvard roommate in Faulkner's *The Sound and the Fury* (1929): "Calling Shreve my husband. Ah let him alone, Shreve said, if he's got better sense than to chase after the dirty little sluts, whose business. In the South you are ashamed of being a virgin. Boys. Men. They lie about it" (78).

Yet eighteen-year-old Carl does not appear ashamed before this rite of passage but rather *after* its completion. Upon returning to the ship, "he undressed swiftly, ripping his clothes off, ripping off a button" (*Collected* 888), and scours away any evidence of "the sex difference" (888, 877). Sexual anxiety stems not from his undershirt-clad dancing with George aboard the ship but rather from his furtive encounter with the prostitute on shore. With Carl "moping," "mooning" (890), and refusing even to look toward the city for days, reconciliation transpires almost as a confession—not for his momentary lapse but for his ongoing repulsion. George consoles Carl, who "was just trying not to puke," with a graphically gynophobic reference: "'Oh,' I says, 'the smell. It don't mean nothing. . . . It ain't that they smell bad . . . it's just the Italian national air" (892). Hence Noel Polk's contention that, "women in [Faulkner's] fiction are nearly always associated not just with shame and sex but also with filth, excrement, pain, and death" (150). Carl's immediate, prolonged reaction is twofold: collapsing into violent illness and retreating into monastic silence. Here and elsewhere, the text "keeps trying to deny homosexuality in ways that reassert it" (Parker 79). The aftermath of Carl's sexual initiation further unsettles gender and sexual boundaries; such repositioning, however, occurs within the transient, portable space of the ship.

Multiplying Narrators and Mobilized Accounts

Perhaps one central episode—even more so than transoceanic voyages, narrative ruptures, rites of passage, or repeated departures from and returns to the ship—warrants locating "Divorce in Naples" as a tale that wanders: George's arrest and subsequent imprisonment. Structurally and thematically, the incident, configured as Carl's betrayal and George's incarceration, is made central, for the ensuing consequences destabilize their previously idealized relationship. Faulkner pulls not from his own experiences in Italy for this incident, but instead borrows from those of his traveling companion. The historical occasion—a daytime arrival in Genoa, Italy (Sunday August 2 1925), an evening of debauchery, and a night passed in the "vermin-infested Palazzo Ducale jail" (Blotner, 1984 156)—starred not Faulkner but one William Spratling.

Various accounts of the incident feature multiple, even competing, narrators: the unnamed shipmate who "left [Carl, George, and the woman] and went back to the ship" (*Collected* 882), assorted Genoa journalists, literary agent Ben Wasson, biographers Blotner and Joel Williamson, and Spratling himself. The episode spirals ever outward, crossing national and international borders, blending fact and fiction, moving backward and forward through time. The odd trajectory of the real-life Spratling affair peculiarly mirrors an abiding uncertainty at the core of "Divorce in Naples." The short story reanimates yet another permutation and additionally reveals "clear relations with an American experience and background despite [its] foreign setting" (Skei, *Novelist* 98). Even while transpiring elsewhere, such slippages and generic flux trouble discourses at home.

Facts surrounding the August 2, 1925, arrest, Massimo Bacigalupo's research demonstrates, circulated widely in the local Genoa papers. Whereas the *Corriere Mercantile* reports the capture of "American citizen William P. Sparthing [sic]," deeming him an "impudent and disrespectful person," *il Secolo XIX*'s "Exploits of a Drunken Foreigner" states, "a foreigner, one William P. Spartling [sic] . . . spat on a roll of Italian banknotes which he had thrown on the ground and stupidly stamped on, while making irreverent remarks about Italy" (qtd. in Bacigalupo 323, 324). Spratling's identity markers—both name and traits—shift from impudent American citizen "Sparthing" to threatening drunk foreigner "Spartling." *Il Caffaro* simply lumps him among the "Foreign Rabble" (324–25).

Yet the Spratling episode roams farther still, traversing not only geographies but also moving forward through time via postcard, fiction, memoir, and biography. Faulkner appropriates the affair, initially by naming himself the crime's perpetrator. As Ben Wasson recalls in his memoir, "He had sent me a postcard telling of being incarcerated briefly for vagrancy" (75). The title of Wasson's memoir, *Count No 'Count: Flashbacks to Faulkner*, in fact conjures the multidirectional effects of such spiraling—not only flashbacks but also flash-forwards. In two other versions of the incident, Faulkner's unpublished novel "Elmer" and "the unpublished story he extracted from it," Bacigalupo explains, "the episode is moved from Genoa to the more literary Venice" (321). Of course, "Divorce in Naples" shifts locations yet again. Just as he takes latitudes with Italian geography, so Faulkner readily transforms actual events into the stuff of fiction, heightening those fractures between the real and the imaginary.

Even among presumably factual accounts, conspicuous fissures abound. Over forty years later in 1966, Spratling reflects upon that infamous evening in "Chronicle of a Friendship," originally published in the *Texas Quarterly*. He remembers, "by about 2:00 a.m. I had been led out between two carabinieri, with Napoleon hats, and driven off through the dark streets to jail. . . . Far away and in the confusion of the dance floor Bill [Faulkner] and my other shipmates were unaware of the incident" (Spratling 14). Following his release, Spratling recalls, Faulkner was outwardly miffed, unsympathetically "remark[ing] that I 'no longer looked so vulgarly healthy,'" and visibly annoyed at "having missed such an experience himself" (15). Details such as the "Napoleon hats" eerily overlap with Faulkner's tale, first published three decades earlier. To what extent was Spratling influenced by fictionalized adaptations already in circulation? According to the publisher's foreword to *Sherwood Anderson and Other Famous Creoles* (1967), he planned "to make several minor revisions" before the book was rereleased, yet his untimely death in an automobile accident (August 1967) precluded their implementation. Noticeably absent from Spratling's "Chronicle" and Faulkner's postcard is any mention of a homosexual liaison. According to Williamson, "Spratling told Faulkner that while he was in jail, he participated in a homosexual act. Later, when Faulkner told Ben Wasson about the incident," he "presumably . . . did not tell Ben about a sexual encounter" (202). Despite such excision, Gary Richards points out, "Faulkner, knowing the link between incarceration and same-sex acts, even if it remained unacknowledged to Wasson, *did* share the anecdote, alter the identities of the participants, and hint at a desire to be similarly transgressive for the 'experience' it would provide" (26). In three variations of the tale—Spratling's "Chronicle," Blotner's 1984 one-volume biography, and Williamson's *William Faulkner and Southern History* (1993)—the author reportedly curses over the lost "experience."

Returning to Faulkner's short story, George's jailhouse experience, despite thorough descriptions of his rank cell and unpleasant incarceration, does not mention any sexual escapade. While the temptation is to read this omission as reflective of Faulkner's own anxiety over homoeroticism and/or as a calculated effort to sanitize the story for public consumption, the effect is to uphold George's fealty to Carl. Analyzing the troubling "bite" of same-sex eroticism in Faulkner's second novel, *Mosquitoes* (1927), Minrose Gwin persuasively proposes that "Faulkner found the terrain, especially the male homoerotic terrain, of the queer abject treacherous footing for the successful male writer in the U.S." (139). Comfortably situated on a foreign shore, "Divorce in Naples" seemingly reaffirms a "tender and gossamer relationship" (Skei, *Novelist* 120). George remains true even in the midst of opportunity and Carl's devastating duplicity. Their dancing romance, in place of frantic dark-alley groping or desperate sexual exchanges in prison, reemerges out in the open, inscribed within an almost chivalric code. Moreover, their union appears wholly contained on the ship. Such placement preserves an otherwise transitioning space as the sacred site of transgressive love. Almost paradoxically, then, both the fixed Italian jail and the passing American ship reorient the boundaries of desire.

"A Gay Faulkner"

In her 2010 introduction to *Faulkner's Sexualities*, Annette Trefzer underscores the intimate ambiguities embedded in the collection's title, which "blurs the lines between the author's body and the body of his work" (ix). Prompted by contributor Gary Richards's study of "the homoerotic plot of Faulkner's [early] fiction and life," she arrives at "the question of a gay legibility—'has there ever been a gay Faulkner?'" (xii, xiii). While not explicitly addressing Trefzer's rhetorical question, Brannon Costello's "Randall Kenan Beyond the Final Frontier" (also published in 2010) nevertheless offers an implicit rejoinder: "Kenan has entered the southern literary canon not just as a 'black Marquez' . . . but also as a 'gay Faulkner'" (127). In addition to their overlapping themes, George Hovis maintains, "Kenan adds the element of explicit homosexual desire to the mix, and, in so doing, draws our attention to how the same element, though already thoroughly latent in Faulkner, must be fully recognized as integral" (252).

Whereas Faulkner relegates to the "'Beyond' category . . . tales with settings beyond the borders of the United States or those that soar beyond the bounds of reality" (Volpe, *Reader's Guide* 6), Kenan foregrounds magic and mysticism, infused throughout his real and fictional topographies. Consider Mercedes McDonald's cover illustration for *Let the Dead Bury Their Dead*. Enlarged from the original hardcover's thumbnail to the 1993 paperback edition's full-page imprint, the image calls forth a fantastic world in which the supernatural seamlessly coexists with the everyday. A centrally looming prophet figure bears a blade, a book, and a baby; flames morph into thorny vines (or spiny tails of a mythical creature); a distant floating house, set ablaze, glows overhead. Kenan offers additional context: "The bedrock of what people think of as Southern literature is 'realism.' . . . In truth I don't see social realism and so-called magic realism as being counter. I see them as being able to co-exist" (Rowell 145). Staging his intervention directly in American cultural, social, historical, and political discourses, Kenan intercedes from within Tims Creek's southern environs.

Unlike "Divorce in Naples," which seemingly privileges romanticized love, Kenan's "Run, Mourner, Run," with its epigraph lifted from Rainer Maria Rilke's "Archaic Torso of Apollo" (1908), immediately foregrounds the virile male body and quivering sexual desire. The quoted verse draws from the sonnet's closing lines, *"for there is no place that / does not see you. You must change your life"* (qtd. in Kenan 163), but the story invokes more than a final stirring charge. Even without encountering "his legendary head" (Rilke 1), the speaker asserts that this remnant, a brilliantly beaming muscled torso lit from within, "gleams in all its power" (5). Mesmerized by "the curved breast . . . [that] dazzle[s]" (6) and "the translucent cascade of the shoulders" that "glistens" (10–11), the beholder seems pulled toward the center of male sexual agency, its primal magnetism "a smile run through the placid hips and thighs / to that dark center where procreation flared" (7–8). Certainly this visual catalogue—luminous torso, breast, hips, thighs, groin, and shoulders radiating sexual energy—resonates with Dean Williams's corporeal memory: "those tender fingers exploring the joints and hinges of his body; as a wet, warm tongue outlined, ever so lightly, the shape of his gooseflesh-cold body" (Kenan 176).

Ephemeral Visions, Bounded Realities

For Dean, a poor white factory worker, suspended somewhere between boyhood and manhood, the prospect of truly changing his life belongs in the realm of fairy tales. "Run, Mourner, Run" opens and closes at roughly the same moment in time, presenting the same image of Dean adrift in a tire, "swing[ing] back and forth, back and forth" (Kenan 163). Although his twenty-three-year-old "legs, now lanky and mannish, drag the ground," he wistfully remembers being five years old, pushed by his daddy "higher and higher . . . his heart pounding, his eyes wide" (163). While Carl insists upon differentiating between the fifteen-year-old "kid" who "hadn't been nowheres [sic] then" and the man who has "been to sea three years" (*Collected* 880, 878), Dean seems more at ease with childhood's relative simplicity. As a boy, "he read the fairy stories and nursery rhymes . . . over and over" (Kenan 164); as a man, he almost compulsively returns to the soothing world of Mother Goose. His seduction of Raymond Brown is presented as two "boy[s] wanting to play" (171); several evenings later at a Raleigh gay bar, Dean and Ray enjoy "playing the game now, old and familiar . . . like checkers, like Old Maid" (173).

Throughout the story, Kenan's central character drifts between the oppressive banality of daily struggle and his far-off dreams of a better life, dreams that lift and list steadily out of reach. Treks to the grocery store for Bisquick, ripped paper bags spilling their sad contents, a broken-down Ford Torino perpetually in need of fixing, and insurmountable bills from his mother's surgeries all bespeak financial hardship. Through the figure of Dean, Kenan spotlights issues of racial, sexual, and class differences. Desperation and feelings of entrapment highlight poverty's relentlessness. Yet "once upon a time—what now seems decades ago rather than ten or fifteen years—Dean had real dreams. . . . If pigs could fly and foxes could talk and dragons were for real, then surely he could be anything he wanted to be" (164). Pulled between the fantasy of escape and the socioeconomic reality of being stuck in place, Dean again turns to fairy tales. Such daydreams elevate him beyond the unremitting tedium of noisy, dusty shift work at the International Spinning Corporation, of waiting for another dinner of "canned peas, rice, Salisbury steak" prepared by his mother (164), of "one-night stands with nameless truckers in nameless truckstops and bored workers at boring shopping malls" (184). Only in the world of nursery rhymes can Dean imagine marrying Mr. Punchinello (170), project a time "*when I am king and you shall be queen*" (172), celebrate remembering and being remembered (177), or fantasize the endless possibilities "*if all the world was apple pie*" (190).

As he approaches Dean Williams, then, Percy Terrell thinly cloaks his envy of Raymond Brown, speaking instead in terms of land acquisition. Terrell, "driving his big Dodge truck," talks vaguely of commercial interests; Dean, "sitting in the cab of that truck, groceries in his lap (his Ford Torino had been in need of a carburetor that day)" (165), listens to Percy's pitch. The premise of their conversation is one of exchange: payment offered for services rendered. Or, as Percy phrases it, "Son, I think I got a job for you" (165). The contrasts between Percy Terrell, "the richest white man in Tims Creek" (167), and Dean Williams, who must "trade on . . . his looks" (170), are striking. The wealthy business owner and young blue-collar laborer, "nothing more than poor white trash: a sweet-faced, dark-haired faggot" to Percy (166), have little reason to interact apart from this scheme to out—and thus oust—"the richest black man in Tims Creek" (167).

Kenan's language makes the jockeying for power, position, and place obvious. Dean revels in his "audience with the [white] king" (166). "King" Terrell hatches an elaborate plan to quash "the one colored undertaker . . . something of a *prince*" in Tims Creek (167; emphasis added). As Sheila Smith McKoy astutely points out, "Kenan structures the plot so that white males proclaim Brown's manhood as well as his place in the community, which is secure despite the fact that he is a black gay man" (33). Of course, Terrell's anger is wrapped up in this question of place—not simply the "homeplace" Brown declines to sell, but the undertaker's refusal to remain conveniently in his place. Consider Percy's vulgar self-justification: "They're blocking me. . . . Niggers shouldn't own something as pretty as Chitaqua Pond" (166). A pawn in the scheme, Dean appears oblivious to the subtle machinations of power. With his dreams of being a doctor, a lawyer, and an Indian chief having long since faded, he can only marvel at Percy's offer, "more a dream or less a dream?" (168). When Percy dangles the bait, promotion to foreman and a six-thousand-dollar raise, the boy who is forever swinging, watching, and waiting grasps at a possible escape route: "you must change your life" (Rilke 14).

Home and Exile

Unlike "Divorce in Naples," in which the overall trajectory, despite internal flashbacks, moves forward through time, "Run, Mourner, Run" seemingly portrays a closed circuit: on the story's first and final pages, Dean Williams simply sways from a sycamore tree. Yet just as ship voyages can herald shifting boundaries, so Kenan reveals that remaining in place can challenge an outmoded, intractable social order. Caught in a triangulated economic web, Dean appears wedged between a white man's desire to consume and a black man's desire to preserve. His betrayal is forced by economic necessity. Tragically, the only location where he finds momentary reprieve, the homeplace, and the only lover with whom he glimpses possibility, Ray Brown, are violently stripped away. An invasive cacophony of jeering men, whirring Polaroid, and growling dogs breaches the formerly inviolate space of transgressive love. Such irrevocable violation occurs in two parts: first, the vicious judgment, "fucking queers, fucking faggots" (179); later, news of a quiet sale, the mythic "homeplace" reduced finally to "a tiny piece of property over by Chitaqua Pond" (184). In the devastating aftermath, Dean remains powerless to alter the nightmare he unwittingly facilitated: "numb and naked, curled up in a tight ball like a cat," unable to "wake up. Stop dreaming" (182). But for one glorious month, time seemingly stands still.

Rooted in the southern landscape, the familial "homeplace" emerges as a fleeting source of safety, stability, and sanctity for the lovers. Although Dean and Ray initially collide in public places, McTarr's Grocery Store and The Jack Rabbit, they return to the privacy of the countryside, "down narrow back roads, through winding paths, alongside fields, into woods, into a meadow Dean had never seen before, near Chitaqua Pond" (175). The nearly ninety-year-old homestead, here anchored in the rural topography, exists at the center—not only the locus of white desire for control but also the heart of black resistance to oppression. African American feminist scholar bell hooks (Gloria Jean Watkins) discusses "homeplace" in these very terms, as a radical site of (political) resistance, the source of subjectivity, "a safe place" (42), and "a space where we return for renewal and self-recovery" (49). Ray's "brief tour of the house where he had grown up" (Kenan 176) inadvertently emphasizes these qualities, as individual rooms—the kitchen, the pantry, the living room, the bathroom, and the bedroom—signify familial history and safeguard transgenerational memory.

Similarly stressing the degree to which home mingles concrete and symbolic attachments, African American poet Brenda Marie Osbey explains that, "To be from someplace is not merely to have lived there for some time. Home is memory and blood, dust and air. It is also to be from and of that particular people. To be possessed by that history" (41). Slowly brought into the sacred "homeplace," an awestruck Dean encounters visual, tactile testimony to the family's enduring presence, including "the deep enamel sink and the wood stove . . . the neat rows of God-only-knows-how-old preserves and cans and boxes . . . the gaping fireplace where Christmas stockings had hung" (Kenan 176). Here, in the same room where "measles had been tended and babies created," Ray reverently undresses Dean. Beneath an antique "quilt made by Ray's great-grandmother," they "joined at the mouth" (176), transcending the boundaries of time and space.

Despite inscription within a mythic "homeplace," Dean and Ray's passionate affair, which flagrantly subverts racial, class, and sexual borders, inevitably succumbs to outside forces—in this case, betrayal and blackmail. Ray unconsciously underscores the ephemeral quality of their union when he quotes Walt Whitman's "A Glimpse": "There we are two, content, happy in beauty together, speaking little, / perhaps not a word" (Kenan 178). Temporally, this "glimpse, through an interstice caught" (Whitman 1) remains fixed in springtime's ecstatic overflow, "the daffodils and the crocuses and the blessed jonquils" (Kenan 177–78). Ensconced in a temporary safe haven, a poor, inconsequential white boy and a wealthy, respected black man may twine together, set apart from the stringent social codes governing Tims Creek. Yet Ray

Brown—husband to Gloria, church deacon, undertaker, and successful business owner—remains vulnerable by virtue of his standing in the community.

Thus, once his ties to Ray have been severed, hastened by the ruinous sale of the family home, Dean Williams is thrust into permanent exile: "for here there is no place" (Rilke 13); life is evacuated of meaning. "Run, Mourner, Run" in fact forecasts Dean's compulsory banishment. Even as he "trembled and tingled and clutched" in sexual pleasure, Dean also experiences terror, haunted by the "voices of old black men and old black women screaming for his death, his blood, for him to be strung up on a Judas tree, to die and breathe no more" (Kenan 177).

The Judas tree simultaneously recalls lynching in the South, evokes aimless tire swinging, and signifies cruel betrayal. The tree's attendant images cross borders. Specifically referencing Dean's swing, Suzanne Jones likewise emphasizes "this contemporary image of strange fruit hanging from a southern tree, [that] conjures up, even as it reverses in a way, old images of black men lynched after rumored offenses to white women" (160). While an ancestral presence often connotes powerful rootedness, as in Toni Morrison's configuration, with "timeless people whose relationships to the characters are benevolent, instructive, and protective" (343), Dean is profoundly disoriented. The clamoring voices and his discomfort reflect the conspiracy afoot, yet his feelings of displacement prefigure eternal expulsion: "You get the hell out too" (Kenan 182). After Percy Terrell's conquering invasion, with Ray Brown overthrown and the land obtained, Dean Williams is utterly bereft, having "sensed the enormity of what he had done" (182). The exile that follows, "some strange limbo, some odd place of ghosts and shadows," emerges as a nonplace indeed (187).

Reading to the End

Having taken up "Virginia Woolf's admonition that you should begin as near the end of a story as possible to create a tautness . . . focus. Compression" (Rowell 137), Kenan inadvertently raises a provocative question: how to interpret the vexed endings of "Run, Mourner, Run" and "Divorce in Naples." Both he and Faulkner allude to the difficulty of crafting short stories, linking the form and its demands to poetry. While Faulkner expresses his anxious frustration in terms of his feelings (or lack thereof) for the genre, Kenan identifies the writer's struggle to sustain unity within a compressed space. Skei further elucidates, "One of the chief characteristics of the short story, whether told to an audience or written, seems to be its orientation toward an end" (*Reading* 35). What, then, of these elusive endings?

"Run, Mourner, Run" closes in late October, leaving Dean Williams to face "a road of ghosts": poignant regrets and painful losses (190). Having fulfilled his treacherous agreement with Percy Terrell, he has "waited six months. Twenty-four weeks. April. May. June. July. August. September" (184). Days pass, time accumulates, yet nothing changes. Dismissed as a "pathetic white-trash faggot whore" (187), Dean is severely beaten, his punishment for daring to challenge Percy Terrell. A glorious month of expanded dreams is summarily reduced to a twenty-dollar bill, the "price of a blowjob" (187–88). Despite locating this site of transgressive love in the rural South, Kenan remains a realist. Unlike fairy tales, there are no happy endings here. Repeatedly breaching racial, class, and sexual borders often produces devastating consequences. Finding no heartfelt reconciliation, readers are left instead with an image of profound heartbreak. Dean Williams, in exile, is:

> Waiting for the world to come to an end. Waiting for this cruel dream world to pass away. Waiting for the leopard to lie down with the kid and the goats with the sheep. Waiting for everything to be made all right— cause I know it will be all right, it has to be all right—and he will sit like Little Jack Horner in a corner with his Christmas pie and put in a thumb and pull out a plum and say: What a good, what a good, O what a good boy am I. (Kenan 191)

Having merged his identity with Little Jack Horner, Dean is seemingly erased from the narrative. This heartrending regression strikes the tragic register where Kenan imparts his harsh invective, scathingly launched against any community that stigmatizes difference.

Compared to such eschatological overtones, "Divorce in Naples" concludes under far more auspicious circumstances: Carl and George reunited "in decorous embrace, their canvas shoes hissing in unison" (*Collected* 892–93). Perhaps the potential verbal slippage between "in decorous" and "indecorous" alludes to the story's final ambiguity. After the supposed divorce, what does the future hold for the two dancing seamen? Carl, having broken his nearly twenty-day silence, has made an all-important request: "When we get to Galveston, I want you to buy me a suit of these pink silk teddy-bears that ladies use. A little bigger than I'd wear, see?" (893). George previously has agreed to the favor, yet the question remains: for whom has Carl selected women's underwear? Faulkner closes the story amid uncertainty. Williamson has argued that Carl is "transiting to a heterosexual mode" (389), in which case the Naples prostitute, paid already for the sexual transaction, becomes the gift recipient. In this love triangle, however, two other possibilities emerge that uphold the story's central romance. The notion of either burly George or saintly Carl clad in a pink teddy might seem indecorously silly. Yet to substitute ambivalence for certainty contradicts the tale's penchant for rupture. Perhaps this final voyage opens the possibility of shifting Carl and George's "decorous embrace" from floating periphery to the Texas shore.

Ongoing oscillation—the voyaging ship and an unhinging psyche—leave "Divorce in Naples" and "Run, Mourner, Run" vexingly unsettled. In reading to the end of these stories, readers, along with Carl, George, Dean, and Ray, are left suspended, perhaps not waiting "for the world to come to an end" (Kenan 191), but certainly hoping for a different one. Kenan's transfiguration of the "homeplace" into a site of crossover over may ring progressively, yet Dean Williams loses grievously in the transaction, brutally shoved back into a painfully circumscribed place. Faulkner, despite what Michael Zeitlin terms his "unmistakably transgressive and polymorphous desire" (69), seemingly retreats from openly exploring homoerotic desire in his later fiction. Both writers gesture toward a provocative potential, yet a truly reinvigorated southern American landscape—a place where Carl and George or Dean and Ray may dance freely, flickers in the margins.

Works Cited

Bacigalupo, Massimo. "New Information on William Faulkner's First Trip to Italy." *Journal of Modern Literature* 24.2 (2000): 321–25. Print.

Blotner, Joseph. *Faulkner: A Biography*. New York: Random, 1974. Print.

___. *Faulkner: A Biography—One-Volume Edition*. New York: Random, 1984. Print.

Carothers, James B. *William Faulkner's Short Stories*. Ann Arbor: U of Michigan Research P, 1985. Print.

Costello, Brannon. "Randall Kenan Beyond the Final Frontier: Science Fiction, Superheroes, and the South in 'A Visitation of Spirits.'" *Southern Literary Journal* 43.1 (2010): 125–50. Print.

Gilroy, Paul. *Against Race: Imagining Political Culture beyond the Color Line*. Cambridge: Harvard UP, 2000. Print.

Faulkner, William. *Collected Stories*. 1950. New York: Vintage, 1995. Print.

___. *Selected Letters of William Faulkner*. Ed. Joseph Blotner. New York: Random, 1977. Print.

___. *The Sound and the Fury*. New York: Vintage, 1990. Print.

Ferguson, James. *Faulkner's Short Fiction*. Knoxville: U of Tennessee P, 1991. Print.

Gwin, Minrose. "Did Ernest Like Gordon?: Faulkner's *Mosquitoes* and the Bite of 'Gender Trouble.'" *Faulkner and Gender*. Ed. Donald M. Kartiganer and Ann J. Abadie. Jackson: UP of Mississippi, 1996. 120–44. Print.

Gwynn, Frederick L., and Joseph L. Blotner, eds. *Faulkner in the University*. Charlottesville: UP of Virginia, 1995. Print.

Hooks, Bell. *Yearning: Race, Gender, and Cultural Politics*. London: Turnaround, 1991. Print.

Hovis, George. *Vale of Humility: Plain Folk in Contemporary North Carolina Fiction*. Columbia: U of South Carolina P, 2007. Print.

Inge, Thomas M., ed. *William Faulkner: The Contemporary Reviews*. New York: Cambridge UP, 1995. Print.

Jones, Suzanne W. *Race Mixing: Southern Fiction since the Sixties*. Baltimore: Johns Hopkins UP, 2004. Print.

Kenan, Randall. "An Interview with Randall Kenan." Interview by Charles H. Rowell. *Callaloo* 21.1 (1998): 133–148. Print.

___. *Let the Dead Bury Their Dead and Other Stories*. New York: Harcourt, 1992. Print.

Ladd, Barbara. "Dismantling the Monolith: Southern Places—Past, Present, and Future." *South to a New Place: Region, Literature, Culture.* Ed. Suzanne W. Jones and Sharon Monteith. Baton Rouge: Louisiana State UP, 2002. 44–57. Print.

Massey, Doreen. *Space, Place, and Gender.* Minneapolis: U of Minnesota P, 1994. Print.

McKoy, Sheila Smith. "Rescuing the Black Homosexual Lambs: Randall Kenan and the Reconstruction of Southern Gay Masculinity." *Contemporary Black Men's Fiction and Drama.* Urbana: U of Illinois P, 2001. 15–36. Print.

Morrison, Toni. "Rootedness: The Ancestor as Foundation." *Black Women Writers: 1950–1980.* Ed. Mari Evans. New York: Anchor, 1984. 339–45. Print.

Osbey, Brenda Marie. "Writing Home." *Southern Literary Journal* 40.2 (2008): 19–41. Print.

Parker, Robert Dale. "Sex and Gender, Feminine and Masculine: Faulkner and the Polymorphous Exchange of Cultural Binaries." *Faulkner and Gender.* Ed. Donald M. Kartiganer and Ann J. Abadie. Jackson: UP of Mississippi, 1996. 73–96. Print.

Polk, Noel. *Children of the Dark House.* Jackson: UP of Mississippi, 1996. Print.

Richards, Gary. "The Artful and Crafty Ones of the French Quarter: Male Homosexuality and Faulkner's Early Prose Writings." *Faulkner's Sexualities.* Ed. Annette Trefzer and Ann J. Abadie. Jackson: UP of Mississippi, 2010. 21–37. Print.

Rilke, Rainer Maria. *Ahead of All Parting: The Selected Poetry and Prose of Rainer Maria Rilke.* Trans. Stephen Mitchell. New York: Modern Library, 1995. Print.

Skei, Hans. *Reading Faulkner's Best Short Stories.* Columbia: U of South Carolina P, 1999. Print.

___. *William Faulkner: The Novelist as Short Story Writer.* New York: Columbia UP, 1985. Print.

Spratling, William, and William Faulkner. *Sherwood Anderson and Other Famous Creoles.* Austin: U of Texas P, 1967. Print.

Trefzer, Annette. "Introduction." *Faulkner's Sexualities.* Ed. Annette Trefzer and Ann J. Abadie. Jackson: UP of Mississippi, 2010. 54–72. Print.

Trinh, T. Minh-Ha. "Other than Myself/My Other Self." *Travellers' Tales: Narratives of Home and Displacement.* Ed. George Robertson, et al. New York: Routledge, 1994. 9–26. Print.

Towner, Theresa M., and James B. Carothers. *Reading Faulkner: Collected Stories.* Jackson: UP of Mississippi, 2006. Print.

Volpe, Edward. *A Reader's Guide to William Faulkner: The Short Stories.* Syracuse: Syracuse UP, 2004. Print.

___. "A Tale of Ambivalences: Faulkner's 'Divorce in Naples.'" *Studies in Short Fiction* 28.1 (1991): 41–45. Print.

Wasson, Ben. *Count No 'Count: Flashbacks to Faulkner.* Jackson: UP of Mississippi, 1983. Print.

Williamson, Joel. *William Faulkner and Southern History.* New York: Oxford UP, 1993. Print.

Zeitlin, Michael. "Faulkner, Marcuse, and Erotic Power." *Faulkner's Sexualities.* Ed. Annette Trefzer and Ann J. Abadie. Jackson: UP of Mississippi, 2010. 54–72. Print.

Faulkner and the Bible: A Haunted Voice_____

Norman W. Jones

Many of William Faulkner's stories exemplify the "southern gothic," a subgenre that takes elements of southern culture and history as key ingredients in a dark mixture of decayed settings, twisted psychology, and grotesque affronts to an everyday sense of order and morality. One of the most widely known of such Faulkner stories, "A Rose for Emily," shocks the reader with the revelation that an eccentric old lady who represents a bygone era with its genteel values actually engages in a horrific parody of social traditions, sharing a bed each night with the corpse of the man she murdered. Similarly, one of Faulkner's most famous and critically acclaimed novels, *Absalom, Absalom!* (1936), is a ghost story: It centers on a midnight expedition to discover who or what is haunting a now-decrepit and abandoned mansion that once dominated an antebellum plantation.

Absalom helps illustrate why an understanding of Faulkner's uses of gothic conventions can help one better understand even those of his stories that are less obviously gothic. In *Absalom*, one finds that a key to Faulkner's representations of southern culture in the early twentieth century is the metaphorical sense of being haunted by the past: "the deep South" he describes as "dead since 1865 and peopled with garrulous outraged baffled ghosts," and Quentin Compson must listen "to one of the ghosts which had refused to lie still even longer than most had, telling him about old ghost-times" (4). The "ghost" metaphor articulates a sense of belatedness, of living after the fall, after the defeat of the South in the Civil War. At the beginning of *Absalom*, Faulkner describes the voice of Miss Rosa Coldfield as being haunted by this history: "The ghost mused with shadowy docility as if it were the voice which he haunted where a more fortunate one would have had a house" (4). The novel raises the possibility that the particular ghost referred to here, Thomas Sutpen, the antebellum patriarch who originally built the haunted house at the center of the novel, might indeed be haunting his old house. Yet the image of a ghost haunting not a house but the actual voice of a living person potentially reveals something crucial about Faulkner's own authorial voice—not only in *Absalom* but in many of his other stories as well. Faulkner's narrative voice is often metaphorically haunted not only by southern history but also by the Bible.

Absalom tells the story of Thomas Sutpen, a legendary plantation owner in antebellum Mississippi who amasses a fortune from nothing—creating his hundred-square-mile plantation as if by divine fiat, "the *Be Sutpen's Hundred* like the oldentime *Be Light*" (4). Sutpen is motivated primarily by his horror at having realized when he was a young boy that his family resided near the very bottom of the socioeconomic hierarchy. Despite his rags-to-riches success, his fortune and his plantation eventually fall into ruin in the aftermath of the Civil War. The war comes to symbolize Sutpen's own house divided against itself as his son, Henry, rejects his father and repudiates his birthright—echoing not only the New Testament parable of the "house divided," famously used by Abraham Lincoln to describe the Civil War, but also the Old Testament conflict between David and Absalom alluded to in the novel's title. Henry, the only male heir to his father's estate, goes on to cement his apostasy by murdering the man he loves, Charles Bon—Henry's half brother as well as his sister Judith's fiancé—which echoes the Absalom–Amnon–Tamar story told in 2 Samuel 13. Henry afterward flees in shame, never to be seen again by his father. The novel opens in 1909, with the inheritors of this history telling and retelling it to each other. Rosa, an older woman, wants Quentin, a college student, to accompany her on a midnight adventure to the now decrepit Sutpen mansion, which is referred to as a "haunted house" (174). The novel is structured as a complex ghost story: From the beginning, the narrative lures the reader with the mystery of the haunted house, but only in its closing pages does it reveal what Rosa and Quentin discovered there.

It is no coincidence that Faulkner chose to allude to the Bible in the title of this novel that explores and develops the image of being haunted as a metaphor for the relationship between past and present in the early twentieth-century South. The biblical intertext emphasizes the ways in which Faulkner's meditation on southern history does not confine its significance to the South alone but also lays claim to a much broader sense of history writ large, so to speak. Invocations of the Bible constitute one of the rhetorical strategies by which the local aspires to a more universal resonance in Faulkner's work. In *Absalom*, for example, Faulkner derives a fictional tale from what he famously referred to as his "own little postage stamp of native soil," and he turns it into a grand epic of mythic proportions by casting his antebellum plantation patriarch, Sutpen, as a latter-day King David, whose hard-won ascendancy comes to symbolize the story of an entire people—the South, much as David in some measure represents Israel. David's fall from being the greatest king of Israel to having his rule challenged and nearly toppled by his own son, Absalom, becomes the collapse of Sutpen's would-be dynasty as his son similarly rejects and repudiates his father.

Yet there is a more subtle way in which Faulkner's complex invocations of the Bible can be productively understood as evincing much the same relationship with his writing as that between the early twentieth-century South and its antebellum past, such that Faulkner's narrative voice itself may be heard, in a sense, as a voice haunted by the Bible. This might seem a strange claim to make, primarily because Faulkner's writing style is so different from that of the King James Version of the Bible (the KJV), which is the version he knew best. While the KJV favors concrete diction and grammatically simple and direct sentences, Faulkner's style in *Absalom* and elsewhere favors abstraction, circumlocution, and hypercomplex grammatical structures. Likewise, neither Faulkner's expansive Latinate diction nor his complex narrative structures are characteristic of the KJV. In short, Faulkner's stories do not imitate these aspects of the Bible; his uses of the Bible are subtler and more interesting than mere imitation would allow. Instead, many of his works create the sense of a ghostly echo of the KJV—not an obvious repetition but the evocation of multiple yet vague resemblances. Direct allusions to the Bible pervade Faulkner's stories: Jessie McGuire Coffee documents almost four hundred such direct allusions in the novels alone (129–30). Thus, for readers who possess even a basic knowledge of the Bible, the spectral biblical intertext haunting Faulkner's narrative voice gets raised perhaps first and most conspicuously by these direct allusions. Once the ear (or eye) becomes attuned to that set of frequencies, however, the KJV can begin to be heard as a kind of ghostly presence in Faulkner's narrative voice itself—a voice at once present yet absent in the sense of being repeatedly suggested but not clearly or fully possessing its own authoritative voice in the text.

This "ghostly" sense of the Bible reflects one of the ways many readers of Faulkner's day (and our own) think of the Bible, particularly the King James Version. Indeed, by the early twentieth century, the KJV was experienced by many as a kind of ghostly book in four specific ways: (1) new historical studies of the Bible undermined a sense of its unity; (2) scientific advances conflicted with the biblical picture of the natural world; (3) technological advances made the modern world seem far removed from biblical times; and (4) linguistic changes had rendered the language of the KJV increasingly arcane.

To elaborate, first, a scholarly method known as the "higher criticism" rose to prominence among English Bible readers in the nineteenth century and created for many a sense of distance between the biblical past and the modern present. Developed primarily in Germany, the higher criticism implicitly undermined the authority of the Bible as a sacred text by analyzing it according to the same standards that would be applied to any other historical document. It especially aimed to distinguish what was historically verifiable in the Bible from what might be merely mythological. In light of this approach, many biblical narratives appeared historically questionable or even doubtful, which undermined an older, more traditional sense that these narratives offered reliable historical accounts. The Bible could instead be seen as a mosaic of often disparate ancient texts that had been edited together in complex and subjective ways. For many modern readers, the Bible stories thus seemed to be at once there and not-there in the sense that the higher criticism implied that the true history behind these stories was available only indirectly in the Bible itself, hinted at but also obscured by layers of retelling and editing.

Interestingly, Faulkner's own personal Bible (inscribed by his mother, Maud Falkner, on October 1, 1904, when Faulkner was six years old) includes extensive notes and appendixes informed by the higher criticism.[1] While there is no firm evidence available to establish whether Faulkner studied this material or what he thought of it, it was an extensive part of this Sunday-school Bible that remained with him throughout his life. The appendixes include, for example, Julius Wellhausen's documentary hypothesis, which holds that the Pentateuch (the Five Books of Moses) was not written by Moses but is an edited compilation of various narratives that were originally independent of one another.

The literal authority of the Bible was widely seen (by both its supporters and detractors) as being undermined not only by the higher criticism but also by modern scientific developments, as emblematized by the 1925 Scopes Monkey trial. Many still felt the Bible spoke in clear and authoritative tones; others felt it did not. Yet accounts of the trial often pay little attention to those who found themselves in the middleground between these two positions—those who were unsure whether the stories in the Bible were literally true (say, in its account of a six-day creation) but who, at the same time, were not ready to consign the Bible to the trash bin, either. Faulkner's stories invoke the Bible in ways that speak especially to such readers—perhaps even more so in the twenty-first century when not only the authority of the literal meaning of the Bible continues to be questionable for many people, but also now that biblical literacy has decreased so dramatically that many people have only a vague sense of the contents of the Bible but nevertheless often accord it a sense of respect. The Bible possesses some kind of authority for such people, but that authority is not entirely clear.

In addition to the scientific advances of Faulkner's day, it is important to note also that technological advances were rapidly changing the look and feel of daily life to such an extent that the world described in the Bible came to seem radically different from that of modern times. It was not merely a case of increased urbanization in the United States. As many of Faulkner's stories document, rural areas, too, were slowly but irrevocably being transformed by new technologies—"patented electric gadgets for cooking and freezing and cleaning" (*Intruder in the Dust* 118). Only a century earlier, there had been far fewer technological differences between the world inhabited by most Bible readers and the world depicted in the Bible. As the twentieth century wore on, the world depicted in the Bible came to seem remote and archaic in unprecedented ways.

Finally, as if metaphorically representing the scholarly, scientific, and technological lights by which the Bible could appear archaic, the very language—the sound—of the KJV was becoming increasingly archaic, too. The second epigraph Ernest Hemingway chose for his 1926 novel, *The Sun Also Rises*, attests to this change by implicitly contrasting Hemingway's spare, modern style with the KJV rendering of Ecclesiastes: "The sun also ariseth, and the sun goeth down, and hasteth to the place where he arose" (7). Yet even for Hemingway in *The Sun Also Rises*, the world-weary words of Ecclesiastes speaks with a vague yet still vaguely powerful sense of oracular authority. For both Faulkner and Hemingway, despite their markedly different writing styles, the sound of the KJV seems suggestive of an ancient, even otherworldly voice from the past. Indeed, what scholars typically describe as the simple, direct, and concrete diction and syntax of the KJV is often not so simple and clear to nonacademic modern readers.

One should note that even in 1611, the language of the KJV was not that of ordinary speech but already had a slightly strange, archaic feel: It was not precisely an older form of English but its own unique amalgam that included genuine archaisms alongside strange new Hebraized English. Examples of once-unfamiliar Hebrew idioms made familiar by the KJV include "by the skin of my teeth," "to stand in awe," "put words in his mouth," "rise and shine," and "a fly in the ointment." Older forms of English now enshrined as KJV "church English" were already falling out of use in 1611, such as "thee," "thou," and the "-eth" suffix (as, for example, in Luke 22:21, "Behold, the hand of him that betrayeth me is with me on the table").

To illustrate some of the distinctive stylistic and structural features of the KJV, consider the following passages from 2 Samuel in which David learns of the death of his son, Absalom. First, the story is told sparsely, using few brush strokes, as it were, to paint emotions: "And the king said unto Cushi, 'Is the young man Absalom safe?' And Cushi answered, 'The enemies of my lord the king, and all that rise against thee to do thee hurt, be as that young man is.' And the king was much moved, and went up to the chamber over the gate, and wept" (2 Sam. 18:32–33). The event is told in just a few lines; Cushi's answer is not explicit or direct, and David offers him no reply. The sense is conveyed, but we are invited to read between the lines for more details. As the story unfolds further, it focuses on a psychological drama that develops from ironic, unexpected reversals: The king mourns for the traitor; victory becomes defeat; and the servant, Joab, corrects the master, David. In David's famous lament, the curious irony is that Absalom sought to overthrow his father and might well have killed him if David and his army had not fought back, but David's words belie his earlier actions: "O my son Absalom, my son, my son Absalom: would God I had died for thee, O Absalom, my son, my son" (2 Sam. 18:33). This irony is not lost on the people, who are cast as one character: "Victory that day was turned into mourning unto all the people: for the people heard say that day how the king was grieved for his son. And the people gat them by stealth that day into the city, as people being ashamed steal away when they flee in battle" (2 Sam. 19:2–3). Note how the simile (fleeing in battle) drives home the ironic reversal: They were victorious in battle but now retreat as if in defeat.

Joab admonishes his king in a stately rhythm that caries prophetic undertones: "Thou has shamed this day the faces of all thy servants, which this day have saved thy life, and the lives of thy sons and of thy daughters, and the lives of thy wives, and the lives of thy concubines, in that thou lovest thy enemies, and hatest thy friends. . . . For this day I perceive, that if Absalom had lived, and all we had died this day, then it had pleased thee well" (2 Sam. 19:5–6). The sentences are composed of rather brief phrases (the many commas visibly mark this pacing), and the cumulative enumeration ("lives of thy sons . . . daughters . . . wives . . . concubines") and contrasting antithesis ("lovest they enemies, and hatest thy friends") serve to keep the rhythm slow and measured. Joab's prophetic undertones rise to the surface as he seems to bear witness against David on behalf of God himself: "I swear by the LORD, if thou go not forth . . . that will be worse unto thee than all the evil that befell thee from thy youth until now" (2 Sam. 7). Finally, and most obviously, the vocabulary in the above passages is often archaic—*thee*, *thy*, *doth*, *hatest*, and *gat*.

Now consider the similarities between these stylistic and structural features of the KJV and those of the following passage from Faulkner's *Absalom*. First, while Faulkner's writing style might seem anything but sparse, he often creates such densely multifaceted psychological complexity that the effect is a kind of packed economy that forces the reader to read between the lines:

> It seems that this demon—his name was Sutpen—(Colonel Sutpen)—Colonel Sutpen. Who came out of nowhere and without warning upon the land . . . and built a plantation—(Tore violently a plantation, Miss Rosa Coldfield says)—tore violently. And married her sister Ellen and begot a son and a daughter which—(Without gentleness begot, Miss Rosa Coldfield says)—without gentleness. Which should have been the jewels of his pride and the shield and comfort of his old age, only—(Only they destroyed him or something or he destroyed them or something. And died)—and died. Without regret, Miss Rosa Coldfield says—(Save by her) Yes, save by her. (And by Quentin Compson). (5)

Here, the narrative foregrounds Rosa's and Quentin's different investments in the Sutpen story such that the passage becomes a densely layered representation not only of Sutpen but also of Miss Rosa and Quentin (who seems to be speaking with her and being corrected by her as he speaks). Note, too, that in addition to creating a legendary or mythic sense of history (Sutpen is a "demon" who "tore" a plantation from the land as if it were built in a single blow), the passage emphasizes ironic psychological reversals: Sutpen's pride, his jewel, ended up destroying him, or being destroyed by him, as may be said of the relationship between David and Absalom; despite his disappointments, however, Sutpen died "without regret." More obviously, the passage echoes the KJV in its use of the archaic *begot*. Robert Alter argues that Faulkner regularly uses this and other thematic keywords from the KJV, such as birthright, curse, land, flesh and blood, bones, dust, and clay (86). Even the use of *shield* and *comfort* echo the KJV's frequent uses of these words, as in Genesis 15:1 ("I am thy shield") and Psalm 119:50 ("my comfort in my affliction").

Finally, the rhythm of the above passage is built on the same kind of short phrases and cumulative enumeration characteristic of the KJV whereby, as Maxine Rose explains, "each phrase or clause explains or increases or enlarges upon the meaning of the previous one(s)" (139). Compare it with the opening of Genesis in the KJV, which uses the word *and* to translate the Hebrew connective transliterated *waw*, thus creating a paratactic (coordinating) rather than hypotactic (subordinating) grammatical structure in English in order to recreate the parataxis of ancient Hebrew:

In the beginning God created the heaven and the earth. *And* the earth was without form, and void, *and* darkness was upon the face of the deep. *And* the Spirit of God moved upon the face of the waters. *And* God said, "Let there be light": *and* there was light. *And* God saw the light, that it was good: *and* God divided the light from the darkness. *And* God called the light Day, and the darkness he called Night. *And* the evening and the morning were the first day. (Gen. 1:1–5, emphasis added)

In the passage from *Absalom*, Sutpen "came out of nowhere . . . and built a plantation . . . And married . . . and begot a son and a daughter . . . and died" (5).

This type of cumulative effect sometimes takes on a more structured form in biblical Hebrew, as is most clearly evident in the parallelism of the Psalms: each verse consists of two or more statements that work together in one of three ways. They can be synonymous (the second restates the first), as in the second verse of Psalm 149: "Let Israel rejoice in him that made him: let the children of Zion be joyful in their King." They can be synthetic (the second builds on the first): "Let them praise his name in the dance: let them sing praises unto him with the timbrel and harp" (Ps. 149:3). Or they can be antithetical (the second contrasts with the first): "let the wickedness of the wicked come to an end, but establish the just" (Ps. 7:9). Rose argues that Faulkner's sentences often create cumulative patterns that echo the parallelism of ancient Hebrew poetry (140–43). Consider the following passages from *Absalom*, in which the past is described as being hidden from the present—inaccessible yet still present in an insistent and mysterious way (like a ghost): "It's just incredible. It just does not explain. Or perhaps that's it: they dont explain and we are not supposed to know. We have a few old mouth-to-mouth tales; we exhume from old trunks and boxes and drawers letters without salutation or signature" (80). The first two sentences synthetically build on one another; the third and fourth sentences similarly offer synthetic repetitions (they do not explain, we are not supposed to know; we have old tales, we exhume old letters). Then, the passage creates a series of pairs: "*men and women* who once *lived and breathed* are now merely *initials or nicknames* out of some now incomprehensible affection which sound to us like *Sanskrit or Chocktaw*" (80, emphasis added). Finally, we get an antithesis which, in the context of this particular narrative, suggests a further echo of ancient Hebrew parallelism: "They are there, yet something is missing" (80). Not one of these examples is sufficient to establish that the narrative definitely echoes the KJV; even taken together, they do not create enough of a regular and extended pattern to be considered a clear imitation of the KJV. Yet in the context of this novel that announces the KJV as a crucial intertext, these stylistic features create (at least for those who possess a basic knowledge of the KJV) a vague echo of the KJV in the diction and sentence structure of Faulkner's narrative voice itself.

These formal echoes draw significance not only from the more direct allusions to the KJV but also from its ghostly thematic presence-yet-absence in one of the central conflicts faced by the characters: the tension between what might be described as a "law ethic" and a "love ethic." *Absalom* casts this tension in strongly biblical terms, drawing from the David-and-Absalom story as well as from New Testament accounts of clashes between Jesus and the Pharisees. In the David story, the law condemns his rebellious son Absalom as a traitor who sought to overthrow his king, but David rejects the primacy of that legal standard: David's lament ignores his son's culpability and instead asserts the primacy of his identification as a loving father over that of a wronged king. Sutpen, by contrast, makes no such lament, which renders the novel's title rather ironic. Colonel Sutpen is no King David. The novel's biblical allusions in this vein serve to highlight the disjunction between its story and the Bible at least as much as the similarities between the two. Indeed, when Sutpen tries to rectify the "mistake" in his "design" (his plan to become a wealthy plantation patriarch), he makes the additional mistake of consulting a "legally trained" mind rather than considering that his woes might be the result of a more profound "retribution": the "sins of the father come home to roost"—particularly the sin of repudiating his first marriage on racist grounds (215, 219–220). Sutpen faces the kind of dilemma depicted repeatedly in the New Testament as a conflict between the law and love (the former associated especially with the "scribes and Pharisees" of Matt. 23:1–36): the question of healing or working on the Sabbath (Mark 3:1–6, Mark 2:23–8), of having dirty hands at dinner (Mark 7:1–23), of associating with Samaritans (Luke 10:25–37), and of befriending tax collectors and sinners (Mark 2:13–17). Yet it never seems to occur to Sutpen to choose anything but the law. Appropriately enough, Rosa, who sees him as her nemesis, styles herself "love's . . . advocate" (117).

The tension between love and the law shapes the central conflicts of all of the major characters in *Absalom*. Throughout the novel, major characters face critical and revelatory moments of decision—what might be termed "conversion" challenges (given the novel's biblical intertext) that force them to change their perspective and consider changing their behavior. These potential conversion narratives are reminiscent of the account in Acts 9 of Paul's experience on the road to Damascus when suddenly a bright light blinds him and precipitates his conversion from being the strictest observer of the law to one who sees that even the ancient circumcision covenant can be abrogated by God's love. In one such moment in *Absalom*, Bon (Sutpen's estranged son) feels as though a "jigsaw puzzle" suddenly "[fell] into pattern," revealing "at once, like a flash of light, the meaning of his whole life" (250). Quentin and his college roommate, Shreve, also imagine that Sutpen and his son Henry each must have experienced such a conversion challenge in their lives (186, 284–86). Going further, it can be argued that the entire novel constitutes an account of Quentin's own conversion challenge as he realizes the significance of what he and Miss Rosa discovered in the haunted Sutpen mansion. As Charles R. Wilson explains, the "central theme of southern religion is the need for conversion in a specific experience that will lead to baptism, to a purified new person"; put simply, this "need is to be born again" (59). It should come as no surprise that the call to conversion serves as a central theme in *Absalom*. (Faulkner's formative denomination was Methodist, which, despite literary critics' emphasis on the influence of Calvinist theology in his work, departs strongly from Calvinism in its emphasis on free will and personal spirituality [Wilson 60]).

In keeping with the irony of the novel's title, the conversion challenges depicted in *Absalom* all end in failure by biblical standards. Not one character chooses love wholeheartedly. Even Rosa, who thinks of herself as love's "advocate," seems consumed instead by a vengeful bitterness. Likewise, Wash Jones, who kills Sutpen because of Sutpen's heartless treatment of Milly, Jones's granddaughter, serves as no biblical champion of love: Faulkner pointedly reminds the reader of the nineteenth century's hateful Bible defense of slavery by way of Jones, who believes "the Bible said" black people should be enslaved because they are "cursed by God" (226). It is in this sense that the characters are thematically haunted by the Bible. They find themselves challenged by a biblical call to choose something deeper and truer than the law—what Faulkner, in his 1941 story, "The Tall Men," describes as "our backbone," which is apparently missing from the "investigator" whose blind devotion to the law leaves him "all fogged up with rules and regulations" (59). Yet this something deeper and truer, this backbone of the human species that is associated in *Absalom* with the Bible, remains a ghost to the major characters because it is at once there and not-there: They are forced to confront it but cannot accept it—especially the "passages of the old violent vindictive mysticism" that seem relevant only to the likes of Rosa's fanatical and self-destructive father (64). Ultimately, man-made laws seem more real, and the major characters choose to trust such laws (literally and metaphorically) instead of the vague, shadowy, archaic alternative. These characters do not have conversion experiences; they experience conversion challenges, but, like the rich young man in Matthew 19 who finds the price of entering the kingdom of heaven unrealistically high, these characters turn "away sorrowful" (Matt. 19:22). Indeed, this is how Faulkner casts the South itself (in keeping with the biblical trope whereby Israel is often represented as a single character): Like the man described in Matthew 7 who built his house on unsteady sand instead of on a solid rock foundation, "the South . . . erected its economic edifice not on the rock of stern morality but on the shifting sands of opportunism and moral brigandage" (209). The major characters in *Absalom*, like the young man in Matthew 19, cannot accept the conversion challenge but cannot completely dismiss it, either—by the end of the novel, Quentin is left feeling irrevocably haunted (in tones reminiscent of another gothic classic, Edgar Allan Poe's "The Raven"): "Nevermore of peace. Nevermore of peace. Nevermore. Nevermore. Nevermore" (298–99).[2]

If the central "ghost" metaphor in *Absalom* may be productively applied to Faulkner's uses of the Bible in that novel, this metaphor also offers a productive trope for understanding the role of the Bible in many of his other works as well. While a thorough analysis would require its own volume, Faulkner's 1929 novel, *The Sound and the Fury*, provides an instructive example by which to guide further exploration. So far, this introduction to Faulkner's uses of the Bible has focused on the Bible rather than on Christianity per se (with the exception of a brief note on the centrality of conversion experiences in southern religion). Turning to *The Sound and the Fury* affords the opportunity to explain why Christianity—especially considered in terms of systematic theology—is arguably not the most useful lens through which to analyze Faulkner's work. Scholars have long debated Faulkner's representations of Christianity, and the scholarship on *The Sound and the Fury* may serve as a microcosm of these debates. Some argue that the novel ultimately forwards a Christian perspective; others believe that it is not fully Christian but more vaguely and generally hopeful; still others affirm that it offers no hope whatsoever. For this last group, the bleakness of the title (which alludes to Macbeth's famous soliloquy in act 5, scene 5 just after he learns of his wife's death, in which he describes life as "a tale / Told by an idiot, full of sound and fury, / Signifying nothing"), and the bleakness of the first three sections of the novel cannot be saved by the famous Easter service in the fourth and final section.

John Hunt contends that Faulkner presents readers with a nihilistic skepticism whereby not only are traditional religious beliefs called into question but also all meaning at even the most basic level finds itself threatened with utter negation (174–75). Faulkner takes this threat seriously but counters it, according to Hunt, with a "theology of tension" that amounts to a "tension between Christian and Stoic visions" (169).

While this argument helps clarify key elements of the major conflicts in *The Sound and the Fury*, Hunt concedes that the argument also "strain[s] [Faulkner's] fiction by theological language" (176). Indeed, it strains the stories too far, as do most attempts to locate articulations of systematic theology in them. Put simply, to ask about the role of theology in Faulkner's stories is to ask the wrong question. These stories do not speak that language. Instead, as Wilson argues, the religious world of Faulkner's stories is primarily that of "folk religion," which is "beyond theology": It is created by the actual beliefs and practices of "plain folk, the poor whites and blacks" in the South; in this context, the Bible "possessed a near mystical attraction . . . even in dissent, it was the source of all authority" (63, 67–68). One therefore gets more useful answers from Faulkner's stories if one asks about the role of the Bible in them. They may not speak theology, but they definitely speak Bible.

The Sound and the Fury tells the story of a family in decline. The first three sections of the novel give the first-person perspectives of three brothers, each in turn, on the Compson family and their respective places in it. Each brother fixates on his only sister, Candace (nicknamed Caddy), whose romantic adventures are seen as having disgraced the family. Each brother harbors a special, personal sorrow or grudge related to Caddy. In the novel's fourth section, Dilsey, the black housekeeper and cook who works for the Compson family, finds herself revived and transported by an Easter Sunday church service.

Faulkner was repeatedly drawn to the imagery of Holy Week; *The Sound and the Fury* and his 1954 novel, *A Fable*, offer the clearest examples of this. *A Fable* emphasizes the crucifixion and the events leading up to it in the Passion narrative far more than the resurrection (not unlike the Gospel of Mark account that ends at 16:8). This is arguably true of *The Sound and the Fury*, as well: Despite the Easter ending, the effect is not entirely or even strongly hopeful. Some have tried to see the youngest Compson brother, Benjy, as a Christ figure, but while his role is in keeping with the biblical scapegoat, it is not that of the

Passover lamb—no one is saved by his suffering. The second-oldest brother, Jason, is a Macbeth-like figure in that he seems unconsciously self-destructive as he pursues his will to power. Quentin, the oldest, is quite consciously self-destructive; while some have read him as a Christ-like figure, a martyr dying for his ideals, there is no redemption in his story, which means he is ultimately more like Sophocles' tragic Antigone than a true martyr. Indeed, his section suggests that his lack of faith, at least in part, is what leads him to commit suicide. He equates "Jesus walking on Galilee," the miracle of walking on the water, with George "Washington not telling lies"—both are myths (51). Quentin cannot believe in a God of time who transcends time, but he cannot stand not believing, either: "It's not when you realize that nothing can help you—religion, pride, anything—it's when you realize that you don't need any aid" (51). By committing suicide, Quentin becomes, in a sense, his father's definition of a false Christ, who "was not crucified: he was worn away by a minute clicking of little wheels" (49). Christ did not transcend time, according to Quentin's father, and neither does Quentin: Time goes on with or without him, as the rest of the novel pointedly reminds readers.

Even so, as Hunt claims, the narrative casts this nihilistic skepticism as deeply troubling, and one cannot ignore the Easter service that dominates the novel's fourth and final section. Some have suggested that such religious imagery merely reflects Faulkner's region and era. Faulkner himself, in one of his interviews at the University of Virginia, explained that the religious culture of the South was "a part of [his] background": "It has nothing to do with how much of it I might believe or disbelieve—it's just there" (qtd. in Wilson 61). Even so, there is too much of it, too carefully crafted, to be dismissed; in addition to setting the novel during Holy Week, there are more direct allusions to the Bible in *The Sound and the Fury* than in any of his other novels (Coffee 129). The biblical references (direct and indirect) are deliberately and insistently ambiguous in complex ways, functioning together as a ghost that haunts this novel both formally and thematically.

Readers whose ears are attuned to the KJV hear this long before the narration of the actual Easter service. Leaving aside the direct allusions to the Bible in the novel's first three sections, the opening of the fourth section exemplifies the more subtle ways in which the narrative voice in *The Sound and the Fury* is often haunted by the KJV. First, note the biblical keywords, *dust* and *flesh*, in the opening sentence: "The day dawned bleak and chill, a moving wall of gray light out of the northeast which, instead of dissolving into moisture, seemed to disintegrate into minute and venomous particles, like dust that, when Dilsey opened the door of the cabin and emerged, needled laterally into her flesh" (165). The commas give a visible marker of the slow, biblical pace of the sentence. To use dust as a simile for rain might seem paradoxical (dry as wet), except in the context of the biblical sense of mortality implied by both rain (the rain in Genesis 7 brings death to those not on Noah's ark; also, the rain is "venomous," suggestive of the serpent whose treachery led to the curse of death) and dust: "for dust thou art, and unto dust shalt thou return" (Gen. 3:19).

Second, note the mythic depiction of a rather mundane morning. The rain conjures images of death; as the passage continues, concrete images continue to serve, as they so often do in the KJV, to symbolize grand abstractions: "as though muscle and tissue had been courage or fortitude which the days or the years had consumed until only the indomitable skeleton was left rising like a ruin or a landmark" (165). Similarly, the ground just outside the cabin door is not ground but "earth," and it suggests the mythic history of an enslaved people (not unlike the Israelites), destitute "generations" whose unshod feet passed there: "The earth immediately about the door was bare. It had a patina, as though from the soles of bare feet in generations" (165).

One also finds, as in *Absalom*, the use of paired adjectives that create the effect of cumulative enumeration: "muscle and tissue," "courage or fortitude," "the days or the years," and "a ruin or a landmark" (165). The use of "and" in the following passage has a similar effect: "Dilsey opened the door . . . *and* emerged. . . . She wore a stiff black straw hat perched upon her turban, *and* a maroon velvet cape with a border of mangy and anonymous fur above a dress of purple silk, *and* she stood in the door for a while with her myriad and sunken face lifted to the weather, *and* one gaunt hand flac-soled as the belly of a fish" (165, emphasis added). Here too, paired adjectives create a biblical sense of cumulative enumeration: "mangy and anonymous," and "myriad and sunken." Faulkner goes on to describe Dilsey as wearing a "gown . . . in color regal and moribund": here, the syntactical inversion "noun + adjective" in "color regal" (and in "hand flac-soled") is a Hebraism atypical in English but characteristically appearing in the KJV as a "noun + of + noun" construction, such as "men of strength" rather than "strong men" in Isaiah 5 (165).[3]

Again, however, all this is not to say that the opening of the fourth section—let alone all of *The Sound and the Fury*, which is written in four distinctly different styles—imitates or even sounds like the KJV. Parts of the novel vaguely echo the KJV, sometimes more strongly, sometimes less so. Many of these echoes might be missed if not for the direct biblical allusions and thematic incorporation of southern religious culture. All of these elements, taken together, collectively haunt the narrative in an ambiguous and often ambivalent way—troubling it as an ancient, specifically premodern, opposition to the modern threat of nihilistic skepticism that also troubles the narrative both formally and thematically.

Unlike in *Absalom*, *The Sound and the Fury* includes characters who choose wholeheartedly to disregard the law (metaphorically or literally) in the name of something to do with honor and love—something vaguely to do with the Bible, the narrative suggests—characters who have backbones. So Dilsey takes Benjy to her church despite her daughter's protests that this violates social codes of conduct concerning race and (dis)ability. Dilsey's response is that these unofficial codes are in conflict with God and so cannot stand. The codes hold that Benjy "aint good enough fer white church" because of his developmental disability, while a black church "aint good enough fer him" because of his race; this would leave no church for Benjy to attend, which outcome Dilsey rejects: "de good Lawd dont keer whether he bright er not" (181). She suggests God also does not care whether Benjy is white or not—a brave position to take in 1920s Mississippi.

The sheriff to whom Jason turns at the end of the novel similarly shows backbone. When Jason solicits the sheriff as "a commissioned officer of the law" to help Jason track down his niece who has run away with a large sum of money (which was meant for her upkeep but has been embezzled by Jason), the sheriff refuses to help him: "You drove that girl into running off, Jason. . . . And I have some suspicions about who that money belongs to that I dont reckon I'll ever know for certain" (189). Jason specifically accuses the sheriff of flouting the law by refusing to help: "This is not Russia, where just because he wears a little metal badge, a man is immune to law" (189). Yet the sheriff refuses nonetheless.

These characters implicitly undermine a Calvinistic insistence on the utter depravity of all human beings, but the stronger thematic resonance with the rest of the narrative is less theological than biblical: They are faced with a biblical conflict between a "law ethic" and a "love ethic," and they must make a choice. They choose the latter, but as in the Bible, even the heroes (such as David) are far from perfect. Indeed, Faulkner's stories on the whole seem most interested in the imperfect, those for whom this kind of ethical choice is anything but a foregone conclusion.

Inasmuch as the Bible may be said to haunt much of Faulkner's work, this suggests one of the many reasons why his stories have spoken so powerfully to so many readers: A sense of the Bible as ghost—as an archaic yet still vaguely prophetic text—became widespread in the twentieth century and is still prevalent today. The ambiguous and ambivalent echoes of the Bible in Faulkner's narrative voice resonate with various ways in which modern and even postmodern people wrestle with that ancient text. The gothic metaphor is useful because it helps articulate Faulkner's implicit reversal of the expected order of things:

The Bible in his work is paradoxically and somewhat grotesquely dead and not dead at the same time, at once premodern and modern. Faulkner's stories often insist that the Bible continues to speak to us, whether or not we will listen to it, while also insisting that what the Bible has to say to the modern world is anything but clear or simple.

Notes

1. The author would like to thank William Griffith, Curator and Director of Rowan Oak, as well as his colleagues, Hannah McMahon and Caroline Croom, for their generous assistance in making Faulkner's personal Bible available for study.
2. Regarding this and other gothic similarities between Faulkner and Poe, see Shoko Itoh's "Poe, Faulkner, and Gothic America."
3. See Hammond, 45–51.

Works Cited

Alter, Robert. *Pen of Iron: American Prose and the King James Bible*. Princeton, NJ: Princeton UP, 2010. Print.

Coffee, Jessie McGuire. *Faulkner's Un-Christlike Christians: Biblical Allusions in the Novels*. Ann Arbor: U of Michigan Research P, 1983. Print.

Faulkner, William. *The Sound and the Fury*. 1929. New York: Norton, 1994. Print.

___. *Absalom, Absalom!* 1936. New York: Vintage, 1991. Print.

___. "The Tall Men." 1941. *Collected Stories of William Faulkner*. Ed. Erroll McDonald. New York: Vintage, 1995. 45–61. Print.

___. *Intruder in the Dust*. 1948. New York: Vintage, 1991. Print.

Hammond, Gerald. *The Making of the English Bible*. Manchester: Carcanet, 1982.

Hemingway, Ernest. *The Sun Also Rises*. New York: Simon, 1926. Print.

Hunt, John W. *William Faulkner: Art in Theological Tension*. Syracuse, NY: Syracuse UP, 1965. Print.

Itoh, Shoko. "Poe, Faulkner, and Gothic America." *The Faulkner Journal of Japan* 3 (Sept. 2001): n.p. Web. 11 Aug. 2012.

Rose, Maxine. "Echoes of the King James Bible in the Prose Style of *Absalom, Absalom!*" *Arizona Quarterly* 37.2 (1981): 137–48. Print.

Wilson, Charles Reagan. *Judgment and Grace in Dixie: Southern Faiths from Faulkner to Elvis*. Athens: U of Georgia P, 1995. Print.

"A Summer of Wistaria": Old Tales and Talking, Story, and History in *Absalom, Absalom!*

Hans H. Skei

Absalom, Absalom! (1936) is widely regarded as the greatest southern novel and has long been seen as one of Faulkner's most difficult and complex narratives, taking language and storytelling to the limits of achievement.[1] *Absalom, Absalom!* is a novel from which readers can slowly re-create a continuous and chronological story so that it makes sense and even then only to a certain extent. Readers must work with the different narrators in an attempt to reach beneath and beyond all secrets, gossip, hearsay, and unfinished narratives to see how the text constitutes its meaning—and only then look for possible interpretations.

In its first chapters the novel appears to tell a story of which the basic elements are parts of the mythical past of Jefferson and Yoknapatawpha County. Quentin Compson has heard the story so often that he hardly knows why he listens to it once more. Yet for various reasons he is compulsively engaged in every aspect of the legend about Thomas Sutpen. It is almost as if he has inherited some sort of responsibility for everything that went wrong, perhaps because his grandfather, General Compson, was Sutpen's first and only friend in Jefferson. Then the narrative changes. The reader joins Quentin and his roommate at Harvard, Shreve McCannon, a few months after the events narrated in the opening chapters.

Pure and simple storytelling, no matter how advanced and speculative it may seem, comes to an end. It is replaced by speculation and surmise and guesswork, with construction of what could have happened rather than reconstruction of what actually happened. History must be given narrative form to be accessible, but the different and subjective, not to say prejudiced, versions of Sutpen's story in *Absalom, Absalom!* must not be seen only as an attempt to "get it right." Nor is it just a worthwhile failure when it proves impossible to find all facts or to understand the motivations behind this or that act of courage or cowardice. The novel, almost inadvertently, asks questions about how the past can be anything but a fallible reconstruction in retrospect, given narrative form and becoming a literary artifact. In the end, the limitations of narrative, language, and storytelling seem clear when it comes to conveying something simple, significant, and true. Yet the novel and the story it tells finally undercut the doubts and misgivings readers experience while reading.

Critics, such as Peter Brooks, either have called Faulkner's technique "incredulous narration,"[2] or they have found that the author has become a postmodernist writer, adding a metafictional level to all the other layers of the text, when Quentin and Shreve have to speculate and conjure up possible interpretations, since they lack information or evidence (See McHale 8–11).[3] Although it has not been applied to this novel in any serious ways, modern theories of unnatural narration, unnatural voices, and antimimetic narration may prove to be of some help in the much needed study of who sees and who narrates, what they tell and what they keep secret, and what is kept secret from them.[4]

Absalom, Absalom! is not only an intricate attempt to tell a complex story of Sutpen's design and his rise and ultimate fall. It is almost as much Quentin Compson's story. Given both its biblically allusive title and references to and parallels with Greek tragedies, one must also search beneath the problems of multiple and extremely subjective narrators to investigate the sense of doom or destiny and even tragedy—Sutpen's as well as the South's. The novel as a whole seems to indicate that tragedy is inevitable, given the curse of slavery and the readiness by almost everybody to enslave others. Blackness is a pervasive presence in this work—perhaps more so than in any other of Faulkner's books, with the possible exception of *Go Down, Moses* (1942).[5] The patriarchal structure of a society with strong traditions and conservative values, and the very limited and insignificant role women are allowed to play within such a structure, is of great importance in almost all aspects of the events to which readers slowly and fragmentarily gain access. All these matters have been approached by other critics, and most of them have been treated with great intelligence.[6] Yet the little awareness of who tells what (and who knows what at which point in the long span of time the novel covers) reduces the value of many analyses and interpretations.

Despite the multiple narrators and the apparent authority given to Quentin as narrator from chapter six onward, readers must ask how it is possible to reduce (or deauthorize) the eyewitness account of Miss Rosa, and should question or at least problematize the reliability of Mr. Compson's part of the storytelling. Mr. Compson is at least one remove from the story as it happened and has been told what he knows by his father, who had some of the information from Sutpen himself. When Quentin changes from listener to teller, from narratee to narrator, he has some fresh knowledge that Miss Rosa has been instrumental in providing, but otherwise he is at a great distance in time and space from what took place at Sutpen's Hundred. Since this temporal distance is clearly problematic, readers must pay close attention to the distribution of narrative voice and to the comments, direct and indirect, by the outside narrator who appears as a voice and a force that set the principles of the whole narrative and distribute narrative authority among the four narrators of the Sutpen story. Even when one of these narrators speculates or surmises, textual commentary on what stories are made of, abound:

> We have a few old mouth-to-mouth tales; we exhume from old trunks and boxes and drawers letters without salutation or signature, in which men and women who once lived and breathed are now merely initials or nicknames out of some now incomprehensible affection which sound to us like Sanskrit or Chocktaw; we see dimly people, the people in whose living blood and seed we ourselves lay dormant and waiting, in this shadowy attenuation of time possessing now heroic proportions, performing their acts of simple passion and simple violence, impervious to time and inexplicable. (*AA* 80)

These words are spoken by Mr. Compson, to whom the whole Sutpen story is incredible. As for Miss Rosa, Mr. Compson distrusts her narrative but also insists that women lead beautiful lives. Rosa Coldfield is central in the events that lead up to the final revelations at Sutpen's Hundred, and she is also the only one who knew Sutpen and many, if not all, aspects of life at the plantation. She has been a burden on the genteel families in Jefferson but also a kind of hereditary obligation for them, which explains why she can summon Quentin Compson and ask him to take her out to the ruined mansion at Sutpen's Hundred. Her narrative is doubted or set aside by the other narrators who have less firsthand knowledge than she does, possibly because she is a woman in a patriarchal society or because she is one of the many hysteric unmarried women in Faulkner's fiction. She opens the novel as its first narrator and is introduced by the outside narrator in the dim and dusty room that her father called the office. She brings the Sutpen mystery to conclusion even if many elements of the Sutpen story still seem inconclusive. The letter about her death frames the Quentin/Shreve section of the novel, and in the 160 pages that intervene between the opening and the closure of the letter, the pervasive smell of wisteria may well be felt by the reader all the time. There are many references to her "summer of wistaria"—Faulkner's spelling—in the past as well as in the present of the narrative. The distance between the "summer of wistaria"—the hot September days in Mississippi—and the iron cold winter air in the North hints at an almost impossible distance in understanding people, ways of life, and society itself from both the outside and such distance. Quentin may need his roommate as a corrective to the story he tells, but the deeper layers in the Sutpen story seem to slip away from Shreve. On the other hand, Quentin may need the distance and the exile to see his home and the people closest to him in a new and different light from when he was summoned to Miss Rosa's house. There he is forced to listen to her version of the story of Thomas Sutpen, whom she can only refer to as "the demon." Later, he takes her out to the decaying plantation house at Sutpen's Hundred to add to everything he has been told and experienced as a young boy. He may possibly even find the ultimate key to a story that in the end leaves so much to the reader to try to piece together to make sense.

Readers should not shift emphasis completely from the others, who are allowed to tell their version of parts of the Sutpen story in the novel. The novel's four different narrative voices and the characters behind them—indeed everything in the text—are transmitted by an outside narrator. This narrator is not to be equated with the author himself, although experienced readers of Faulkner's novels may well hear the master's voice above and beyond the stories read or heard. Thus, even if the novel, to an unusual extent, also makes use of listeners, readers, and narratees (those to whom a story is directed or told) who later try to reconstruct the story they have been told, I would not go as far as Peter Brooks. He claims that "the voice of the reader has evicted all other voices from the text" (304). What is clear in Brooks's analysis, and touched upon by other critics, including Joseph R. Urgo and Noel Polk, is the importance of metafictional elements in the book—that is, instances where the text comments on itself as narrative, as writing, as storytelling. The reader's active participation in the creation of the text cannot be overlooked, and the many comments on storytelling itself—in combination with letters, inscriptions on gravestones, and different remembrances of a past that cannot really be recaptured or reconstructed—are all metafictional elements that may contribute greatly to understanding the text.

Faulkner admitted that this novel had been particularly difficult to write, and he also more or less confessed that there were problems in the text that he had not thought through and to which readers could never expect to find "correct" answers (*Faulkner in the University* 281). He admitted this when answering questions more than twenty years after the book's publication, and he actually went on to speculate further on the motives behind some of the curious actions and activities in the novel. But he always insisted that *Absalom, Absalom!* is Sutpen's story: "The story of a man who wanted a son and got too many, got so many that they destroyed him" (71). He admitted, cautiously, however, that it is also "the story of Quentin Compson's hatred of the bad qualities in the country he loves" (71). Asked almost the same question later, Faulkner still insisted that the novel tells Sutpen's story, but he added a few remarks regarding Quentin's contribution in the novel that are both telling and revelatory with regard to the other narrators: "Every time any character gets into a book, no matter how minor, he's actually telling his biography—that's all anyone ever does, he tells his own biography, talking about himself, in a thousand different terms, but himself" (275).

Before discussing the narrative complexities of the book, a brief outline of what has so far been referred to as Sutpen's story may be useful. Thomas Sutpen suddenly turns up in Jefferson, Mississippi, in 1833. He has a horse, two pistols, the clothes he wears, and apparently nothing else. Later readers learn that he was born in the mountains of western Virginia in 1807 and that as a young boy he had been turned away from the front door of a plantation house by a black man and told to enter by the back door. He makes up his mind to settle things by having his own mansion and becoming a wealthy man. He happens to hear of plantations and get-rich-quick schemes in the Caribbean, and it is from Haiti he returns in 1833. Somehow he gets the deed to an enormous piece of land from an Indian chief and then brings in a French architect and a wild group of Haitian slaves. An enormous mansion is built on the plantation known now as Sutpen's Hundred. He marries Ellen Coldfield, who bears him two children, Henry and Judith, but he also has a black daughter, Clytie. Henry becomes close friends with a young man who seems a little old to begin his studies, Charles Bon, and brings him home to Sutpen's Hundred to visit. Nothing actually seems to happen, but Judith and Charles are soon engaged. This is where the past is not even past, but an active ingredient in the present: Charles is Sutpen's son with his first wife Eulalia, who was from Haiti and may have a drop of black blood.

Then the Civil War begins in 1861, and Thomas Sutpen, Henry, and Charles join the Confederate army. They all survive the war, but Henry kills Charles at the gate to Sutpen's Hundred when they return home, and then Henry disappears. Ellen has died during the war, and her much younger sister, Rosa Coldfield, has lived in the house to take care of her niece, Judith, who is older than she is. Sutpen makes such an indecent proposition to Rosa that she leaves immediately. Sutpen tries to save what can be salvaged from a plantation now in ruins and is helped by his overseer, Wash Jones, until Wash also experiences the ultimate humiliation from his master and kills him in 1869. The story is carried forward and told and retold in the late summer of 1909, as the novel begins, in the midst of a pervading smell from the wisteria vine blooming for the second time that particular summer. The story comes to a climactic end some weeks later. The narration concludes a little later, in January of 1910, as Quentin receives a letter from his father regarding Miss Rosa's death.

This could be a simple, dramatic, and perhaps even melodramatic story, but it has the elements of high tragedy, with a grand design and heroic efforts to create a fortune and a dynasty. These ambitions motivate a man whose innocence and belief in his own strength and will are without limits. Quentin's grandfather insists that Sutpen's "trouble was innocence" (*AA* 179) and elaborates on that innocence later on, "that innocence which believed that the ingredients of morality were like the ingredients of pie or cake and once you had measured them and balanced them and mixed them and put them into the oven it was all finished and nothing but pie or cake could come out" (211–12). Accordingly, Sutpen does not ask of his first and only friend, Quentin's grandfather, where he did wrong, since he does not think in such terms, but rather "where did I make the mistake in it [his design]" (212). He must ask others where he made his mistake, because he cannot possibly understand what went wrong, since he had a design and carried it out according to plan, using the courage he knew he had and the shrewdness he acquired as he went along. So where is his tragic flaw to be found—in some weakness of character, bad luck, or his blind acceptance of a system that had imbedded within it the curse of slavery?

Readers should be reluctant to use the word "tragedy" in literary criticism, particularly when dealing with a novel. Yet even the Greek tragedies can be said to be little more than sad stories of commonwealths and kings, and even in the most perfect of them, Sophocles's *Oedipus the King* (ca. 429 BCE; English translation, 1715), almost nothing happens except messengers coming and going. Everything has already occurred and so is past and must be rethought, reconstructed, and reinvestigated in an attempt to find where it all went wrong. Fate or destiny may have little to do with it, and in the case of Thomas Sutpen, he may not even be aware of such terms, even though three generations of male Compsons may philosophize over them.

"Tragedy" is relevant as a term for people of high standing, to allow for a fall from on high. Does Thomas Sutpen fill such a role? Yes and no. Faulkner himself said that Sutpen wanted to show that he "could make himself a king and raise a line of princes" (*Faulkner in the University* 98).[7] The author also reminds readers that Sutpen had a grand design (and should in no ways be compared with the base ways of a Flem Snopes) and that he was close to getting it realized. The design was within his reach, but something in his past that he thought was settled caught up with him and created a situation that comes as close to "tragedy" as modern literature can expect to achieve.[8] Dreams of a dynasty, a grand design, built on the sins of the past and infested by incest, fratricide, miscegenation—this is material for high tragedy or, in the hand of a lesser artist, for a gothic novel—which *Absalom, Absalom!* to a certain extent is.[9]

Narrators and Narration in *Absalom, Absalom!*

In the volume on *Absalom, Absalom!* in the Reading Faulkner series, Urgo and Polk present a useful glossary and commentary on this text, now and then also offering interpretive help or at least suggestions and speculations regarding inconsistencies and even inadequate motivation or explanation for actions and events. They begin by explaining and discussing the title (a quote from 2 Samuel 18:33 in the Bible), one that they struggle to apply to Sutpen and his sons. Most remarkable is their reference to critic Bernice Schrank, who in a 1975 article called the novel's title the first "authorial contribution to the text," noting it as "distinct from the four narrators" (qtd. in Urgo and Polk 3). Fortunately, the commentators take this to mean that there is a narrator working in the novel who is not one of the novel's characters, a point really too obvious to deserve mention. They also find that "the fourth narrator is apparent from the novel's opening but may be recognized as intrusive for the first time at 7:4" (Urgo and Polk 3)—referring to the sentences "*Without regret, Miss Rosa Coldfield says—(Save by her) Yes, save by her. (And by Quentin Compson) Yes. And by Quentin Compson*" (*AA* 5). This is all bewildering. *Absalom, Absalom!* is not a novel where authorial intrusion or intervention is a part of the narrative system.

Though Urgo and Polk talk about an outside narrator, that narrator is the fifth, not the fourth. The discrepancy may relate to the fact that some critics see Shreve as a listener or a narratee, a sounding board for Quentin's compulsive and existentially important storytelling. There is little reason to reduce Shreve's function. Even if he always retells and also revises what Quentin already has told, he is still an active narrative voice, who, innocently or unaware, also comments on the very story material and the way it is narrated through his questions and his attempts at being funny, using ridicule and irony, when the South is beyond even his imagination.

Valuable and incisive comments on the narrative mode in the novel are given by Urgo and Polk when they discuss the whole italicized passage leading up to the quote above. Some of the questions they raise are related to the thematic interpretation, but more important, they suggest that the intruding voice in this passage may be the narrator's. This seems absolutely correct, but then they move on to speculate that it might be Shreve's voice (Urgo and Polk 8–9). Readers should be cautious and think twice about seeing the first chapters of the book as something they definitely are not—part of the narrative give and take that much later takes place between Quentin and Shreve, far removed from the summer of wisteria and the home state that Quentin loves, not because of its virtues, but despite its faults and shortcomings.[10]

The narrative clearly and decisively changes gears when chapter six introduces Shreve and Quentin in their room at Harvard. This chapter breaks completely with the narrative pace and tone in the preceding one, which is Miss Rosa's long and winding tale about her life at Sutpen's Hundred after she was fetched there by Wash Jones immediately after Henry's killing of Charles Bon. Readers might even hold that the narrative mode changes so much that the novel is in two parts: five chapters of storytelling by Miss Rosa and Mr. Compson in their own voices, within a framework of commentary, evaluation, interpretation, and speculation by the outside narrator, before all the elements of the Sutpen story later are told, retold, and added to by Quentin and Shreve and by factual knowledge not divulged in the early chapters. But the novel must be seen as a whole and then the differences appear much smaller, as the text deals with the same story material in reiterated attempts to understand. Little by little the reader gets to know what happened but must read the text closely and reflect on which questions the text invites, which questions it permits, and which questions it seems to oppose or to resist. Readers notice how the many versions of the Sutpen story reflect each teller's interest and involvement in it and may be tempted to feel free to create their own versions. Even if this is what all readers do in some manner or other, literary critics have to stick closely to the text and carry out the reflexive reading that this novel in particular undertakes.

The transition from chapter five to chapter six in the book demonstrates the changes in narrative technique and signals a departure from relatively straight storytelling and attempts at reconstruction to construction, guesswork, conjecture, and speculation. The change can be seen at work on many levels. The student friends at the newly established university in Oxford, Mississippi, in the late 1850s, Henry and

Charles have their doubles in Quentin and Shreve at Harvard in 1909. They are some fifty years and a long spatial distance apart, but they are still parallel and, some critics undoubtedly would say, convey the same homoerotic overtones. The setting moves from a room penetrated by the smell of wisteria to a strange room with "a strange lamplit table in Cambridge" with its "strange iron New England snow" (*AA* 141). But on this table, lying on an open textbook, is the letter from Quentin's father, dated Jan 10, 1910. "Attenuated" (one of Faulkner's favorite words) up from Mississippi, the letter carries with it "that dead summer twilight—the wistaria, the cigar-smell, the fireflies" (141). The scene has changed and the narrative register is dramatically different from the earlier chapters, but these aspects must be seen as necessary tools to get a complex story told and, finally, to make it signify.

A final note on the narrative complexities of *Absalom, Absalom!*: Urgo and Polk find in the text "a narrative instability that the reader must tolerate to be able to read the novel with any understanding" (9). They find passages that warn "against looking for and finding a stable narrative voice," and they find that the narrators, who are so obsessed with the Sutpen story, not only regret "the legacy of slavery and racism, but the epistemological legacy which undermines all things stable and renders history unrecoverable" (9). This is a good point, but once again Faulkner attempts the impossible and, by another "splendid failure" in this novel (*Faulkner in the University* 77), gets his story told, if only indecisively and through circumvention. Miss Rosa (no doubt helped by the outside narrator in choice of words, rhythm, and understanding) reflects on memory and her reflections become yet another comment on the text to which she contributes:

That is the substance of remembering—sense, sight, smell: the muscles with which we see and hear and feel—not mind, not thought: there is no such thing as memory: the brain recalls just what the muscles grope for: no more, no less: and its resultant sum is usually incorrect and false and worthy only of the name of dream. (*AA* 115)

Thematic Significance

Absalom, Absalom! is written in a language that oscillates between beautiful, lyrical passages and intensely dramatic episodes in which movement, speed, and violent action are described. In between are long sections of self-conscious narration, often filled with symbols and literary references, in cynical or slightly desperate and hollow words. Since some facts obviously can be established whereas other elements cannot be accounted for or explained, the central narrative voice becomes that of an inquisitive investigator, always asking questions, brooding, wondering, thinking—and so it is in the deep structure of the novel's linguistic and narrative order that "truth" may be sought after, no matter how elusive it is.

Absalom, Absalom! is a novel, a fictional account, a work of art, and as such it offers a profound search for connections, causes, explanations, and motivations for the rise and fall of a family in the South before, during, and after the Civil War. It tells the story of Thomas Sutpen's rise from rags to riches but involves so many other people that it must be seen as the story of a family and, in many ways, as a condensed version of certain aspects of southern history.

As seen already, the author himself always insisted that *Absalom, Absalom!* is the story of Thomas Sutpen and his "design." Faulkner apparently thought of Sutpen as a pitiable human being because he was ruthless and self-centered, not really a member of the human family. In the novel and in many critical discussions of it, Sutpen's innocence has a central place. What does it mean that he was and remained innocent even after all the vicious and outlandish things he did? The question points to Sutpen's conviction that he could get what he wanted if he was strong enough and wanted it enough. He had the courage and the determination and shrewdness he knew was required to realize his grand design, but he did not at all understand his fellow human beings. It is a simplification to think in terms of the American Dream, and it is beyond the mark to think in philosophical terms such as the "will to power" or the like. Sutpen is innocent, and perhaps even amoral, since he cannot see that he ever did anything wrong. Thus, he remains perplexed about why his design failed, backfiring on him, and about what he had done wrong. His innocence probably also gave him courage, first as a boy of fourteen to leave the country to become rich and later as a soldier during the war. Innocence and a limitless belief in his own capacities go hand in hand not only to create out of nothing an enormous mansion on a hundred square miles of land but also to be heedless and commit wrongs to which his innocence blinds him. He built his house and laid the groundwork for a dynasty on sand, doing as other planters but on a bigger scale. He had to lose it all because his empire was built on a system that could not and should not be allowed to last.

Sutpen's design is carried out as a kind of revenge on those whose house he was not allowed to enter by the front door as a young boy. It is not a joke from fate or blind destiny when his downfall also is a result of revenge—that of his son Charles, either because Sutpen has not accepted him fully or because Charles wants to avenge his mother, whom Sutpen had paid off. Miss Rosa and Quentin, who both "regret" much about Sutpen, seem to want revenge in subtler ways. Thus, they try to come to grips with the legacy that he has left them in the twentieth century and that still threatens to ruin their lives.

"Summers of Wistaria" and the Burden of Southern History

With its fragmentary and investigative narrative by characters with numerous preconceived ideas about Sutpen, *Absalom, Absalom!* excels in rumors, gossip, assumptions, and guesses about his life and his grand design. More than just a great plantation, Sutpen's design required recognition and respectability—something that money normally will not buy and something that he never obtained. In Miss Rosa's eyes he was never a gentleman and could never become one. If her story is to be trusted, the respectability he tried to achieve by marrying her much older sister, Ellen, is of no significance. Miss Rosa is probably the least reliable of the many unreliable narrators in the novel, but she contributes with a personal and intimate knowledge of the Sutpen story that none of the other narrators can provide. The attempts at reconstructing the past finally demonstrate how impossible it is to reach exact and trustworthy knowledge, even about one single individual, and as a whole, the novel shows how unreliable memory is, how subjective any narrative of past events tends to become.

There are certain objective facts also about Sutpen's life—facts that are the same in all the versions of his story—birth and marriage and death, events from the Civil War, tombstones marking the beginning and end of life and the grief, true or false, of the bereaved. Even if there may be small discrepancies—even between the novel proper and the added "Genealogy"—these facts are shared by the narrators, but they provide a framework for interpretation and speculation where the facts are of little help. Despite the outside narrator's deliberate withholding of crucial information—what Quentin learned when he and Miss Rosa went out to Sutpen's Hundred in September 1909—Quentin and Shreve have as much of a complete story about Thomas Sutpen as it seems possible to have. So, even if they must resort to conjecture and speculation about what might have happened, this is where the novel comes to a close. Nothing more will be told, but readers should be well equipped to reflect on what they have read and should be aware of who has told them what.

Particular attention should be paid to Miss Rosa's narrative, since what she tells is refuted and even discarded by other narrators, notably by Mr. Compson and Quentin. Shreve, in his turn, mostly jokes about her and the way Quentin has obeyed her wishes. Miss Rosa is in fact one of the most pitiable characters in the novel, and her precarious position, both in relation to the Sutpen story and to the narrative as a whole, deserves closer scrutiny. She remembers a summer of wisteria when she was fourteen, and this summer is repeated and intensified in a new summer when the wisteria vine blossoms for the second time outside the window of her house. One might hold that the smell of wisteria follows the whole narrative and is brought into the "iron cold" New England winter both with the letter to Quentin from his father and, indelibly, in Quentin's memory and troubled existence. Miss Rosa also plays a significant part in the overall structure of the novel. Not only do readers hear her story first, but it is really her initiative that gets the whole story going—the summoning of Quentin first to tell him a story that he already knows most of, but also to join her on a trip to Sutpen's Hundred in order to lay the past to rest by finding the "ghost" living there. In fact, Rosa Coldfield suggests that the story she can tell is material suitable for stories and maybe even a book:

> So maybe you will enter the literary profession as so many Southern gentlemen and gentlewomen too are doing now and maybe some day you will remember this and write about it. . . . Perhaps you will even remember kindly then the old woman who made you spend a whole afternoon sitting indoors and listening while she talked about people and events you were fortunate enough to escape yourself when you wanted to be out among young friends of your own age. (*AA* 5)

Absalom, Absalom! is a difficult book to read, and it offers the reader serious challenges on almost all levels. It is very much a southern novel. By indirection and along byways it depicts a way of life and a social system's destruction almost from within, despite what the Civil War brought about. Nonetheless, the novel also shows admirable qualities in men and women, white and black. Courage, compassion, and endurance in Faulkner's world are qualities so important that less admirable character traits are overlooked. Somehow the South seems impossible to understand, even for Quentin, the young southern gentleman studying at Harvard, who has inherited the burden of southern history and struggles to cope with it as it becomes part and parcel of his personal problems, too. For Shreve McCannon the South is beyond comprehension, but his attempts at understanding are important in order to reconstruct as much as possible of what Quentin knows of the Sutpen story. However, Shreve will never come to understand that there exists something more, beneath or above, racism, slavery, and injustice. The vices of the South are abundantly clear, but the values and strengths escape the Canadian. This is why he, in the final paragraphs of the novel, has a question to ask of his roommate:

> "Now I want you to tell me just one thing more. Why do you hate the South?"

> "I dont hate it," Quentin said, quickly, at once, immediately; "I dont hate it," he said. *I dont hate it* he thought, panting in the cold air, the iron New England dark*: I dont. I dont! I dont hate it! I dont hate it!* (*AA* 303)

Perhaps this novel tells readers that they must get away from the sentimental summers of wisteria to be able to see what happened in the South in a clearer light and with a new perspective. It also indicates, however, that it will always be difficult for someone who is not deeply rooted in the soil and traditions of the South ever to understand what happened there and, as in the case with Thomas Sutpen's rise and fall, seems to have happened with tragic and inevitable necessity.

Absalom, Absalom! demonstrates fully the old saying that it takes a lot of history to create a little fiction. The book narrates a tragic story about Thomas Sutpen and his, and a whole region's, legacy of injustice, inequality, slavery and an understanding of race and class that proves wholly destructive. To Quentin Compson, history is what hurts, and the burden of southern history has never been given better fictional representation than in this novel.

Notes

1. All references to the novel come from *Absalom, Absalom!: The Corrected Text* (1986), and the book's title is abbreviated "AA" for in-text citations.
2. Rosa Coldfield talks about "the raging and incredulous recounting" in the novel itself (*AA* 130).

3. I discuss the validity of McHale's arguments in "The Function of Metafictional Elements in William Faulkner's Fiction" in *Faulkner and Other Southern Writers* (41–48).
4. For a useful introduction to the study of "unnatural narration" see Richardson. "Unnatural narration" in general refers to postmodern experimental narratives, in particular those narrated in ways that break completely with conventions or traditions of the novel. In many ways it is similar to theories of metafiction but takes them many steps further, insisting that structuralist narratology does not account for everything found in avant-garde fictions.
5. This is the subject of a well-written article by Thadious M. Davis, included in Hobson. "Blackness" is central in many of Faulkner's novels but is of little or no significance in at least half of them.
6. The most helpful casebook on this novel is Hobson's.
7. Discussed at some length in *Faulkner and Other Southern Writers* 44–45.
8. For an early but still valid and valuable discussion of *Absalom, Absalom!* in relation to the tragic experience, see Cleanth Brooks.
9. Millgate comments on some of the gothic elements in the novel, comparing it with *Jane Eyre* and *The House of the Seven Gables* (162–64).
10. This corresponds to Faulkner's conclusion of "Mississippi," his fictional essay about his home state: "you dont love because: you love despite; not for the virtues, but despite the faults" (*Essays* 43).

Works Cited

Brooks, Cleanth. "History and the Sense of the Tragic." *William Faulkner: The Yoknapatawpha Country*. New Haven: Yale UP, 1963. Rpt. in Hobson 17–46. Print.

Brooks, Peter. "Incredulous Narration: *Absalom, Absalom!*" *Reading for the Plot: Design and Intention in Narrative*. New York: Random, 1984. 286–312. Print.

Davis, Thadious M. "The Signifying Abstraction: Reading 'the Negro' in *Absalom, Absalom!*" Hobson 69–106. Print.

Faulkner, William. *Absalom, Absalom!: The Corrected Text*. New York: Random, 1986. Print.

___. *Essays, Speeches, and Public Letters*. Ed. James B. Meriwether. New York: Random, 1965. Print.

___. *Faulkner in the University: Class Conferences at the University of Virginia, 1957–1958*. Ed. Frederick L. Gwynn and Joseph Blotner. Charlottesville: UP of Virginia, 1959. Print.

Hobson, Fred, ed. *William Faulkner's Absalom, Absalom!: A Casebook*. New York: Oxford UP, 2003. Print.

McHale, Brian. *Postmodernist Fiction*. New York: Methuen, 1987. Print.

Millgate, Michael. *The Achievement of William Faulkner*. New York: Vintage, 1971. Print.

Richardson, Brian. *Unnatural Voices: Extreme Narration in Modern and Contemporary Fiction.* Columbus: Ohio State UP, 2006. Print.

Skei, Hans H. *Faulkner and Other Southern Writers: Literary Essays*. Oslo: Novus, 2004. Print.

Urgo, Joseph R., and Noel Polk, eds. *Reading Faulkner:* Absalom, Absalom!*, Glossary and Commentary*. Jackson: UP of Mississippi, 2010. Print.

Faulkner and Film: The 1950s Melodramas_____

D. Matthew Ramsey

Back in the early 1980s as an eager undergraduate English major interested in the works of William Shakespeare, I often found myself defending the practice, and the value, of analyzing and discussing films based on Shakespeare's plays to my skeptical peers and some wary literature professors. After all, as I had come to understand it, every performance of Shakespeare was an *interpretation*, each performance of a play (including a filmed version) offered many different interpretations, and this multiplicity was an important part of the beauty and timelessness of Shakespeare. I was fascinated by Roman Polanski's brutal *Macbeth* (1971); Laurence Olivier's Freudian *Hamlet* (1948) and his colorful, "meta" and patriotic *Henry V* (1944); and Franco Zeffirelli's sensitive, lyrical *Romeo and Juliet* (1968)—all the while recognizing how each altered, added, or eliminated elements of Shakespeare's originals. Also, I believed that some of my fellow students and professors were being overly conservative. Did they not realize there is no agreement about the "authentic" versions of Shakespeare's plays? Had these people not heard of the "death of the author"? Or Stephen Greenblatt, New Historicism, and the emphasis on context instead of originating "genius"? Because of my love for film and what I was learning in certain classrooms, I was less prone than some to privilege the written word over the cinematic text, a combination that gave rise to what became the principle fascination of my academic life: the richness of the relationship between literature and film.

My high-minded ideals were soon tested, however, when I started graduate school and was drawn to the study of another canonical author, William Faulkner. It took me a long time to figure out that I could pursue my interests in Faulkner and film simultaneously. My initial exploration of the overlap was less than promising. The only films I had seen connected to Faulkner were a couple of those he helped Howard Hawks write while working in Hollywood: *To Have and Have Not*

(1944) and *The Big Sleep* (1946). Faulkner criticism at that time was of little help. The only sustained academic works on Faulkner and adaptation were Bruce F. Kawin's *Faulkner and Film* (1977) and Gene D. Phillips's *Fiction, Film, and Faulkner* (1988), and most of the films they discussed were not available on VHS. (Some of the films remain unavailable on DVD.[1]) What little criticism there was on adaptations of Faulkner's works was often dismissive of film versions of Faulkner's novels and short stories, particularly the canonical ones.

When I finally managed to catch a late-night showing of Martin Ritt's 1959 color, CinemaScope version of *The Sound and the Fury*, all of my prior open-mindedness about film versions *interpreting* a literary text went out the window. I *hated* it. I saw no value in the film and could not imagine suggesting we watch the film in the Faulkner seminar I was then taking. I cannot blame this reaction entirely on Kawin and Phillips, though they did not help matters any. Kawin, a film scholar by training, was one of the first critics to make note of the cinematic elements of Faulkner's literary output, and to suggest that film was fully capable of capturing the "spirit" of Faulkner's work. His assessment of the Jerry Wald–produced *The Sound and the Fury* holds the film accountable for falling short of that potential:

> It is one thing to feel, like Hawks, that a film ought to tell a story clearly and in chronological order, and another to have the talent to do that job well. In the case of Jerry Wald, such conservatism could become obnoxious (as well as pretentious and low-brow) when coupled with what was at times an extraordinary lack of artistic *and* commercial intelligence. . . . The husband-and-wife team of Irving Ravetch and Harriet Frank, Jr. [the screenwriters]—apparently had some kind of respect for Faulkner's work. . . . But they shared with Wald his initial assumption that the only part of *The Sound and the Fury* that *could* be brought or was worth bringing to the screen was its plot. And they did a poor job in even that department. (21)

Phillips is a bit more understated and measured, but it is clear that he also regarded the film as insufficient: "Though some film reviewers found the positive outcome of the film [its happy ending] touching, it is no match for the Faulkner original" (161). Other than some tepid newspaper reviews, this was about all of the critical work on the film then available. No one was writing about it from a film-studies perspective—it was several years more before people began to see director Martin Ritt as worthy of sustained analysis. *The Sound and the Fury* was essentially a film lost to both Faulkner criticism and to film criticism.

At age twenty-five I lamented, much like Kawin, the failure of artistic ambition to try to replicate or to approximate the intricate narrative structure, psychological complexity, and fragmentation found in Faulkner's 1929 modernist masterpiece. My training in literary narrative theory and modernism made such an oversight seem fatal. Point-of-view, focalization, unreliable narration, mythical and literary allusions—all felt inadequately addressed. Despite my interest in film, the "commercial" versus "artistic" chasm seemed unbridgeable when it came to the adaptation of *The Sound and the Fury*. As Martin Halliwell notes, "William Faulkner offers a classic illustration of the stand-off between the US film industry and literary modernism," in large part because Faulkner's more experimental works are seemingly incompatible with "the dominant tenets of classical Hollywood film—seamless worlds, linear narratives, a stable hierarchy of characters, humanist ideology, and tidy resolutions" (91).

Lacking much knowledge of classical Hollywood cinema and studio-era history, particularly of the 1950s, I also had relatively little knowledge of stars Joanne Woodward, Margaret Leighton, and Ethel Waters. I knew Yul Brynner as Pharaoh Rameses, a gunfighter in black, or the king of Siam, characters that did not seem compatible with Jason Compson. My favorite character from the novel, Quentin, was missing, and his "equivalent"—an alcoholic, middle-aged Uncle Howard (played by John Beal)—was for a young viewer no substitute for the novel's tortured, suicidal college student. Finally, the machinations necessary to provide a "satisfying" resolution by suggesting a future romantic relationship between the film's Quentin (Woodward, playing Caddy's daughter) and Jason (who in the film is not related to Quentin by blood) seemed ludicrous. Just as my attitude toward Shakespeare adaptations reflected the dual training I received as an undergraduate (with a literature major and a film studies minor), my graduate school training in Faulkner criticism and narrative theory shaped my somewhat cynical, skeptical response to film adaptations of Faulkner's works. It was not until I started intensive film work focused on cultural studies and adaptation studies that I began to see value in putting the literary and filmic Faulkner in dialogue.

Nearly thirty years after my undergraduate experiences, I have noticed that the vast majority of students in my university courses have no idea who Faulkner even is, or why they should be studying him. Sometimes, a description of "A Rose for Emily" will ring a bell, and maybe one or two will have read one of the other oft-anthologized short stories, such as "Barn Burning," "Dry September," or "Spotted Horses." If my students have had experience with a Faulkner novel, it is typically one they found particularly inaccessible—usually *As I Lay Dying* (1930) or *The Sound and the Fury* (1929). This experience ensured no further exploration would occur. I have long thought that the initial challenge when it comes to teaching Faulkner is to give students a point of entry, a context that allows them to see the accessibility of a notoriously difficult author. That notoriety offered a starting point for me that I can no longer take for granted.

The momentary blip of Oprah Winfrey's 2005 "Summer of Faulkner" aside, in the early years of the twenty-first century, Faulkner's work has rarely made it into the mainstream of American culture. An attitude of fear, and perhaps avoidance, toward Faulkner's texts remains. As high school and college teachers clamor to show the latest Hollywoodizations of Jane Austen and Shakespeare—and even other "tough" authors such as Henry James and fellow modernists Virginia Woolf and F. Scott Fitzgerald—in order to get their students to "engage," few educators seem interested in doing the same for Faulkner. The possible reasons for this are numerous: canonical dead white male; southerner; conflicted attitudes toward race, gender, and sexuality; and expanding curricula that is less "elitist" about including popular culture in the classroom. The assumption there is that Faulkner has had little to do with popular culture, and is squarely located in the "Literature" with a capital "L" camp. As such, his works have often been crowded out of the pedagogical marketplace by more contemporary, "accessible," or multicultural alternatives. Yet such logic ignores Faulkner's own engagement with popular-culture forms, and the beauty and complexity of his literary and film output—factors that make him particularly worth teaching in the current climate.

Developments on the media horizon may offer exciting new opportunities for popular engagement with Faulkner's works. In November of 2011, a deal between HBO, the William Faulkner Literary Estate, and *Deadwood* and *NYPD Blue* showrunner David Milch was announced, an arrangement that includes the television rights to nineteen Faulkner novels and 125 short stories.[2] Less than a year later, in August of 2012, it was announced that James Franco would be producing and directing, on location in Mississippi, a Hollywood adaptation of William Faulkner's 1930 novel *As I Lay Dying*.

The prospect of a new intersection of Faulkner and popular culture can beckon us to explore other facets of a career that was rich in such intersections. Faulkner worked as a screenwriter in Hollywood intermittently throughout the 1930s, 1940s, and early 1950s, his career in film fading just as his literary reputation was being cemented. His last screen credit was on the Howard Hawks epic *Land of the Pharaohs* (1955), which disappointed at the box office; he won the Nobel Prize for Literature in 1949 and Pulitzer Prizes for *A Fable* in 1954 and *The Reivers* in 1962.

Thus, for a period of the 1950s, Faulkner was arguably the hot Hollywood film and television property (perhaps rivaled only by Tennessee Williams), not as a screenwriter, but as a source of material to be adapted. Despite his lionization as a literary great, during the 1950s, Faulkner was arguably most familiar to the general public through the Hollywood and television adaptations being made of his novels and short stories. Several weekly television drama series, including *Lux Video Theatre*, *Camera Three*, *Playwrights '56*, and *Climax!*, regularly aired hour-long programs ("telefilms") based on literary works. According to Internet Movie Database, television programs based on Faulkner properties that aired between 1952 and 1956 as part of these series included adaptations of "Honor," "Smoke," "Barn Burning," "An Error in Chemistry," "Knight's Gambit," *The Sound and the Fury*, *As I Lay Dying*, "The Brooch," and "Shall Not Perish." (Like so many programs from the early years of television, these are nearly all lost.)

In addition to Faulkner's television presence, during the late 1950s, three major studio Hollywood adaptations of Faulkner works were released in quick succession—*The Tarnished Angels* (1957), *The Long, Hot Summer* (1958), and the previously mentioned *The Sound and the Fury* (1959). The reputation of all three films is mixed, particularly as far as Faulkner scholars, film scholars, and more casual fans are concerned. Yet later discussions of adaptation, authorship, and intertextuality can help to illuminate the value of putting these adaptations in conversation with each other and with their literary source texts—respectively: *Pylon* (1935); *The Hamlet* (1940), "Barn Burning" (1939) and "Spotted Horses" (1931); and *The Sound and the Fury* (1929). Thinking through cinematic equivalents to literary techniques can help students come to a greater understanding of the literature as well as the challenges and opportunities offered by commercial film. This essay focuses on a few of these Hollywood adaptations as demonstrative of the value of studying Faulkner's literature through film, focusing on the 1950s rather than later releases, such as the 1997 Hallmark Hall of Fame version of *Old Man* and the 1985 two-part NBC version of *The Long Hot Summer*.[3]

As early as 1961, there was within Faulkner criticism a somewhat belated attempt to take Faulkner's film career seriously, but it rested on the argument, subsequently much-discussed, of what the author gained and/or lost during his time writing screenplays in Hollywood.[4] Much less attention has been paid to the Hollywood films based on Faulkner's works that he had no substantive part in. More than any other author, adaptations (or proposed adaptations) of Faulkner's works have been met with intense skepticism, usually based on three factors. The first factor is the general failure of most adaptations to remain "faithful" to the original. The second factor is the difficulty of adapting Faulkner's complicated language to film. In a typical example, one respondent to Anthony Taormina's *Screen Rant* blog entry announcing Franco's plan to take on *As I Lay Dying* comments: "I love Faulkner's novels and *As I Lay Dying* in particular, but frankly I don't see how it is shot as a movie that modern audiences will appreciate without massive changes. The subtlety of Faulkner's writing has always presented enormous challenges to anyone contemplating adapting it for the screen or stage." The third factor: "Why do it?" James Poniewozik for Time magazine wrote: "I'm not exactly sure that Faulkner's stories—dependent as they are on the language on the page to create their worlds—need to be translated for the screen."

Franco for one has been aware of these issues, in particular the implied anxiety about remaining "faithful" to Faulkner's original vision. In a *Los Angeles Times* article by Carolyn Kellogg on *As I Lay Dying*, he is quoted as saying: "'I want to be loyal to the book—my approach is to always be loyal in a lot of ways—but in order to be loyal I will have to change some things for the movie. . . . You want to capture the tone, but you can't work in exactly the same way. . . . Movies just work differently than books.'" Franco knows that Faulkner devotees will be very sensitive to "fidelity" to the source text. Films based on Faulkner's works are particularly prone to attack from an overly formalistic, fidelity-model brand of adaptation studies. Students and educators should seek to complicate such approaches, to suggest that the anxieties surrounding film adaptations of Faulkner's works are misplaced, and to argue that putting film and novel/story in dialogue can reap great benefits.

The fidelity model, which has dominated discussion of Hollywood adaptations of literature in particular, operates on the assumption that adaptation runs only one way—from source text (literature) to screenplay to movie—and measures success solely on how close the film hews to the "essence" of the original. Typically, in this conception of adaptation each subsequent version is viewed as moving further from the "authentic" text and is thus devalued. Because of Faulkner's canonical status and his literary reputation, this condemnation of works adapted from his writing is widespread, even though Faulkner wrote for the movies on and off for three decades; wrote for several mainstream, middlebrow magazines (including the *Saturday Evening Post* and *Scribner's*); and at least one novel, *Sanctuary* (1932), was considered particularly lurid and sensationalist when it was published.

There are several "Faulkners" that can be investigated—modernist with poetic aspirations, southerner, regionalist, screenwriter, short-story writer, novelist, troubled alcoholic, and hack interested in making money. In the main, Faulkner criticism has chosen a select few of these identities and has ignored the rest. Until the twenty-first century, this was particularly true of Faulkner the screenwriter, and the film adaptations based on his works have rarely been studied or taught. The ever-diminishing gap between high and low culture in academic discourse and curricula necessitates a dialogue between literature and film (and not just replacing one with the other). The Faulkner I want to put forward is not a static and unchanging one, or even "one" for that matter. Popular culture is characterized by the process of re-consumption—it keeps changing, keeps re-imagining itself. This is how I encourage students to approach the study of any text. Faulkner's reputation as a difficult, complex, sometimes inaccessible modernist is well-earned. This is precisely why Faulkner should be taught—the difficulties offered by Faulkner's works, as well as his engagement with questions of race, gender, and class. His works also offer a rich testing ground for reductive approaches to the questions raised by literature-to-film adaptations.

Although there has been, particularly in the twenty-first century decade, an increasing interest in film and popular culture within Faulkner studies, many of the concepts that can be taken from adaptation studies have yet to be fully considered.[5] In "Beyond Fidelity: The Dialogics of Adaptation," Robert Stam speaks to the analytic limitations of expecting a film adaptation to "match" or remain "faithful" to its literary source; for students just coming to adaptation and film studies, these are important issues to raise. First, the disappointment (or outrage) viewers often feel:

> The notion of fidelity gains its persuasive force from our sense that some adaptations fail to "realize" or substantiate that which we most appreciated in the source novels. Words such as *infidelity* or *betrayal* in this sense translate our feeling, when we have loved a book, that an adaptation has not been worthy of that love. We read a novel through our introjected desires, hopes, and utopias, and as we read we fashion our own imaginary mise-en-scène of the novel on the private stages of our minds. (54)

Mise-en-scène, a French term that translates into English as literally "putting on stage," is generally used in film studies to indicate what appears in front of the camera—acting, props, costumes, lighting, set design, blocking, etc. What Stam is referring to is how viewers use their imaginations to "picture" moments in the novel, and the unavoidable disappointment felt when a film version does it differently. Stam points out that even if strict fidelity to the source text were desirable (a point this essay will return to), it is questionable that it is even possible:

> The words of a novel, as countless commentators have pointed out, have a virtual, symbolic meaning; we as readers, or as directors, have to fill in their paradigmatic indeterminances. A novelist's portrayal of a character as "beautiful" induces us to imagine the person's features in our minds. Flaubert never even tells us the exact color of Emma Bovary's eyes, but we color them nonetheless. A film, by contrast, must choose a specific

performer. Instead of a virtual, verbally constructed Madame Bovary open to our imaginative reconstruction, we are faced with a specific actress, encumbered with nationality and accent, a Jennifer Jones or an Isabelle Huppert. (55)

Stam calls this relationship between literature and film "automatic difference," and suggests that even if filmmakers set out to create a straightforward, "faithful" adaptation of even a single scene, the realities of film (visual, multitrack, including sound and music) make the issue of fidelity to a single track medium (literature) illusory. No matter how descriptive an author may be, the reader's imagination can never find a perfect match in the realities presented to the viewer.

Most viewers, of course, rarely attend to such minutiae (unless, perhaps, they think a character has been badly miscast—the Russian Brynner, with a wig, cast as southerner Jason Compson in *The Sound and the Fury*, for example). When people speak of a "faithful adaptation," what they typically mean is that to their minds, the plot and themes remain the same, allowing for unavoidable compression or deletion of some material. For the most part, for example, it appears most fans of Suzanne Collins's novel *The Hunger Games* (2008) were content when the 2012 film version was released, satisfied with its faithfulness to the original. Stam, however, questions such assessments, noting that such analyses are essentialist: "It [the notion of fidelity] assumes that a novel 'contains' an extractable 'essence,' a kind of 'heart of the artichoke' hidden 'underneath' the surface details of style. . . . A single novelistic text comprises a series of verbal signals that can generate a plethora of possible readings" (57).

The most important takeaway from Stam and adaptation theorists like him is that literary and film texts cannot be compared in a "faithful or not" way because they are ever-changing, since readers do not exist in a vacuum. Contexts change, and thus how one reads texts is never fully determined simply by what the words say, or what is seen on the screen. What I did not realize when I felt that initial disappointment upon watching *The Sound and the Fury* was that my reaction was complicated by being a better reader of novels than I was of film. I had been trained to understand a modernist novel, and because I wanted the film to replicate what I thought I knew of Faulkner's work, I failed to engage with the film as a film, a provocative and productive interaction between the source material and the genre it was being translated into. At that stage in my life I had little to no appreciation or understanding of the Hollywood melodrama, particularly the "family melodrama," and the ways that subgenre arguably rivals Faulkner's works in providing a complex examination of American society and culture. Despite the seeming "un-Faulkner-like" naïveté, exaggerated emotional content, and predictable happy endings of the melodrama, it is no accident that the decade that featured the most Hollywood Faulkner adaptations was the 1950s.

At first, one might be hard-pressed to see direct thematic or formal connections to Faulkner's preoccupations in Thomas Schatz's description of the basic Hollywood melodrama, popular in the earliest days of the cinema: "Generally speaking, 'melodrama' was applied to popular romances that depicted a virtuous individual (usually a woman) or couple (usually lovers) victimized by repressive and inequitable social circumstances, particularly those involving marriage, occupation, and the nuclear family" (*Hollywood Genres* 222). On the surface these films often appear to confirm the value of the patriarchal, traditional family structure, and have often been dismissed as "women's pictures" and "weepies." But it was in the mid-to-late 1950s, Schatz argues, that the "family melodrama," which came to dominate America's movie screens, evolved to present—to a largely unsuspecting public—subtle, complex critiques of American life:

> Because of a variety of industry-based factors, as well as external cultural phenomena, the melodrama reached its equilibrium at the same time that certain filmmakers were beginning to subvert and counter the superficial prosocial thematics and clichéd romantic narratives that had previously

identified the genre. No other genre films, not even the "anti-Westerns" of the same period, projected so complex and paradoxical a view of America, at once celebrating and severely questioning the basic values and attitudes of the mass audience. (223)

These films include classics such as *Magnificent Obsession* (directed by Douglas Sirk, 1954), *East of Eden* (Elia Kazan, 1955), *Rebel without a Cause* (Nicholas Ray, 1955), *Picnic* (Joshua Logan, 1956), *All That Heaven Allows* (Sirk, 1956), *Giant* (George Stevens, 1956), *Tea and Sympathy* (Vincente Minnelli, 1956), *Written on the Wind* (Sirk, 1957), *Peyton Place* (Mark Robson, 1957), *Imitation of Life* (Sirk, 1959), *Some Came Running* (Minnelli, 1959), and *Home from the Hill* (Minnelli, 1960). By the early 1960s, Schatz argues, it was over: "the melodrama had been co-opted by commercial television" (224),[6] and perhaps not coincidentally, the heyday of Faulkner adaptations was at an end.

The 1950s also brought to American screens the most sustained cinematic exploration of the American South in film history, and the majority of these films are family melodramas. They include *A Streetcar Named Desire* (1951), *Baby Doll* (1956), *Raintree County* (1957), *God's Little Acre* (1958), and *Cat on a Hot Tin Roof* (1958). Schatz argues that the family melodrama, particularly the subset he calls "the family aristocracy variation," finds a natural fit in the South and its continued reliance on the dream of the landed gentry:

These melodramas trace the behavioral and attitudinal traits of succeeding generations. The dramatic conflict is based on a contradictory view of marriage: it is a means of liberation from unreasonable familial demands and also the only way of perpetuating the family aristocracy. . . . The constellation of characters in this variation revolves around an aging patriarch (sometimes close to death), whose wife is either dead or else functions only as a peripheral character who has produced inadequate male heirs and sexually frustrated daughters. (*Hollywood Genres* 235–237)

Two of the three 1950s Faulkner-inspired Hollywood melodramas fit squarely into this "family aristocracy" category: the rise of the Varners in *The Long, Hot Summer* and the fall of the Compsons in *The Sound and the Fury* are "ideological givens" tied to "the socioeconomic climate that is around them" (236). Anxieties about lineage and family obligation abound. In each, the character most clearly faced with these questions of love, marriage, and continuing the family line is played by Woodward—Clara Varner in *The Long, Hot Summer* and Quentin Compson in *The Sound and the Fury*. The viewer's ability to see this connection, among many between the two films (made one year apart), should not be surprising: in addition to Woodward, they share the same studio, producer, director, screenwriters, composer, art directors, costume designer, makeup team, and sound team. A comparison of these films, and the critical reaction to them, opens up further questions about different expectations due to the source materials.

It is clear that the canonical status of the novel *The Sound and the Fury* and its reputation as one of the key texts of American modernism are part of the continued critical backlash or dismissal of Ritt's *The Sound and the Fury*, which continues to suffer almost hyperbolic censure: "While doing pre-production for *The Sound and the Fury*, Ritt said, 'We've now made it a conventional story but preserved the basic quality.' Unfortunately, Ritt, the Ravetches, and producer Wald did not apparently understand what this 'basic quality' is, for their adaptation of Faulkner's masterpiece is one of the most ineffective movies based on a serious literary work" (Adams 145–46). However, when compared to other family melodramas from the 1950s, it certainly does not seem nearly as egregious or as "hopeless" as this criticism suggests. Nor, for that matter, does *The Long, Hot Summer* seem far superior to it. Perhaps, as Phillips argues, part of the reason *The Long, Hot Summer* is considered the superior film (or is at least not as derided as *The Sound and the Fury*) may be down to the less ambitious formal nature of its source texts:

Oddly enough, it was probably the novel's episodic narrative structure, which literary critics had decried when it came out, that made *The Hamlet* easily adapted for film. Several incidents in the novel, some of which had been published separately as short stories before their inclusion in *The Hamlet*, constitute self-contained units. The screenwriters therefore were able to simply pick the episodes they judged noteworthy and drop the rest. (136)

It is not simply *The Hamlet*'s episodic narrative structure that explains *The Long, Hot Summer*'s relatively good reputation. Many critics, and readers, consider the novel less challenging, more "folksy," and more humorous than Faulkner's more modernist, experimental works. Researching the production of these films also suggests that *The Long, Hot Summer* is to some a more satisfying film because it was shot on location in Louisiana, while *The Sound and the Fury* was shot in Hollywood as a cost-saving measure. Adding to *The Long, Hot Summer*'s appeal is without doubt the relationship between stars Paul Newman and Woodward, who were married immediately after production wrapped. Not only is their chemistry onscreen fairly palpable, but the publicity and gossip surrounding the production had an effect on audience response. *The Sound and the Fury*, with only an ambiguous hint of a burgeoning relationship between Brynner's Jason and Woodward's Quentin, does not offer the same pleasures.

Attention to these "extratextual" matters—publicity, marketing, gossip, and the Hollywood studio system (producer-driven, genre-focused, based on contract workers working within studios), can help students better understand the pressures and opportunities of turning a literary property into a Hollywood film. Genre and audience expectations; the star system; and the Production Code, which dictated what could and could not be included in a film's script, are all relevant factors not just for understanding film, but for turning viewers back to Faulkner's literary output. What equivalents might there be for the family melodrama in fiction? What, if any, overlap was there between audiences who were seeking the pleasures offered by the melodrama and those who sought something from Faulkner's works? If one of the conventions of the family melodrama is the "happy ending" (albeit sometimes ambiguous, even "false" happy endings), how do adaptations provide endings far different from those offered by Faulkner? How can this be compared to Faulkner's fiction, prone as it is to return to stories and characters, and which was working under no such obligations to provide happy endings?

The outlier is arguably *The Tarnished Angels*, the first 1950s melodrama based on a Faulkner work, but one which does not fit the family melodrama formula. As such, this critically respected film provides an example of how attending to Faulkner adaptations can open up both literature and film in ways that might prove difficult, or impossible, through any other lens. As noted, the family melodrama has become an important focus in film studies, largely because of the ways it both reaffirms and critiques traditional notions of marriage, the home, family, and gender roles within 1950s society. Despite this interest, and the critical consensus that the questioning and/or subversion of traditional values and beliefs was also of interest to Faulkner, there has been little critical work done on either *The Long, Hot Summer* or *The Sound and the Fury*. This is not true of *The Tarnished Angels*, but almost all of the critical work has come from film studies. The easy answer for the film's much greater critical reputation is its director, Sirk, who became a darling for auteur critics starting in the 1970s.

The Long, Hot Summer and *The Sound and the Fury*, despite all of the changes made from literature to film, still feel somewhat "Faulknerian" in their southern setting, retention of recognizable plot points, and interest in family dynamics. *The Tarnished Angels* seems less connected to Faulkner unless one digs a bit deeper into his reputation at the time. Despite the respectability that comes with a Nobel Prize, during the 1950s, Faulkner was still considered somewhat "daring" and "shocking" in his explorations of the darker side of human existence. It is not terribly surprising, then, that studios might be eager to cash in on Faulkner's name recognition and this surge in interest in the South. The first of the Faulkner adaptations since the serious, racially charged "message picture" *Intruder in the Dust* (1949) was *The Tarnished Angels*. German émigré director Sirk reportedly admired Faulkner's 1936 novel *Pylon* and had wanted to adapt it in the 1930s while working at UFA, Germany's prestige film studio (Halliday 170), but did not receive his opportunity until the 1950s. An understanding of the restrictions and opportunities that come with directing a studio-era Hollywood film based on a slightly controversial, relatively unpopular novel from a major literary figure not only complicates the standard "the book was better" assumptions, but also gives insight into a Faulkner whom students might find approachable.

The film's solid reputation is largely because Sirk was the director, but the reason the film was made in the first place was producer Albert Zugsmith, who brought the idea to Universal-International and helped negotiate the $50,000 deal Faulkner received for the rights to *Pylon*.[7] Zugsmith, generally known as a producer of low-budget exploitation films, is more accurately described by Schatz as "the most flexible and least genre-bound of Universal's unit producers," responsible for science-fiction, film noir, and melodrama masterpieces (*Genius* 469).[8] The novel was of interest to Zugsmith not just because of Faulkner's modernist reputation—equally important was the "exploitative" nature of the source text, along with its scandalous reputation.

The recurring copy on the advertising materials for the film, including posters and lobby cards, proclaims in bold letters "The Book They Said Could Never Be Filmed," and "The Boldest Author of Our Time," which does double duty. It refers to both the perceived difficulty of the novelist's style as well as the novel's "saucy" content (which includes a ménage à trios situation, a sex scene in the cockpit of an airplane, and frequent instances of obscene language). For students first coming to Faulkner, this scandalous (and popular) reputation is worth knowing. The situation for Universal in the 1950s is also relevant. Unlike the modern film industry, during the Hollywood studio era (roughly the 1920s through the 1960s) each studio had its own distinctive style, look, stable of actors and directors, and emphasis on specific genres. Unlike many of its peers, the somewhat weak Universal was throughout the late 1940s and 1950s preparing for the coming dominance of television, creating "a dual agenda of low-cost formula pictures and A-class productions via outside independents" (Schatz, *Genius* 463). The studio that distributed the Academy Award–winning version of *Hamlet* (1948) made most of its money from Abbott and Costello vehicles. This A-list/exploitation duality is one that perfectly fits so many Faulkner texts.

As the above list of southern films suggests, Universal was not particularly interested in the southern film per se, and like *A Streetcar Named Desire*, also set in New Orleans, *The Tarnished Angels* feels much less "southern" than the two adaptations to follow. What Universal was interested in was finding a way to cash in on audience recognition very much separated from Faulkner. According to Phillips, Zugsmith was able to convince Universal to make the film only by bringing together again the key players from the successful 1956 family melodrama *Written on the Wind*—director Sirk, screenwriter Zuckerman, and actors Robert Stack, Rock Hudson, and Dorothy Malone (122). However, as suggested earlier, *The Tarnished Angels* does not quite fit the family melodrama genre, as *Written on the Wind* does, and the social critique Sirk had in mind is quite specific to Faulkner's original novel. Whereas Sirk's melodramas are usually discussed in terms of his examination of social conflict and the contradictions of middle-class American life, *The Tarnished Angels* offers an interesting variant on the melodrama—an emphasis on consumerism and the threat of the crowd that likely had its roots in antifascism, but which shifted to suit the needs of 1950s culture.

One might not automatically associate the Hollywood melodrama with the "Literature" produced by William Faulkner, but as many critics have noted, there are in almost all of Faulkner's corpus melodramatic elements.[9] *Pylon* was published after the more highly regarded

Light in August (1932), and it is one of the few Faulkner novels not set in his fictional Yoknapatawpha County. Faulkner wrote *Pylon* while taking a break from a novel very much about a declining family aristocracy—*Absalom, Absalom!* (1936). *Pylon* takes place in his fictionalized version of New Orleans, New Valois, and revolves around an unnamed newspaper reporter and his encounter with a very unusual "family" connected to a visiting air show. This novel was not particularly popular upon release, has been rarely taught, and has received relatively little critical attention. This could in part be because of its non-Yoknapatawpha setting; its somewhat threadbare, at times lurid plot; or its relative lack of interest in questions of race.

Some critics, however, seem to find the novel lacking because of its perceived melodramatic characteristics, and within Faulkner studies, melodrama has traditionally been ignored or castigated, often because of a conflation of melodrama and "sentimentality" within literary studies. Phillips claims that it "rarely rises about the level of routine melodrama" (120). Lurie argues that, despite including one section titled "Lovesong of J. A. Prufrock," it is not quite modernist *enough*: "Set almost completely in unified space . . . and following a series of events that take place over a circumscribed period of time, *Pylon* makes use of few of the narrative and temporal ruptures that characterize high-modernist experimentation" (16). Edmund Wilson provides a good early example of the attempt to "rescue" Faulkner from the "stain" of melodrama: "The truth is that, from *Pylon*, at any rate, one of the most striking features of his work, and one that sets if off from that of many of his contemporaries, has been a kind of romantic morality that allows you the thrills of melodrama without making you ashamed, as a rule, of the values which have been exploited to produce them" (347–48).

The novel's perceived lack of artistic ambition may in part explain the film adaptation's relatively good reputation, but is that why Sirk might have been drawn to it in the 1930s while working in Germany? Michael Zeitlin's work on *Pylon* suggests an alternative—the novel's "antifascist, analytical power" (97). Zeitlin discusses the specific

1930s anxieties about fascism, both abroad and at home (particularly in the South). His reading of the novel opens up *The Tarnished Angels* to several promising questions, and may indeed make *Pylon* a more interesting text for students. Does the overtly political nature of the novel explain why *The Tarnished Angels* does not quite fit with Sirk's other melodramas? Does this help to explain why *The Tarnished Angels* was Sirk's personal favorite of his films? How are antifascist elements in the novel connected to the film's melodramatic elements? How does Sirk transform the political elements of the source text into a critique of advertising and consumer society? How does the attempt by Faulkner critics to "rescue" him from commercial impulses relate to the way Sirk critics reject the value of melodrama per se in favor of what they perceive as Sirk's subversion of the genre?[10] Future work on the relationship between Faulkner and these 1950s films should take seriously the subversive potentials *and* the pleasures of melodrama in source text and adaptation.

The field of Faulkner studies has come to embrace the importance of intertextuality as a way of thinking about the interrelatedness of texts, highlighting medium, means of production, dissemination, genre, and the mixing of high and low and visual and literary culture. This sort of approach is particularly appropriate for studying Faulkner. Analyzing film and literature in dialogue allows us to lessen the burden of having to approach Faulkner only as literary icon and "Great American Modernist," and it lets students, who at times feel more comfortable talking about visual culture, able to make Faulkner more relevant to their own lives—and more intellectually stimulating in the bargain.

Notes

1. The following Faulkner-related feature-length films (either films for which he earned screenwriting credit or films based on his works) may be difficult to find on DVD or VHS: *The Story of Temple Drake* (1933), *The Road to Glory* (1936), and *Sanctuary* (1961). The following are available on DVD: *Today We Live* (1933); *Slave Ship* (1937); *To Have and Have Not* (1944); *The Big Sleep* (1946);

Intruder in the Dust (1949); *Land of the Pharaohs* (1955); *The Tarnished Angels* (1957); *The Long, Hot Summer* (1958); *The Sound and the Fury* (1959); *The Reivers* (1969); and *Tomorrow* (1972).

2. David Milch, as an English major at Yale University and as a graduate student at the Iowa Writers' Workshop at the University of Iowa, worked with such Faulkner scholars and admirers as Robert Penn Warren, Cleanth Brooks, and R. W. B. Lewis. Milch's daughter Olivia, who also studied Faulkner at Yale, signed on as coordinating producer. See David Itzkoff. "David Milch Strikes Deal to Bring Faulkner Works to HBO." *New York Times* (30 Nov. 2011).

3. First telecast on October 6 and October 7, 1985, this four-hour version complicates the conventional wisdom that more is usually better when it comes to adapting literary works, as it received very mixed reviews. Directed by Stuart Cooper and coscripted by Rita Mae Brown, it stars Don Johnson, Judith Ivey, Cybill Shepherd, Jason Robards Jr., and Ava Gardner. For more on this adaptation, see Phillips (142–46).

4. George Sidney's article "An Addition to the Faulkner Canon: The Hollywood Writings" (1961) represents the first real look at Faulkner's screenwriting career. For later studies of how Faulkner's fiction reveals a complex understanding of cinematic language, and was perhaps influenced by his screenwriting experiences, see Lurie and Urgo.

5. The field of adaptation studies is surging, made most evident by the 2008 founding of the journal *Adaptation: The Journal of Literature on Screen Studies*, the continuing presence of *Literature/Film Quarterly*, and a number of book-length studies and collections of essays. For good introductory examples of book-length studies see McFarlane and Leitch. For recommended collections of essays see Corrigan, Stam and Raengo, Cartmell and Whelehan, and Naremore.

6. It is worth noting that *The Long, Hot Summer* was made into a nighttime drama that lasted on ABC-TV for one season (1965–66), arguably the last melodrama based on Faulkner's works.

7. See Phillips (122).

8. Well-known examples of Zugsmith-produced films include *The Incredible Shrinking Man* (1957), *High School Confidential* (1958), *Touch of Evil* (1958), and *Written on the Wind* (1956).

9. For more on Faulkner's relationship to melodrama, see the chapter "Screening Readerly Pleasures: Modernism, Melodrama, and Mass Markets in *If I Forget Thee, Jerusalem*" in Lurie (129–160).

10. As Willemen states, Sirk is "either praised for making extraordinary films in spite of the exigencies of the weepie as a genre, or else it is the weepie-genre itself which is validated, and Sirk is brought forward as its most accomplished practitioner" (128).

Works Cited

Adams, Michael. "'How Come Everybody down Here Has Three Names?': Martin Ritt's Southern Films." *The South and Film*. Ed. Warren French. Jackson: UP of Mississippi, 1981. 143–55. Print.

Cartmell, Deborah, and Imelda Whelehan, eds. *The Cambridge Companion to Literature on Screen*. New York: Cambridge UP, 2007. Print.

Corrigan, Timothy, ed. *Film and Literature: An Introduction and Reader*. 2nd ed. New York: Routledge, 2012. Print.

Faulkner, William. *Pylon*. 1935. New York: Vintage, 1987. Print.

___. *The Hamlet*. 1940. New York: Vintage, 1991. Print.

___. *The Sound and the Fury*. 1929. New York: Vintage, 1984. Print.

Halliday, Jon. *Sirk on Sirk*. New York: Viking, 1972. Print.

Halliwell, Martin. "Modernism and Adaptation." *The Cambridge Companion to Literature on Screen*. Ed. Deborah Cartmell and Imelda Whelehan. New York: Cambridge UP, 2007. 90–106. Print.

Kawin, Bruce. *Faulkner and Film*. New York: Ungar, 1977. Print.

Kellogg, Carolyn. "You Can Be in James Franco's Film of Faulkner's *As I Lay Dying*." *Los Angeles Times* 8 Aug. 2012. Web. 22 Jan. 2013.

Leitch, Thomas. *Film Adaptation and Its Discontents: From* Gone with the Wind *to* The Passion of the Christ. Baltimore: Johns Hopkins UP, 2007. Print.

The Long, Hot Summer. Dir. Martin Ritt. Perf. Paul Newman, Joanne Woodward, Orson Welles, Anthony Franciosa, Lee Remick. Twentieth Century Fox, 1958. DVD.

Lurie, Peter. *Vision's Immanence: Faulkner, Film, and the Popular Imagination*. Baltimore: Johns Hopkins UP, 2004. Print.

McFarlane, Brian. *Novel to Film: An Introduction to the Theory of Adaptation*. Oxford: Clarendon, 1996. Print.

Mercer, John, and Martin Shingler. *Melodrama: Genre, Style and Sensibility*. London: Wallflower, 2004. Print.

Naremore, James, ed. *Film Adaptation*. New Brunswick, NJ: Rutgers UP, 2000. Print.

Phillips, Gene D. *Fiction, Film, and Faulkner: The Art of Adaptation*. Knoxville: U of Tennessee P, 1988. Print.

Poniewozik, James. "HBO Signs David Milch and His New Partner, William Faulkner." *Time* 30 Nov. 2011. Web. 22 Jan. 2013.

Schatz, Thomas. *Hollywood Genres: Formulas, Filmmaking, and the Studio System*. New York: McGraw, 1981. Print.

___. *The Genius of the System: Hollywood Filmmaking in the Studio Era*. New York: Pantheon, 1988. Print.

Sidney, George. "An Addition to the Faulkner Canon: The Hollywood Writings." *Twentieth Century Literature* 6.4 (1961): 172–74. Print.

The Sound and the Fury. Dir. Martin Ritt. Perf. Joanne Woodward, Yul Brynner, Margaret Leighton, Ethel Waters, Jack Warden. Twentieth Century Fox, 1959. DVD.

Stam, Robert and Alessandra Raengo, eds. *Literature and Film: A Guide to the Theory and Practice of Film Adaptation*. Malden: Wiley, 2005. Print.

Taormina, Anthony. "James Franco Confirmed to Direct *As I Lay Dying*." *Screen Rant*. 12 Aug. 2012. Web. 22 Jan. 2013.

The Tarnished Angels. Dir. Douglas Sirk. Perf. Rock Hudson, Robert Stack, Dorothy Malone, Jack Carson. Universal, 1957. DVD.

Urgo, Joseph. "*Absalom, Absalom!* The Movie." *American Literature* 62.1 (1990): 56–73. Print.

Willemen, Paul. "Towards an Analysis of the Sirkian System." *Screen* 13.4 (1972): 128–34. Print.

Wilson, Edmund. "William Faulkner's Reply to the Civil-Rights Program." *William Faulkner: Critical Assessments*. Vol 4. Ed. Henry Claridge. New York: Routledge, 2000. 347–53. Print.

Zeitlin, Michael. "*Pylon* and the Rise of European Fascism." *Faulkner Journal* 26.1 (2012): 97–114. Print.

Hurling Yourself against the Beautiful: Faulkner and Creativity_____

Amy Weldon

In *The Sound and the Fury* I had already put perhaps the only thing in literature which would ever move me very much: Caddy climbing the pear tree to look in the window at her grandmother's funeral while Quentin and Jason and Benjy and the negroes looked up at the muddy seat of her drawers.

This is the only one of the seven novels which I wrote without any accompanying feeling of drive or effort, or any following feeling of exhaustion or relief or distaste. When I began it I had no plan at all. I wasn't even writing a book. I was thinking of books, publication, only in the reverse, in saying to myself, I wont have to worry about publishers liking or not liking this at all. . . . One day I seemed to shut a door between me and all publishers' addresses and book lists. I said to myself, Now I can write. Now I can make myself a vase like that which the old Roman kept at his bedside and wore the rim slowly away with kissing it. So I, who had never had a sister and was fated to lose my daughter in infancy, set out to make myself a beautiful and tragic little girl.

—William Faulkner, "An Introduction for *The Sound and the Fury*"

In my senior year of high school, my AP English teacher assigned us *The Sound and the Fury* (1929). Being a classic teacher pleaser and a voracious reader, I dove in. But this was a book like none I had ever seen. I did not understand what was happening, and I did not understand why this William Faulkner did not write the story clearly, in a straight line, like Stephen King. Why did he make us feel so disoriented on purpose, starting with the first paragraph? Why did he tell the story through the voices of three different people before giving us a fourth story in a completely different voice? And why, in spite of all these questions and irritations, did I still finish the book with haunting pictures, and even smells, lingering in my head: honeysuckle drifting over a porch swing where Caddy sits with her lover, Benjy stumbling over the frozen ruts of barnyard mud, the old buggy swinging around the right of the Confederate monument. Why did I still sense that something important *was* going on in this novel and that it was worth trying to understand? How could it ever be "good" to say something mysteriously, indirectly, and visually rather than just telling someone what you meant? Yet somehow, I knew that it was "good" that Faulkner had written it that way. And I knew it was better than good. It was necessary.

Many years later, after I had gone on to become an English professor, to write novels and essays and stories of my own, and to teach *The Sound and the Fury* to my own students, I realized that my favorite way to approach this novel is a creative-writerly one: I draw on the way all of us—particularly writers—imagine and remember the stories and pictures we carry in our minds and the way we try to render them into words. This approach leads us into the heart of what gives this novel its strange power. If you have ever had an experience or emotion that is linked with a visual picture in your head, and you have struggled to describe it to others, either in writing or in spoken language, you already have a sense of what motivated Faulkner to write this book and of what made him keep trying through the filters of four narrative perspectives.

As a teacher, I can give my students historical contexts, technical narrative terminology (like "stream of consciousness"), and other facts to help them understand *The Sound and the Fury*. But increasingly, that is not enough for me or for them. Terminology does not describe the way this book creates an imaginative world and wraps it completely around us, asking us to pay a new and heightened kind of attention, but rewarding us with an experience of total immersion in other people's lives. And it does not help us understand why we should read this book or why it is important. This novel has a quality of challenge and foreignness that rewards us for approaching it on its own terms, letting it call us up out of and beyond ourselves. Any great art stretches the boundaries of our own mental worlds and gives us greater empathy and vision and joy in just this way. And so to understand *The Sound and the Fury*, it is useful to think about making art as Faulkner might have thought about it and as writers still do. As a writer, it is useful to think about how and why you might—as Faulkner did—keep hurling yourself against some beautiful and mysterious thing, trying to get it into words.

At first, you might well wonder why you are being asked to enter into the worlds of the Compson family, which is enmeshed in circumstances different from those most of us know: dysfunctional and embittered lives in the long post–Reconstruction southern twilight that had not really ended even by World War II. Of the four Compson siblings, one is mentally handicapped, in his thirties, and with the mental age of four. Another is intelligent but neurotic and is driven to suicide by his own ideals and his own perceived failure to live up to them. A third is grasping and greedy and is driven by the desire to make a fortune off somebody else while protecting his own interests at all costs. And the fourth—the luminous, loving, openhearted girl around whose memory all three of her brothers revolve—is the absent presence of the novel: the sister whose sensuality becomes both the reason for the family's shame and the type of human connection that none of them can achieve. But if you settle in and read carefully, letting this book wash over you, you will see several important writerly principles at work through these characters, and you can learn things from Faulkner that will help your own writing, both critical and creative.

Faulkner's fellow southern writer Eudora Welty explains in her essay, "Is Phoenix Jackson's Grandson Really Dead?" that the writer should become "at one" with reality as the character understands it. In other words, you have to work from inside the particular quality of your character's lived experience, seeing the world through his or her eyes and, to some degree, setting yourself aside. This requires an act of imagination that feels positively muscular, like lifting or stretching, because it calls upon your own physical memories and senses too. It takes practice and time, but when you do it, it is unmistakable.

Faulkner does this on every page of the novel and positions the reader deeply inside the skins of Benjy, Quentin, and Jason; he lets the reader walk closely beside Dilsey, and one must adjust the lenses of one's own vision in order to see through theirs. It takes a little while to get in, to shift over to the foreign space of another separate person's mind and heart and body. But once in, we are given the needed clues to keep ourselves there, if we only pay attention. Finishing *The Sound and the Fury* feels like waking from a dream because we have been inside and sharing the writer's dream, called out of the familiar territory of our own minds and preoccupations by his appeal to the senses and emotions we share with him and his characters.

With a closer look at one of the most intense passages in the novel— Quentin's confrontation with Caddy in the branch (in the "June Second, 1910" section), one can see and even feel how this artistic empathy works and is created, word by word, on the page:

> then she talked about him clasping her wet knees her face tilted back in the gray light the smell of honeysuckle there was a light in mothers room and in Benjys where T.P.. was putting him to bed
>
> do you love him
>
> her hand came out I didnt move it fumbled down my arm and she held my hand flat against her chest her heart thudding
>
> no no
>
> did he make you then he made you do it let him he was stronger than you and he tomorrow Ill kill him I swear I will father neednt know until afterward and then you and I nobody need ever know we can take my

school money we can cancel my matriculation Caddy you hate him dont you dont you

she held my hand against her chest her heart thudding I turned and caught her arm

Caddy you hate him dont you

she moved my hand up against her throat her heart was hammering there

poor Quentin (95)

Unbroken for nine pages, this tension has been coiled at the heart of Quentin's section all along, as he and his sister both become aware that his frantic need to "save" her from a soiled sexual reputation misunderstands the nature of sexual, or any, experience—and that this misunderstanding is born of codes of southern genteel masculinity, emotional confusion, and love. We can enter so closely into Quentin's stream of thought because the physical markers of the distance between reader, writer, and writer's imagined world have dropped away: Punctuation, capitalization, paragraph indentations, and even apostrophes are gone in order to shorten the distance between the inside of Quentin's mind and our own as much as words on a page can manage. And these prose markers have been replaced by physical ones—sensations and gestures: She sets his hand on her heart to feel it beat; he holds the point of the knife at her throat; he is dizzied by the smell of honeysuckle. The stream of Quentin's memory—and of the time that keeps running forward, carrying both him and Caddy away from this moment he cannot forget—is embodied by the stream of water in which he and Caddy are immersed. By giving us such a physical mirroring of the invisible, which we can imagine with our own senses if we have ever been immersed in a stream, Faulkner helps us participate in the dissolving of boundaries between two bodies and minds and in the shared history and mindset of these two siblings. (They share so close a connection that when "her muscles gathered I sat up," with no separation between the gestures even on the page.) The abstract presence of emotions becomes, then, bodily and real. We even see where he tries to distract himself from the tension of hearing Caddy talk about her lover, Dalton Ames, by looking at the house, because—to his dread and delight—he and Caddy are totally alone. We are inside the ongoing flow of Quentin's thought as it surrounds and encompasses a memory of almost unbearable intimacy that spills out and engulfs him. We are engulfed. We, too, can barely stand the intimacy and tension, even as we cannot look away. And it all happens because of a string of little black marks on a page. It is a mysterious, and miraculous process.

Here is what I tell my own students when they first encounter *The Sound and the Fury* and are puzzled by what seems, like a wall of strangeness on the page, words that make little or no literal sense: "Through the fence, between the curling flower spaces, I could see them hitting." What? Where are we? With Benjy's, and the novel's, first words, we have been deliberately alienated and deliberately cast adrift into the foreign space of not just another person's mind, but the mind of a person who processes memory and language in different ways than many of us do. Consider this: Faulkner is trying to render onto the page consciousness itself, the way it feels to be inside a person's head, where what is happening this instant and what did happen at different times in the past and what we hope will happen are always coexisting, shooting off one another, bouncing forward and backward. If Faulkner had had the Internet, he might have written this novel in a series of hyperlinks where clicking on the words *Caddy's shoe* might take you back not only to words describing Benjy's first possession of the shoe but also a picture or video of the shoe itself, thereby taking you through the same routes Benjy's consciousness travels in reencountering that shoe, which, like the force of Caddy's loss, is new and sorrowful to him every time.

Benjy does not frame memories as "past" or "present," "then" or "now." His interior world—like the artist's, perhaps—is a series of strong mental images with strong feelings attached to each one, and when one reminds him of another, he slides involuntarily between them. The reader has to rely on external markers of time (Who is the servant attending Benjy? Is Caddy or Miss Quentin in the house?) to place these images in a narrative order that is recognizable, both eliding and emphasizing the differences between the way the reader and Benjy understand reality. But to Benjy, as to our own consciousnesses, all these images are coexisting in the same place, exploding into imaginative life at the same time. In consciousness, everything is all and is always happening at once. Think about the way it feels inside your own head at any given time—present concerns and new ideas colliding and reminding you of past ones, which remind you of ideas from the deeper past, which bring you back to the present almost instantaneously. Yet to render this reality on the page, Faulkner has only language, in which words follow one after another and add up their meanings in a straight line. Therefore, he has set himself a pretty big challenge—to overcome a basic mismatch between his tool, which is language, and the consciousness that he is trying to use that tool to represent. Consciousness does not run in a smooth, straight line. It is more like a mirror ball that is hanging and turning, glittering and throwing out light in all directions at once. But language adds up, word by word.

Yet something about this near-impossible effort seems worth trying to Faulkner because something about this story is irresistible to him to tell. What makes it irresistible is bound up in that first image of the little girl in the tree, quoted at the beginning of this essay. For reasons that perhaps Faulkner himself never fully understood, and quite probably did not want to (writers cannot always fully articulate everything they are doing in their work, and the smart ones let that be a mystery), the mental picture he carried of Caddy climbing the pear tree—the seat of her drawers innocently and heartbreakingly dirty from playing in the same branch where Quentin will later place a knife at her throat—

carried so much poignancy and power to him that it was a picture he could not forget, a story he had to try to tell. "Images hold the meaning of our lives," the poet and memoirist Nick Flynn has written. "Without images we have no memory; they give the past shape, keep the memory" (15). Think about your own mental gallery of powerful, meaningful images, which may be memories of people or places, pictures from dreams, moments in which someone looked at you or said something you cannot forget. That is the power of the imagined image the little girl has for Faulkner. That is why he keeps trying to nail that emotion to the page, although, as you know if you have ever tried to describe your own precious images to another person, this effort is really hard.

That image has a type of magnetic force connected to your own deep convictions, memories, and longings. For Faulkner, as illustrated in his introduction to *The Sound and the Fury*, that image is the image of a "beautiful, doomed little girl" climbing a pear tree to seek and to know the truth, as her brothers and her friends are afraid to do. She wants to see the forbidden, the scary, the wondrous and the awful for herself. She wants to see her grandmother's funeral. So she climbs. The less courageous, standing on the ground, can see her creek-mudded underwear, a sight both innocent and, in light of the adult Caddy's continued sensual seeking, sadly premonitory. Faulkner had already lost a baby daughter of his own. Like many southern men, he grew up with a nearly cultlike fascination and suspicion of womanhood—wondering about the unique ways women see and know, the reasons they should be respected and the reasons, many men thought, they would always be just a little weaker than men—never quite as good—more "sinful" and fallible. The artist in Faulkner was drawn to the truth and not the prejudices in this mix, to the mystery: Women became connected for him with mystery, with loss and death, and with the deeper things you see in life once you have lost someone dear or wanted something terribly. The novelist is always looking for ways to see deeper into that mystery.

This fact leads to a third "lesson" from *The Sound and the Fury*: It is not only normal but necessary to work in the dark as a writer, to be comfortable with mystery and not knowing, to let the story develop like a Polaroid photograph before your eyes. (An excellent book on writing, Anne Lamott's *Bird by Bird* (2007), develops this "Polaroid" analogy even more helpfully.) It is simply not true that you "have to know where you are going" as a writer in order to write something, no matter what that is. You discover what you have to say by trying to write it. You discover what you really feel in trying to get it down. This comes through practice and the regular work of multiple drafts over time. If you get serious enough about this process, you tend to get impatient with pretty much everything that is not your writing or does not contribute to it. Controversially, if a little sarcastically, invoking his favorite poem, Faulkner described the lengths a writer will go for his work: "If a writer has to rob his mother, he will not hesitate; the 'Ode on a Grecian Urn' [Keats] is worth any number of old ladies" (qtd. in Blotner 619). Perhaps this is an extreme way to deal with the interruptions of families and their claims on us. But what are the interruptions we are more susceptible to, the latest viral YouTube video, Facebook friends' status updates? Even writers enjoy distractions such as these, but writers must stay mindful of what they cost. Centering your life on your work and on the experiences that truly feed your writing—physical activity, conversations with friends and family, reading—tend to make you impatient (in a good way) with the trivial stuff and help you to minimize it or even cut it out.

Once you get involved with a significant project—as Faulkner also describes, in "shut[ting] a door between myself and all publishers' addresses and book lists"—you find that your work needs to proceed with something like self-forgetfulness. Writing with one eye on an audience can be necessary, because every audience shapes what we say and how we say it, but when we are struggling to say something beautiful and true, we cannot afford to keep asking "will a publisher like this? Will my friends and family like this? Will this make me famous?" Letting yourself be drawn away into dreams of fame dilutes the quiet, patient intensity of the search for the form your material is really trying to take through you. Also, it keeps you worrying about concerns (money, fame, who will your agent be) that in the long term, in the grand scheme of things by which art is measured, really do not matter. Think of any one-hit musical wonder or reality-television star of the last few years. Will we still remember in ten more years who that person is? It is doubtful. (And if you question this, ask people ten or twenty years older than you about their own "one-hit wonders.") Nonetheless, that person, by the world's standards, was "successful" and made money and became famous. But what kind of fame did that person achieve? What kind of art and what kind of life was really made?

By contrast, when Faulkner wrote *The Sound and the Fury*, he had already published three novels, the second of which was less successful than the first, and the third of which he was having trouble getting published at all. So he released—in a sense that seems near-spiritual—the idea of success as the literary industry defines it and simply said "now I can write" without worrying about the idea of success. When *The Sound and the Fury* was published, it was not well received either, nor was it recognized by more than a few as the masterpiece it is. Yet look at how it is regarded now.

Like the shift of imaginative gears required to enter into the skin of another person, real or imaginary, adjusting our notions of truth and beauty in art and being in it for the long game can take a bit of effort. But you do not make anything worthwhile without it. Like living a good life in general, making good art involves figuring out your own beliefs, desires, and urges as routes to your own best and most generous self and then acting on them—not in constantly adjusting yourself to what you think "the market" needs or requires and trying to hit a moving target that is not really worth hitting anyway. You have to be willing to be alone with this thing you are trying to make, this thing that you love and that no one else might understand. Be alone with it and be quiet in the manner of someone who is helpless and humble before something whose beauty and wonder are difficult to describe. The artist needs to have a serious appetite for mystery, for comfort with the unknown.

Perhaps this appetite for mystery is why Faulkner did not give Caddy her own section. Often what we love or long for is wordless and is a sort of luminous presence (or absence) in our minds. We keep returning to it, trying to touch it even as it escapes our grasp. Caddy is this kind of presence in her family's life, and the lack of a section in her voice is Faulkner's way of respecting that. We get to imagine her, to dream of her, and long for her (just as her three brothers do in their own ways) and contemplate how our own family relationships—the ways we mythologize or resent or forgive family members—can either distort or enable the flourishing of our own selves and personalities. In their own ways, none of the brothers can see Caddy as a whole and independent person, separate from the family and from themselves. They try repeatedly to explain themselves to us, revealing in the process only how deeply they have built their self-images upon their own ideals of their sister's, and their family's, purity.

For example, Jason at first seems, despite his unforgettable opening line ("Once a bitch always a bitch, what I say") the most objective and clear, the easiest to understand, the most uncomplicated, and perhaps the most tempting to sympathize with. But as Jason's section proceeds, Faulkner moves carefully through the layers of his consciousness by showing us his moods and traits: greed and stinginess, casual xenophobia, a hypocrisy that can excuse his keeping a mistress but not his niece's or his sister's sexual activity, a grudging hatred of the family duties he still holds himself to. Faulkner also shows the troubling and highly informative ways that these layers connect to one another. If Quentin was most closely connected to their father and his stories of faded Compson family grandeur, Jason is bound to their mother and to her competing mythologies of how the Bascombs (her own people) are better, how Jason and all of them have been cheated by life, and how she and Jason (but particularly herself) have been owed something better by the world than what they have been given. He is her captive audience for a symphony of complaints, passive aggression, and neurosis ("codependency," we might now say) that grow darker until, almost in spite of ourselves, we feel sorry for Jason, even as we might also find ourselves laughing at his over-the-top attempts to control his niece. We see, as he does not, how his warped adult self has grown out of the overlooked small boy with his hands in his pockets and how emotionally stunted and resentful the clash between his perceived duties to the family and to himself have made him.

Caddy is the catalyst for Jason's most revealing moments and deepest feelings, as she is for all the other brothers. The scene in the "April Sixth, 1928" section in which Jason reencounters her at their father's funeral long after she has fled the Compson home for good shows us in midparagraph that his memory leaps directly to the funeral at the very word *Father* from the apparently unrelated topic of Caddy's letters, suggesting that this remains for him a deep and unacknowledged wound:

> When they begun to get it filled up toward the top Mother started crying sure enough, so Uncle Maury got in with her and drove off. He says You can come in with somebody: they'll be glad to give you a lift. I'll have to take your mother on and I thought about saying, Yes, you ought to brought two bottles instead of just one only I thought about where we were, so I let them go on. Little they cared how wet I got, because then Mother could have a whale of a time being afraid I was taking pneumonia.
>
> Well, I got to thinking about that and watching them throwing dirt into it, slapping it on anyway like they were making mortar or something or building a fence, and I began to feel sort of funny and so I decided to walk around a while. (127)

"Feeling sort of funny" is an understatement of grief, but it is all that Jason, locked inside his own furious reticence, can muster to us or to himself. He is the youngest of four children, feeling that their father always preferred Caddy and Quentin and that Benjy absorbed most of whatever emotional energy was left. He has been left behind by his own mother and uncle at his father's grave where there is no one else to take him home and where he is forced to watch and listen to earth being "slapped" onto his father's coffin. (He cannot even bring himself to say "coffin" or "grave.") To avoid that sound, he hides under dripping trees until the gravediggers are gone, and when he comes out, there is Caddy, whom he does not even need to name: "I knew who it was right off, before she turned and looked at me and lifted up her veil" (127). Simply and directly, "we shook hands" (127). Just for an instant, reconciliation seems possible. Yet almost in spite of himself, Jason's resentment about the job Caddy's former husband Herbert promised and failed to give him—which he is held against Caddy ever since, perhaps as a convenient label for more complicated feelings—surges forward: "You dont mind anybody. You dont give a dam about anybody" (127). Caddy continues to respond with gentleness—"I'm sorry about that, Jason"—and then comes close to defusing his anger completely with her own vulnerability:

> "I dont want anything," she says. She looked at the grave. "Why didn't they let me know?" she says. "I just happened to see it in the paper. On the back page. Just happened to."
> I didn't say anything. We stood there, looking at the grave, and then I got to thinking about when we were little and one thing and another and I got to feeling funny again, kind of mad or something, thinking about now we'd have Uncle Maury around the house all the time, running things like the way he left me to come home in the rain by myself. (127)

From word to word, you can see Jason floundering at the quicksand edge of feelings he cannot name, then casting about until he hits a familiar line of grievance (Uncle Maury) and follows it back onto his most familiar emotional ground (anger). Grievances fuel his passage through the world and his dealings with family, and anger is a kind of engine that lifts him up and speeds him over the surfaces of other psychological waters that are darker, deeper, sadder, and full of the kinds of pain with which he is completely unequipped to deal. How many times have we sought refuge in anger in just this way? And how many times have we realized all over again that the way we recoil from (or reconcile with) our families or loved ones so often mirrors the way we try (or fail) to do these things within ourselves? It is Jason's tragedy that he can never realize or accept this—can never move beyond the self-willed reflex of anger—and so he continues to be an instrument of hurt to everyone he encounters: his sister Caddy, his niece Miss Quentin, the loyal family servant Dilsey, and even his brother Benjy. Nonetheless, if we read his section carefully, we can see, as he cannot, that he is just as deeply marked as any of his siblings by their shared history and memory, even if he refuses to acknowledge it.

The Sound and the Fury is important because, like any great art, it has the potential to make you a better person. Watching Jason skirt the edges of his own pain and take refuge in cruelty; feeling indignant at the way Dilsey is relied upon and misunderstood by the family; sympathizing with Benjy's mute, bewildered longing for the sister he loves—all these things make us better, gentler, and wiser people. That is reason enough to pick up this novel and let it work its mysteries on you.

Works Cited

Blotner, Joseph. *Faulkner: A Biography*. New York: Vintage, 1991. Print.

Faulkner, William. *The Sound and the Fury.* 1929. Norton Critical Ed. Ed. David L. Minter. New York: Norton, 1994. Print.Flynn, Nick, and Shirley McPhillips. *A Note Slipped under the Door: Teaching from Poems We Love*. New York: Stenhouse, 2000. Print.

Welty, Eudora. "Is Phoenix Jackson's Grandson Really Dead?" *The Eye of the Story: Selected Essays and Reviews.* New York: Vintage, 1990, 159–62. Print.

RESOURCES

Chronology of William Faulkner's Life_____

1897	William Faulkner is born as William Falkner in New Albany, Mississippi, the oldest of four brothers.
1902	The Falkners moves to Oxford, Mississippi.
1905–14	Faulkner attends Oxford Grade School, then Oxford High School.
1914	Faulkner begins friendship with Phil Stone, who becomes his mentor and critic. He drops out of school.
1916	Faulkner visits University of Mississippi campus frequently, but is not enrolled; his writing is influenced by Algernon Charles Swinburne and A. E. Housman.
1918	Faulkner tries to enlist in the US Army but is rejected. He is accepted into the Royal Air Force in Canada and travels to the Recruits' Depot in Toronto and enters active service the next day; he receives his discharge without having served overseas. He changes name from Falkner to Faulkner and returns to Oxford.
1919	Faulkner's poem "L'Apres-Midi d'un Faune" appears in *The New Republic*, his first published writing. He enters the University of Mississippi as a special student and begins publishing poems in *The Mississippian* and *Oxford Eagle*.
1920	Faulkner joins The Marionettes, the university drama club. He withdraws from the university.
1921	Faulkner presents Estelle Franklin with a gift volume of poems, *Vision in Spring*. He works as a clerk in a New York City bookstore.
1921–24	Faulkner serves as postmaster at University of Mississippi.
1922	Faulkner's poem "Portrait" is published in the *Double Dealer* of New Orleans.
1922–24	Faulkner serves as scoutmaster.

1924	Faulkner is removed as scoutmaster and resigns as postmaster. Stone sends in *The Marble Faun* to Four Seas Co., which agrees to publish it for $400.
1925	Faulkner contributes to the New Orleans *Times-Picayune* and the *Double Dealer*, and he travels in Europe for six months.
1926	*Soldier's Pay* is published by Boni & Liveright. Faulkner writes a hand-lettered gift book of poems, *Helen: A Courtship*, for Helen Baird. He collaborates with William Spratling, while living in New Orleans, on *Sherwood Anderson and Other Famous Creoles*.
1927	*Mosquitoes* is published. *Flags in the Dust* is rejected by publishers.
1928	Faulkner lives in New York for three months.
1929	*Sartoris* is published. Faulkner marries recently divorced Estelle Franklin in College Hill, Mississippi, and he works in the university power plant. *The Sound and the Fury* is published by Jonathan Cape and Harrison Smith.
1930	Faulkner begins publishing stories in national magazines. He also purchases Rowan Oak, an antebellum house and land. *As I Lay Dying* is published.
1931	Faulkner's daughter, Alabama, is born. She lives only nine days. *Sanctuary* and *These Thirteen* are published.
1932	Faulkner begins writing for MGM in Culver City, California. *Light in August* is published by Harrison Smith and Robert Haas.
1933	*A Green Bough* (poems) is published. Faulkner's daughter, Jill, is born.
1934	*Doctor Martino and Other Stories* is published. Faulkner works for three weeks at Universal Studios.
1935	*Pylon* is published. Faulkner has an assignment at Twentieth Century-Fox, where he meets Meta Dougherty Carpenter, beginning an intimate intermittent fifteen-year relationship.

1935–37	Faulkner works at Twentieth Century-Fox a total of eighteen months.
1936	*Absalom, Absalom!* is published by Random House.
1938	*The Unvanquished* is published, and its screen rights are sold to MGM. Faulkner buys land and names it Greenfield Farm.
1939	Faulkner is elected to the National Institute of Arts and Letters. *The Wild Palms* is published.
1940	*The Hamlet* is published.
1942	*Go Down, Moses* is published. Faulkner reports for a five-month segment of a long-term Warner Bros. contract.
1942–45	Faulkner works at Warner Bros. a total of twenty-six months.
1946	*The Portable Faulkner*, edited by Malcolm Cowley, is published by Viking Press.
1947	Faulkner teaches six classes at University of Mississippi.
1948	*Intruder in the Dust* is published, and its screen rights are sold to MGM. Faulkner is elected to the American Academy of Arts and Letters.
1949	*Knight's Gambit* is published. *Intruder in the Dust* is filmed in Oxford.
1950	Faulkner receives American Academy's Howells Medal for Fiction and the 1949 Nobel Prize in Literature *Collected Stories of William Faulkner* is published.
1951	*Notes on a Horsethief* is published. Faulkner receives the National Book Award for Fiction for *Collected Stories* and the Legion of Honor in New Orleans. *Requiem for a Nun* is published.
1951–54	Faulkner works on and off as a scriptwriter for Howard Hawks.
1952	Faulkner travels to France, England, and Norway.

1954	Faulkner travels to Europe, Egypt, South America, and New York.
1955	Faulkner accepts National Book Award for Fiction for his novel *A Fable*, and he speaks at the University of Oregon and Montana State University. *A Fable* wins the Pulitzer Prize. *Big Woods* is published. Faulkner spends a month in Japan for the State Department, as a cultural ambassador, and a month in Europe.
1957	Faulkner stays at the University of Virginia as the writer-in-residence. He travels to Athens for two weeks, as a cultural ambassador for the State Department, and accepts the Silver Medal of Greek Academy. *The Town* is published.
1959	Faulkner breaks his collarbone in a fall from his horse. *The Mansion* is published.
1960	Faulkner accepts appointment to become a University of Virginia faculty member and wills his manuscripts to the William Faulkner Foundation.
1961	Faulkner travels to Venezuela as a cultural ambassador for the State Department.
1962	Faulkner makes a two-day visit to the US Military Academy at West Point. He travels to New York to accept the National Institute of Arts and Letters Gold Medal for Fiction. *The Reivers* is published. Faulkner dies of a heart attack; he is buried in St. Peter's Cemetery, in Oxford, Mississippi.
1968	*The Faulkner-Cowley File: Letter and Memories 1944–62* is published.
1973	*Flags in the Dust* (which was the original version of *Sartoris*) is published.

Works by William Faulkner

Soldier's Pay (1926)
Mosquitoes (1927)
Sartoris (1929)
The Sound and the Fury (1929)
As I Lay Dying (1930)
Sanctuary (1931)
Light in August (1932)
Pylon (1935)
Absalom, Absalom! (1936)
The Unvanquished (1938)
The Wild Palms (1939)
The Hamlet (1940)
Go Down, Moses (1942)
The Portable Faulkner (1946)
Intruder in the Dust (1948)
Knight's Gambit (1949)
Collected Stories of William Faulkner (1950)
Requiem for a Nun (1951)
A Fable (1954)
Big Woods (1955)
The Town (1957)
The Mansion (1959)
The Reivers (1962)

Bibliography

Aboul-Ela, Hosam. *Other South: Faulkner, Coloniality, and the Mariátegui Tradition.* Pittsburgh: U of Pittsburgh P, 2007. Print.

Adams, Richard P. *Faulkner: Myth and Motion.* Princeton: Princeton UP, 1968. Print.

Aiken, Charles S. *William Faulkner and the Southern Landscape.* Athens: U of Georgia P, 2009. Print.

Atkinson, Ted. *Faulkner and the Great Depression: Aesthetics, Ideology, and Cultural Politics.* Athens: U of Georgia P, 2006. Print.

Baker, Charles. *William Faulkner's Postcolonial South.* New York: Peter Lang, 2000. Print.

Baker, Houston A., Jr. *I Don't Hate the South: Reflections on Faulkner, Family, and the South.* New York: Oxford UP, 2007. Print.

Bauer, Margaret Donovan. *William Faulkner's Legacy: "What Shadow, What Stain, What Mark."* Gainesville: UP of Florida, 2005. Print.

Bleikasten, André. *Faulkner's* As I Lay Dying. Trans. Roger Little. Bloomington: Indiana UP, 1973. Print.

___. *The Ink of Melancholy: Faulkner's Novels from* The Sound and the Fury *to* Light in August. Bloomington: Indiana UP, 1990. Print.

___. *The Most Splendid Failure: Faulkner's* The Sound and the Fury. Bloomington: Indiana UP, 1976. Print.

Blotner, Joseph. *Faulkner: A Biography.* New York: Random, 1984. Print.

Brown, Calvin S. "Faulkner's Geography and Topography." *PMLA* 77 (1962): 652–59. Print.

Brylowski, Walter. *Faulkner's Olympian Laugh: Myth in the Novels.* Detroit: Wayne State UP, 1968. Print.

Buckley, G. T. "Is Oxford the Original of Jefferson in William Faulkner's Novels?" *PMLA* 76 (1961): 447–54. Print.

Clarke, Deborah. *Robbing the Mother: Women in Faulkner.* Jackson: UP of Mississippi, 1994. Print.

Coughlan, Robert. *The Private World of William Faulkner.* New York: Avon, 1953. Print.

Cullen, John B. *Old Times in the Faulkner Country.* Chapel Hill: U of North Carolina P, 1961. Print.

Davis, Thadious M. *Faulkner's "Negro": Art and the Southern Context.* Baton Rouge: Louisiana State UP, 1983. Print.

___. *Games of Property: Law, Race, Gender, and Faulkner's* Go Down, Moses. Durham, NC: Duke UP, 2003.

Duvall, John N. *Faulkner's Marginal Couple: Invisible, Outlaw, and Unspeakable Communities.* Austin: U of Texas P, 1990. Print.

Faulkner, John. *My Brother Bill: An Affectionate Reminiscence*. New York: Trident P, 1963. Print.

Faulkner Studies. Vol. 1–3. New York: Kraus, 1966. Print.

Fowler, Doreen. *Faulkner: The Return of the Repressed*. Charlottesville: UP of Virginia, 1997. Print.

___. *Faulkner's Changing Vision: From Outrage to Affirmation*. Ann Arbor: UMI Research P, 1983. Print.

Fruscione, Joseph. *Faulkner and Hemingway: Biography of a Literary Rivalry*. Columbus: Ohio State UP, 2012. Print.

Glissant, Edouard. *Faulkner, Mississippi*. Trans. Barbara Lewis and Thomas C. Spear. Chicago: U of Chicago P, 1999. Print.

Godden, Richard. *Fictions of Labor: William Faulkner and the South's Long Revolution*. Cambridge: Cambridge UP, 1997. Print.

Gray, Richard. *The Life of William Faulkner: A Critical Biography*. Oxford: Blackwell, 1994. Print.

Gwin, Minrose C. *The Feminine and Faulkner: Reading (Beyond) Sexual Difference*. Knoxville: U of Tennessee P, 1990. Print.

Hagood, Taylor. *Faulkner's Imperialism: Space, Place, and the Materiality of Myth*. Baton Rouge: Louisiana State UP, 2008. Print.

Hamblin, Robert W., and Charles A. Peek, eds. *A William Faulkner Encyclopedia*. Westport: Greenwood, 1999. Print.

Hannon, Charles. *Faulkner and the Discourses of Culture*. Baton Rouge: Louisiana State UP, 2005. Print.

Harris, Robert. *Aviation Lore in Faulkner*. Amsterdam: John Benjamins, 1985. Print.

Howell, Elmo. "Faulkner and Tennessee." *Tennessee Historical Quarterly* 21 (1963): 251–62. Print.

Inge, M. Thomas. *William Faulkner: The Contemporary Reviews*. New York: Cambridge UP, 1995. Print.

Jones, Norman W. *Gay and Lesbian Historical Fiction: Sexual Mystery and Post-Secular Narrative*. New York: Palgrave Macmillan, 2007. Print.

Irwin, John T. *Doubling and Incest/Repetition and Revenge: A Speculative Reading of Faulkner*. Baltimore: Johns Hopkins UP, 1975. Print.

Jehlen, Myra. *Class and Character in Faulkner's South*. New York: Columbia UP, 1976. Print.

Karl, Frederick. *William Faulkner, American Author: A Biography*. New York: Weidenfeld, 1989. Print.

Kartiganer, Donald M. *The Fragile Thread: The Meaning of Form in Faulkner's Novels*. Amherst: U of Massachusetts P, 1979. Print.

Kawin, Bruce F. *Faulkner and Film*. New York: Ungar, 1977. Print.

Kirk, Robert W. *Faulkner's People: A Complete Guide and Index to Characters in the Fiction of William Faulkner*. Berkeley: U of California P, 1963. Print.

Kolmerten, Carol A., Stephen M. Ross, and Judith Bryant Wittenberg, eds. *Unflinching Gaze: Faulkner and Morrison Re-Envisioned*. Jackson: UP of Mississippi, 1997. Print.

Labatt, Blair. *Faulkner the Storyteller*. Tuscaloosa: U of Alabama P, 2005. Print.

Levins, Lynn Gatrell. *Faulkner's Heroic Design: The Yoknapatawpha Novels*. Athens: U of Georgia P, 1976. Print.

Loichot, Valérie. *Orphan Narratives: The Postplantation Literature of Faulkner, Glissant, Morrison, and Saint-John Perse*. Charlottesville: U of Virginia P, 2007. Print.

Lurie, Peter. *Vision's Immanence: Faulkner, Film, and the Popular Imagination*. Baltimore: Johns Hopkins UP, 2004. Print.

Matthews, John T. *The Play of Faulkner's Language*. Ithaca: Cornell UP, 1982. Print.

___. *William Faulkner: Seeing through the South*. Oxford: Wiley, 2009. Print.

O'Donnell, George Marion. "Faulkner's Mythology." 1939. *William Faulkner: Three Decades of Criticism*. Ed. Frederick J. Hoffman and Olga W. Vickery. East Lansing: Michigan State UP, 1960. 82–93. Print.

Parini, Jay. *One Matchless Time: A Life of William Faulkner*. New York: Harper, 2004. Print.

Peek, Charles A., and Robert W. Hamblin, eds. *A Companion to Faulkner Studies*. Westport: Greenwood, 2004. Print.

Polk, Noel. *Faulkner and Welty and the Southern Literary Tradition*. Jackson: UP of Mississippi, 2008. Print.

Roberts, Diane. *Faulkner and Southern Womanhood*. Athens: U of Georgia P, 1994.

Robinson, Owen. *Creating Yoknapatawpha: Readers and Writers in Faulkner's Fiction*. New York: Routledge, 2006. Print.

Ross, Stephen M. *Fiction's Inexhaustible Voice: Speech and Writing in Faulkner*. Athens: U of Georgia P, 1989. Print.

Schwartz, Lawrence H. *Creating Faulkner's Reputation: The Politics of Modern Literary Criticism*. Knoxville: U of Tennessee P, 1988. Print.

Sensibar, Judith L. *Faulkner and Love: The Women Who Shaped His Art*. New Haven: Yale UP, 2009.

Skei, Hans H. *Reading Faulkner's Best Short Stories*. Columbia: U of South Carolina P, 1999. Print.

Smith, Jon, and Deborah Cohn, eds. *Look Away! The U.S. South in New World Studies*. Durham, NC: Duke UP, 2004. Print.

Sundquist, Eric. *Faulkner: The House Divided*. Baltimore: Johns Hopkins UP, 1983. Print.

Urgo, Joseph R. *Faulkner's Apocrypha: A Fable, Snopes, and the Spirit of Human Rebellion*. Jackson: UP of Mississippi, 1989. Print.

Weinstein, Philip. *Becoming Faulkner: The Arts and Life of William Faulkner*. New York: Oxford UP, 2010. Print.

___. *Faulkner's Subject: A Cosmos No One Owns*. New York: Cambridge UP, 1992. Print.

___. *What Else but Love? The Ordeal of Race in Faulkner and Morrison*. New York: Columbia UP, 1996. Print.

Williams, David. *Faulkner's Women: The Myth and the Muse*. Montreal: McGill-Queen's UP, 1977. Print.

Wolff, Sally. *Ledgers of History: William Faulkner, an Almost Forgotten Friendship, and an Antebellum Diary*. Baton Rouge: Louisiana State UP, 2010. Print.

Wolff, Sally, and Floyd C. Watkins, eds. *Talking about William Faulkner: Interviews with Jimmy Faulkner and Others*. Baton Rouge: Louisiana State UP, 1996. Print.

Zender, Karl. *The Crossing of the Ways: William Faulkner, the South, and the Modern World*. New Brunswick, NJ: Rutgers UP, 1989. Print.

___. *Faulkner and the Politics of Reading*. Baton Rouge: Louisiana State UP, 2002. Print.

About the Editor_____

Kathryn Stelmach Artuso (PhD, UCLA) is assistant professor of English at Westmont College in Santa Barbara, California, where she teaches twentieth-century and anglophone literature. A specialist in transatlantic modernism, Artuso's research examines the diasporic intersections between the literatures of Ireland, Africa, the Caribbean, and the American South.

She is the author of *Transatlantic Renaissances: Literature of Ireland and the American South* (2013), which traces the influence of the Irish Literary Revival upon the Southern Renaissance, exploring how the latter looked to the former for guidance, artistic innovation, and models for self-invention and regional renovation. Using the themes of initiation and maturation to anchor the book, Artuso analyzes how the volatile development of young women in revivalist texts often reflects or questions larger growth pangs and patterns, including the evolution of the literary revival itself and the development of a regional minority group that must work within a dominant culture, language, and nation while seeking methods of subversion.

Her articles have appeared in *Studies in the Novel*, *Mississippi Quarterly*, the *Eudora Welty Review*, the *Celtic Studies Association of North America Yearbook*, and the *Lexington Herald-Leader*. In 2011, she was awarded the Ruth Vande Kieft Prize for her article in the *Eudora Welty Review*, "Transatlantic Rites of Passage in the Friendship and Fiction of Eudora Welty and Elizabeth Bowen."

Contributors

Kathryn Stelmach Artuso is assistant professor of English at Westmont College in Santa Barbara, California. She is the author of *Transatlantic Renaissances: Literature of Ireland and the American South* (2013). Her articles have appeared in *Studies in the Novel, Mississippi Quarterly*, the *Eudora Welty Review*, and the *Celtic Studies Association of North America Yearbook*.

Lorie Watkins Fulton is assistant professor of English at William Carey University. She is the author of *William Faulkner, Gavin Stevens, and the Cavalier Myth* (2011) and has published essays in such journals as *The Faulkner Journal, The Hemingway Review, African American Review, The Mississippi Quarterly, The Southern Literary Journal*, and *Modern Philology*.

Karen M. Andrews received her PhD in English and American literature from Claremont Graduate University and is associate professor of urban studies at the Westmont in San Francisco program. She has taught urban studies, English electives, and independent study tutorials at the San Francisco program since 1997. Her doctoral dissertation examined interracial relationships and the legacy of slavery in the works of Faulkner. Among her publications, she has coauthored a book chapter, "San Francisco Urban Program: Encountering America's Future-Tense," in *Transformations at the Edge of the World* (2010), edited by Ronald J. Morgan and Cynthia Toms Smedley.

Taylor Hagood is associate professor of American literature at Florida Atlantic University. He is the author of *Faulkner's Imperialism: Space, Place, and the Materiality of Myth* (2008); *Secrecy, Magic, and the One-Act Plays of Harlem Renaissance Women Playwrights* (2010); and essays in journals such as *European Journal of American Culture, Faulkner Journal, Mississippi Quarterly*, and *Southern Literary Journal*.

Doreen Fowler is a professor of English at the University of Kansas. She is the author of *Drawing the Line: The Father Reimagined in Faulkner, Wright, O'Connor, and Morrison* (2013), a study of the role of liminal figures in the cultural production of racial, gender, ethnic, and other identities, and *Faulkner: The Return of the Repressed* (1997), a psychoanalytic interpretation of Faulkner's major novels. She is the coeditor of eleven collections of essays on Faulkner. She has served on the editorial board of the *Faulkner Journal*, the executive committee of the Faulkner Society, and the executive board of the Society for the Study of Southern Literature.

Patrick E. Horn is an ABD graduate student in English and comparative literature at the University of North Carolina at Chapel Hill. His dissertation analyzes "Narrative

Empathy for 'the Other' in American Literature, 1845-1945." Before attending graduate school, he served as a US Air Force intelligence officer in Iraq, Afghanistan, Turkey, Kuwait, and East Africa.

Jacques Pothier teaches American literature at the Université de Versailles Saint-Quentin-en-Yvelines, where he is the director of the research center Suds d'Amériques and dean of the Institute for Languages and International Studies. He is the vice president of the Institut des Amériques (France) for North America. He has published two books, *William Faulkner: Essayer de tout dire* (2003) and *Les nouvelles de Flannery O'Connor* (2004). His fields of research cover the literature of the South, interactions between the literature and history of the South and Latin American literature, modernism and postmodernism, literature and the visual arts, the theme of space, the epistemology of American studies, and the role of literature in the construction of local or national identities and as privileged field for cultural transfer.

Kieran Quinlan is professor of English at the University of Alabama at Birmingham. He received his BA in philosophy and psychology from Oxford and his PhD in American literature from Vanderbilt. His books include *John Crowe Ransom's Secular Faith* (1989); *Walker Percy, the Last Catholic Novelist* (1996); and *Strange Kin: Ireland and the American South* (2005). He is completing a study of religious issues in Seamus Heaney and Irish culture.

Mark Lucas is Jobson Professor of English at Centre College. He is the author of *The Southern Vision of Andrew Lytle* (1987), the editor of *Home Voices: A Sampler of Southern Writing* (1991), and a contributor to *The Companion to Southern Literature* (1998). He teaches courses in Faulkner, Flannery O'Connor, American literature, and interdisciplinary humanities at Centre College, where he also chairs the English department. His interest in music in addition to literature has given rise to two albums of folk Americana: *Dust* and *Uncle Bones*.

Bryan Giemza is associate professor of American literature at Randolph-Macon College in Ashland, Virginia. He is author or editor of four books, including *Irish Catholic Writers and the Invention of the American South* (2013).

Mary Alice Kirkpatrick is an assistant professor of English at Furman University, where she teaches courses in African American and American literature as well as diasporic and global studies. She has published in the *South Atlantic Review* and contributed to *The North Carolina Roots of African American Literature* (2006). Her current book manuscript, recipient of a W. Dougald MacMillan Award from the University of North Carolina at Chapel Hill, theorizes displacement in contemporary African American and postcolonial works while exploring the intersections between cultural geography, critical race theory, and migratory narrative structures.

Norman W. Jones is associate professor of English at Ohio State University. A specialist in the interplay of literature and religion, he is the author of *Gay and Lesbian Historical Fiction: Sexual Mystery and Post-Secular Narrative* (2007) and is the coeditor of *The King James Bible after Four Hundred Years: Literary, Linguistic, and Cultural Influences* (2010). His work on Faulkner has appeared in *American Literature*.

Hans H. Skei is professor of comparative literature at the University of Oslo, Norway. He has published widely on southern literature, with essays or book chapters on writers such as Eudora Welty, Flannery O'Connor, Shelby Foote, James Lee Burke, Madison Jones, and Cormac McCarthy. He has published three books on Faulkner's short stories—*William Faulkner: The Short Story Career* (1981), *William Faulkner: The Novelist as Short Story Writer* (1985), and *Reading Faulkner's Best Short Stories* (1999)—and edited *William Faulkner's Short Fiction: An International Symposium* (1997). He is coeditor of two volumes on short fiction theory and analysis—*The Art of Brevity* (2004) and *Less Is More* (2008). He also wrote *A Little Lost Village: Reading William Faulkner's "The Hamlet"* (2012). He has translated a number of Faulkner's novels into Norwegian.

D. Matthew Ramsey is chair of the Department of English and coordinator of the film studies program at Salve Regina University in Newport, Rhode Island. He has written and presented extensively on Faulkner's relationship to popular culture, covering such Faulkner-related texts as *The Story of Temple Drake* (1933), "Turn About," *Today We Live* (1933), "Golden Land," and *The Road to Glory* (1936). He is working on an article concentrating on Faulkner's last produced screenplay, Howard Hawks's epic *Land of the Pharaohs* (1955).

Amy Weldon, a native Alabamian, is associate professor of English at Luther College in Decorah, Iowa. Her essays, short fiction, and reviews have appeared in *Best Travel Writing 2012* (2012), *Cornbread Nation 2: The United States of Barbeque* (2004), *Mississippi Quarterly, Shenandoah, Fiction Southeast, A River & Sound Review, The Carolina Quarterly, StoryQuarterly,* and *Southern Cultures*. She regularly blogs on sustainability, spirit, and self-reliance.

Index